Routes of Power

Routes of Power

ENERGY AND MODERN AMERICA

Christopher F. Jones

▌▌▌
▌▌▌ Harvard University Press

Cambridge, Massachusetts · London, England

First Harvard University Press paperback edition, 2016
Second printing

Library of Congress Cataloging-in-Publication Data

Jones, Christopher F.
　　Routes of power : energy and modern America / Christopher F. Jones.
　　　　pages cm
　　Includes bibliographical references and index.
　　ISBN 978-0-674-72889-9 (cloth : alk. paper)
　　ISBN 978-0-674-97092-2 (pbk.)
1. Energy policy—United States—History.　2. Energy
development—United States—History.　3. Power resources—
United States—History.　4. Energy consumption—United
States—History.　5. Transportation—United States—History.
　I. Title.
　HD9502.U52J658 2014
　333.790973—dc23　　　2013035785

For Robert Kohler,
whose intellectual energy
is a wellspring of positive
feedback loops

Contents

Introduction

AMERICANS HAVE BEEN the world's most profligate energy consumers for more than a century. During this period, copious quantities of coal, oil, and electricity have been used to manufacture goods, propel vehicles, illuminate the dark, increase agricultural yields, and provide entertainment. This ever-increasing reliance on energy has helped the United States become the world's wealthiest and most powerful nation. It has also given its citizens unparalleled access to creature comforts. At the dawn of the twenty-first century, Americans can be cool in the summer and warm in the winter, fly thousands of miles in a few hours, savor produce grown on other continents, and choose from a bewildering array of cheap and disposable products. A lifestyle that was once reserved for royalty is now within the reach of most members of the middle class.

And yet, despite the pervasiveness of cheap and abundant energy, most Americans have little cognizance of their energy decisions. Like many members of contemporary industrialized societies, Americans casually flick switches, turn knobs for hot water, and hold nozzles while filling cars with gas. As long as lights turn on, showers are warm, and gas tanks get filled, there is little reason to wonder how much electricity an appliance consumes or where the oil came from. It is only during rare moments of interruption such as electricity blackouts that our deep dependence on energy infrastructures is revealed.[1] The more energy we use, the less we seem to notice. Intensive yet abstract energy consumption is one of the defining features of our age.

Americans have not always lived this way. Despite the familiarity of these patterns, at the turn of the nineteenth century Americans had a profoundly different relationship with energy. Human and animal muscles, water, and wood fulfilled the vast majority of their energy needs. Using one of these energy sources was anything but passive: it required the personal exertion of labor. When Americans needed to heat their homes, they were forced to chop, split, stack, and haul firewood. To grow food and manufacture goods, they used the strengths of their muscles and those of their animals. Even harnessing the power of falling water or blowing wind required human effort to maintain mills and to adjust sails on ships. Energy, by and large, was work. The direct connection between labor and energy gave Americans an embodied experience of their energy choices and provided strong incentives to limit their consumption.

Routes of Power explores how these changes came about and their consequences for the nation's subsequent development. This book demonstrates that the growth of a fossil fuel–dependent world was neither natural nor inevitable. Instead, it was the product of a series of historical decisions that unfolded in a specific time and place. In particular, the construction of large energy transport systems in the mid-Atlantic region between 1820 and 1930 was crucial to creating an energy-intensive world. Canals, pipelines, and transmission wires stimulated and sustained the ever-increasing consumption of coal, oil, and electricity by giving rise to what I call landscapes of intensification. In conjunction with the activities of energy entrepreneurs, economic incentives, and new consumer behaviors, these material alterations of the environment transformed the nation's energy practices. The *roots* of America's energy transitions can be found in the building of *routes* along which coal, oil, and electricity were shipped.[2]

The consequences of these energy transitions went far beyond a simple set of substitutions in fuels. They created a shift from an organic to a mineral energy regime: a fundamental reorientation of the relationships between Americans and their environments that led to new ways of living, working, and playing. As historians E. A. Wrigley and Rolf Peter Sieferle demonstrate, those living in an organic energy regime obtain heat, light, and power by tapping renewable flows of solar energy, largely by growing plants that can be eaten, fed to animals, or burned. Energy is correspondingly limited by the amount of land that can be cultivated and the stamina of human and animal muscles. Early-nineteenth-century Americans, like nearly all those who have lived in an organic energy regime, were predominantly rural farmers; correspondingly, agriculture and commerce were the nation's main economic activities. Though fossil fuels are also the products of solar energy, and therefore organic in origin, they are converted into a qualitatively different type of energy source through millions of years of concentration beneath the earth's surface. When Americans tapped into massive stocks of coal, oil, and other sources of energy to produce electricity, they ushered in a mineral energy regime. In this brave new world, energy could be shipped long distances and used in ever-increasing quantities without cultivating more land or straining the capacity of muscles. This created an energy surplus that stimulated the dramatic growth of manufacturing enterprises, urban populations, and leisure patterns based on consuming energy rather than preserving it.[3]

The switch from an organic to a mineral energy regime has happened in many times and places. This study focuses on the mid-Atlantic region because it was America's mineral energy heartland.[4] In much the same way that changing energy practices in the British midlands and the Ruhr Valley in Germany catalyzed a revolution in British and German energy use, the mid-Atlantic played a disproportionate role in forging new energy practices in the United States.[5] But these changes were not confined by the region's boundaries. As other parts of America and other parts of the world began to observe the personal and economic benefits that accompanied the increased use of coal, oil, and electricity, they began to replicate many of the patterns developed in the mid-Atlantic. By the twentieth century, the similarities between the energy practices of the mid-Atlantic and the rest of the nation were more striking than their differences.

Collectively, these energy transitions transformed the path of America's development. In 1820, the United States was largely a rural and agricultural society characterized by small cities, modest manufacturing capacity, and decentralized governance. By 1930, coal, oil, and electricity had enabled the emergence of cities with millions of residents and thousands of factories, an economy dominated by industrial production, corporations of immense size, new experiences of time and space, and a strong central state. America had, in short, become modern. Crucially, all of these developments depended to a significant extent on replacing the limits of the organic energy regime with the possibilities of continual growth of the mineral energy regime. The history of energy is not simply a story of fuels and engines; it is the history of modern America.

Energy Transitions: Then and Now

Because of the changes analyzed in this book, Americans, as do nearly half of the world's citizens, currently depend on nonsustainable stocks of fossil fuels. Though the consumption of coal, oil, and electricity has provided many benefits, the downsides of these energy practices are becoming more acute. Climate change is the most pressing challenge, as greenhouse gases are threatening to destabilize the ecosystems humans have come to depend on for sustaining life. This concern, amplified by the environmental damages associated with fossil fuels and the negative geopolitical consequences of oil dependence, has encouraged many citizens, scholars, activists, and politicians to promote renewable alternatives. While history rarely repeats itself directly, it offers lessons and insights that can guide those seeking to develop policies for a more sustainable energy future. In particular, *Routes of Power* offers three ideas that challenge conventional thinking about the dynamics of energy transitions.

First, we should pay greater attention to building transport infrastructure to stimulate renewable energy sources. It is common to assume that transitions result directly from advances in production, and most energy analyses privilege such events as the discovery of new coal or oil reserves or the invention of technologies like electrical generators or photovoltaic cells. While these studies have offered many insights, they often leave unexamined the crucial step of getting energy to consumers. This history demonstrates that transport systems were not simply passive conduits between producers and users. Rather, they established landscapes of intensification that both initiated and maintained energy transitions. One way to encourage the growth of renewable energy systems today is to focus on the creation of transmission lines linking consumption centers with those places where the wind blows the hardest and the sun shines the brightest. We do not simply need more wind turbines or solar arrays; we need mechanisms to ship this energy cheaply and abundantly.

A second finding is that America's first energy transitions were often driven by supply rather than by demand. Those seeking to pioneer the coal, oil, and electricity industries frequently found that consumers considered these energy sources expensive, unnecessary, and difficult to use. To create an energy transition, entrepreneurs had to work aggressively to build demand, a task that was only accomplished over the course of decades. While our present challenge is to decrease demand, rather than increase it, this understanding of the past is important because it emphasizes that energy demand is not static. Consumer behaviors respond to external pressures and can be modified over time. More sustainable energy behaviors can be initiated, but maintaining them will require consistent and active encouragement.

Third, this book emphasizes the social dimensions of energy transitions. The rising use of coal, oil, and electricity reconfigured many aspects of American life ranging from where people lived to how they worked to how they traveled. Similarly, we should expect that a widespread shift to renewables will be accompanied by numerous social changes. Yet all too often, conversations about energy transitions focus narrowly on fuels and are dominated by scientists, engineers, and economists. A common assumption is that we can simply replace coal-fired power plants with wind turbines and expect everything else to remain the same. History suggests otherwise. To plan more effective and equitable energy transitions, we need to incorporate a broader range of perspectives. In addition to discussing technological developments and economic costs, we must consider society and culture; humanists, social scientists, and citizens should be at the table alongside technical experts.[6]

But what, exactly, is an "energy transition"? Definitions vary. An energy transition can indicate a shift in fuels (e.g., from coal to oil), a shift in uses of a fuel (e.g., using oil as gasoline to power automobiles instead of as kerosene for illumination), or a shift in the converters used to transform energy from one form to another (e.g., consuming oil in an internal combustion engine instead of an industrial boiler). In some cases, a transition means abandoning a former source of energy, while in other cases a new energy source is added to the mix without eliminating earlier practices. All of these types of transitions were part of the rising use of coal, oil, and electricity between 1820 and 1930, so I will not limit my discussion here to a single type. Rather, I will describe an energy transition as occurring any time a large group of people began to obtain heat, light, and power in a new manner.[7]

This emphasis on energy from the consumer's perspective provides a useful way to track common patterns among three transitions involving notably different sources of energy. The most important distinction is that coal and oil are carbon-based fuels while electricity is a flow of electromagnetic charge that requires some other input of energy to be generated. Each energy source also undergoes a unique preparation for the market. Coal is broken into different-size pieces for particular uses, oil is refined into a variety of consumer products, and electricity has its voltage raised and lowered several times. There are material distinctions as well: coal is a solid, oil a liquid, and electricity a channeled flow of current. Yet two similarities between the three matter the most for the purposes of this study. First, coal, oil, and electricity all depended on transport infrastructure systems to be used in quantities large enough to constitute a notable shift in energy practices. Second, Americans used each of these energy sources to change many of the ways they lived, including how they warmed and lit their homes, traveled between places, and produced goods.

Landscapes of Intensification

Transport systems were essential to America's first energy transitions because of the natural and human geography of the mid-Atlantic. The anthracite coalfields of eastern Pennsylvania, the oil fields of western Pennsylvania, and the falling waters of the lower Susquehanna River were far removed from the places most people lived. An energy transition therefore required one of two options: move people to sites of energy abundance, or bring the energetic wealth of remote regions to urban centers. The first strategy had long historical precedent. It was favored by New England entrepreneurs, for

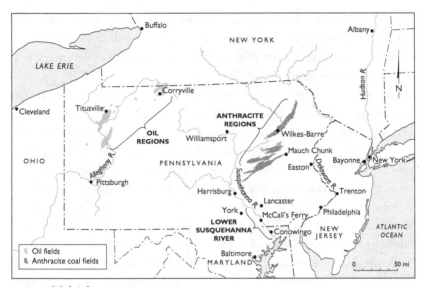

MAP I.1. Mid-Atlantic energy sources.

example, who built factories along stretches of falling water in such rural areas as the Merrimac Valley. Energy pioneers in the mid-Atlantic, however, forged a new path. They decided to ship coal, oil, and electricity long distances. This gave them access to bigger markets but forced them to deal with the fact that shipping large quantities of bulky, heavy, and ephemeral substances across landscapes was, in many ways, as challenging as bringing coal out of the ground, drilling for oil, or running water through turbines.

In its natural state, the environment of the mid-Atlantic did not facilitate the long-distance transport of coal, oil, and electricity. The rivers extending from the coal and oil regions were shallow, choppy, and rarely navigable. Roads were a more reliable option, but overland shipments by wagon were slow and expensive: in 1810, it was cheaper to deliver coal three thousand miles by boat from Britain than to haul it a hundred miles over land.[8] And before electricity, the energy of falling water could not be transported more than a stone's throw from a riverbank. Improved transport options would be needed to stimulate the widespread use of these energy sources in distant places. Over time, mid-Atlantic boosters recognized that coal could be shipped on canals for a tenth or less the cost of wagon shipments; pipelines could move oil for a fraction of the cost of barges; and transmission wires could deliver electricity hundreds of miles away. The mid-Atlantic's first nature may not have been conducive to the long-distance transport of mineral energy sources, but these alterations of the built environment produced a second nature of abundant energy flows.[9]

The ability to connect rural supply sites with urban population centers was an essential first step in pioneering the use of coal, oil, and electricity. But this does not explain why these energy transitions were sustained. Canals, pipelines, and wires also mattered because they gave these processes momentum. Over time, a set of positive feedback loops arose between the building of infrastructure, the economic investments in these systems, the actions of human agents, and new consumption practices. Transport systems made energy transitions not only possible, but likely. They created landscapes of intensification that encouraged prolific energy use.

To understand these linkages, canals, pipelines, and wires must be seen as more than simply material assemblages of earth, water, concrete, iron, steel, and copper. Infrastructures, as historians of large technological systems have demonstrated, are social as well as technological.[10] Cultural values—reflected in financial incentives, state regulations, moral sentiments, and ideas about what constitutes a good life—strongly influence which technologies get built and how they are used over time. Once put in place, technological transformations of the world feed back into social values, augmenting the regulatory, economic, and moral systems in which they were first introduced. This is not a deterministic relationship, but rather one of mutual shaping: social and technological worlds are co-produced.[11]

The economic context in which canals, pipelines, and transmission wires were built played a particularly important role in sustaining the momentum of energy transitions. When coal, oil, and electricity were first introduced into markets, there were relatively few established applications for their use. Having long lived without them, consumers saw little reason to change their practices. Abundant supply exceeded the relatively modest demand. But for the corporations that built these transport networks, the status quo was not an option. They had raised large sums of capital for construction and were under intense pressure to pay off their debts and return profits to shareholders. They could only achieve this goal by maximizing the flows of energy along their pathways. As a result, company officers went to great lengths to generate demand. They sponsored experiments to develop new applications for coal, oil, and electricity; gave free samples and steep discounts to promising users; and built factories to take advantage of surplus capacity. Canal, pipeline, and wire operators were among the region's most prominent energy boosters: agents dedicated to changing consumption patterns. The sunk costs of infrastructure exerted a logic that encouraged boosters to create demand when it did not exist.[12]

The demand-building activities spearheaded by the managers of transport systems highlight a crucial feature of energy transitions: energy demand is malleable. People had lived for centuries without coal, oil, and electricity, and they needed to be convinced that it was worthwhile to alter their practices. This task was further complicated by the fact that switching to a new energy source often required large up-front investments of money as well as effort before the rewards were achieved. Therefore, boosters mattered greatly. Entrepreneurs decided whether and where to build infrastructure systems, convinced factory owners to adopt new energy sources, experimented with processes that gave rise to new industries, and taught consumers how to use coal, oil, and electricity. Most of their names have been lost to the historical record. For every John D. Rockefeller or Thomas Edison, there were thousands of people whose labors were necessary to create our current world of fossil fuel abundance.[13]

Energy transitions were further encouraged by the expansion of transport networks. As consumer demand grew in response to the activities of energy boosters, companies widened and deepened canals, installed pipelines of larger diameter, and erected additional transmission wires. Greater quantities of coal, oil, and electricity could then be shipped at even cheaper prices, thereby reinforcing new behaviors. In a synergistic feedback cycle, cheaper energy helped increase consumer demand, which led to further expansions of infrastructure networks and reductions in cost. Supply fueled demand, demand fueled supply, and increases in the capacity of canals, pipelines, and wires sustained these feedback loops.

Thus were born landscapes of intensification. Canals, pipelines, and wires created a world in which increased energy consumption was both possible and desirable by reordering landscapes, motivating a group of actors to build demand, and sustaining a positive feedback loop between supply and demand. This logic of growth was material, economic, and behavioral. Material transformations of the environment linked remote stocks of energy abundance

with concentrated centers of capital and population. Economic considerations of sunk costs, increasing returns-to-scale, and the desire for profit
provided powerful motivations for human actors to maximize the flows of
energy along these systems. And because many people could reap the benefits of abundant coal, oil, and electricity with relatively few personal costs,
energy-intensive behaviors became more commonplace.

While these landscapes of intensification were powerful, they were also
unequal. Canals, pipelines, and wires privileged certain people and places
over others. These delivery systems were narrow tendrils on the broad
American landscape that provided cheap and abundant energy only in a
very specific geography. The mid-Atlantic was the region in which these
technologies were first built and became most densely layered. As a result,
many in the mid-Atlantic derived greater benefits from these energy transitions than those living in other regions of the United States. But not all
within the mid-Atlantic reaped the same advantages. Some served by canals, pipelines, and wires used their new access to cheap energy to build
profitable industries. A handful of cities were thereby able to increase their
manufacturing output dramatically. The financial gains, however, were
highly concentrated. Factory owners acquired large amounts of wealth
while often paying their workers subsistence wages. The regions in which
coal, oil, and electricity were produced faced extensive ecological degradation while recouping only a small percentage of the economic gain associated with these energy sources. Large swaths of the mid-Atlantic were
not served by transport networks at all, putting these rural residents at an
economic disadvantage compared with their urban brethren. These distributive inequalities were framed by choices over where these technologies
were built, who owned them, and how they were operated. Focusing on the
transport of coal, oil, and electricity reveals many of the spatial politics of
energy transitions.[14]

The Push and Pull of Energy Transitions

The building of landscapes of intensification depended on more than an
ability to manipulate the natural environment. Constructing canals, pipelines, and wires required a significant degree of social support. Fortunately

for the mid-Atlantic's energy boosters, the region's political and cultural environment was largely compatible with their efforts. The region's profit-seeking economic system favored the accumulation of wealth. Politically, many members of state governments in Pennsylvania, New York, and New Jersey promoted policies they believed would stimulate their economies. As a result, they frequently passed measures that gave extensive rights to energy production and transport companies, subsidized scientific surveys of natural resources, and kept energy taxes low. Federal policies, though less important to the coal, oil, and electricity trades than state policies during this time period, also reflected a general support for the growth of an energy-intensive economy.[15] There were, in addition, relatively few cultural norms that stood in the way of exploiting energy resources. Most early Americans of European descent had little objection to using natural resources for their own benefit: subduing nature was both a right and a responsibility.[16]

But there were some countervailing forces. One exception, particularly in the pre-Civil War era, was republicanism, a widespread set of beliefs that offered an alternative perspective on how the nation should develop. Most closely associated with Thomas Jefferson, the republican worldview emphasized the importance of civic virtue, the denial of luxury, and the independence of citizens. The small farmer, able to provide for most of his family's needs by working his land, stood as the paragon of virtue. If industrial production was necessary, republicans believed it should be situated in pastoral rural settings along streams, because urban factories were seen as likely to give rise to a subservient working class. How could a proper democracy function, they asked, under conditions of dependence and inequality like those produced by the dark mills of Manchester and Birmingham? The appeal of republican views likely slowed the rate at which early transitions occurred by leading to policies that limited the rights and privileges granted to canal companies, discouraging the growth of urban manufacturing, and causing many politicians to oppose measures that would promote industrial development. But it did not ultimately stop them.[17]

The extensive ecological damage caused by the production of coal, oil, and electricity served as another possible source of opposition. To be sure, most mid-Atlantic residents in the nineteenth and early twentieth centuries held different attitudes toward the environment than contemporary Americans. Smoke stacks gushing black soot, for example, were often seen as signs of progress, not pollution. Even so, the direct environmental harms of new energy sources were sufficient to be recognized by historical actors as undesirable. Journalists, industry observers, and residents of energy-producing regions knew that coal mines scarred the landscape, oil derricks spilled petroleum into water supplies, and hydroelectric dams ruined fishing grounds. Canal dams and reservoirs flooded fields, pipelines leaked and occasionally exploded, and transmission wires were considered dangerous to have on one's property. These known negative environmental consequences could have led mid-Atlantic residents to limit their hunger for mineral energy sources.

They rarely did. Despite various forms of public opposition, few measures were passed that altered practices damaging to local ecosystems. Over time, the anthracite regions, oil fields, and lower Susquehanna River became sacrifice zones—areas whose environments were forfeited to provide cheap and abundant energy to distant places. Canals, pipelines, and wires played a pivotal role in the creation of these sacrifice zones. The worst environmental damage associated with these energy sources occurred at the sites of production—mines, wells, and dams. Transport infrastructure systems, however, dissociated most consumers from the environmental harms caused by their energy use. Factories in Philadelphia could power their steam engines with anthracite without experiencing landscape destruction in eastern Pennsylvania. Inhabitants of New York City could light their houses with kerosene without ruining their drinking water supply. Merchants in Baltimore could equip their stores with electrical appliances without suffering from the loss of the local fishing industry along the Susquehanna River. In other words, canals, pipelines, and wires gave users little incentive to care or worry about how their energy was produced. As is true for the overwhelming majority of Americans today, nineteenth- and early-twentieth-century consumers could increase their demand without having to face many of the environmental costs entailed by their actions.[18]

Finally, despite the encouragement of energy boosters, countless individuals resisted the spread of coal, oil, and electricity. Millions continued to heat their homes with wood after coal had been introduced. Citizens voted for politicians who did not support the granting of extensive rights to private energy companies. Some farmers in western Pennsylvania preferred a pastoral life to the chaos of the oil boom and refused to let prospectors drill on their land. Fishermen protested the damming of the Susquehanna River because it would block the migration of shad. In these and many other ways, some residents of the mid-Atlantic took actions that stemmed the growth of mineral energy sources.

Collectively, though, the force of these various oppositions was more than offset by the pull of landscapes of intensification and their compatibility with the region's economic, political, and cultural values. Once it developed strength, the logic of growth proved remarkably durable. When canals, pipelines, and wires were first constructed, it was easy for mid-Atlantic residents to choose to live without coal, oil, or electricity. Over time, however, they no longer faced the same choices. Urban residents, merchants, and manufacturers came to depend on ever-increasing supplies of mineral energy to support their way of life. They became locked in a world of intensive energy consumption.

We can think of dependence as technological, economic, and behavioral.[19] A broad range of possible choices about how, when, where, and even whether to employ an energy source is available at the early stages of technological developments. Once a technology is actually constructed, however, flexibility diminishes rapidly and the range of choices is significantly narrowed. In economic terms, large sunk costs offer financial incentives to maximize the use of existing systems and decrease the economic viability of alternative approaches. Users also invest in secondary technologies such as stoves, steam engines, and appliances that lock in the need for continued energy inputs. And at a behavioral level, consumers learn to use new energy sources, become habituated to them, and finally come to depend on their constant supply.

Some of the mechanisms by which people in the mid-Atlantic came to depend on coal, oil, and electricity were straightforward. The expansion of the iron, steel, and aluminum industries created an ongoing demand for large inputs of energy to continue their operations. As the number of residents and factories housed by cities began to increase, they required far more energy than organic sources could supply. Other factors were more indirect. Over time, for instance, the number of firewood merchants declined as anthracite became the dominant fuel for home heating. This made it increasingly difficult for urbanites to heat their homes with wood, even if it was their preference. As electric streetcars made it practical for people to

move to houses miles from commercial centers, suburbanites needed mechanized transport to get to offices and stores. Slowly and unevenly, most
mid-Atlantic residents came to depend on mineral energy sources.

In theory, mid-Atlantic residents could have chosen to give up coal, oil,
or electricity at any point. But the costs became significantly greater over
time. In 1820 the economic and social life of the mid-Atlantic would have
hardly been affected by the absence of anthracite coal. By 1930, however, a
societal decision to forgo coal, oil, or electricity would have destroyed the
region's foundations. Cities would no longer have been able to support their
populations, industries would have collapsed, people could not have traveled to the remaining jobs, and the region would have fallen behind other
areas economically. Even the relatively slight reductions in mineral energy
availability for civilian purposes during World War I were sufficient to disrupt a wide range of activities. Stepping into a world of abundant coal, oil,
and electricity has proven easier than stepping out of one.

Human agents were essential to energy transitions, but as the infrastructure of a mineral energy regime took hold in the mid-Atlantic, the options
available to its citizens and planners narrowed. Failure to win support from
entrepreneurs, investors, politicians, boosters, or consumers at the early stages
could have derailed an energy transition. But several decades later, altering
the momentum of intensification would have required the coordinated actions of numerous powerful agents to amass huge quantities of capital to
construct alternate systems, to initiate significant changes in government
policy, or to foster widespread alterations of social practices. Energy transitions are not natural or inevitable, but once they begin, they can be extremely
durable.

Organic and Mineral Energy Regimes

The shift from an organic to a mineral energy regime has been one of the
most consequential transformations in the relationships between humans
and their environments in world history. In the mid-Atlantic from 1820 to
1930, it enabled a wave of changes including the development of an industrial economy, huge cities, motorized transport systems, giant corporations,
and large government bodies. In our present day, coming to terms with the

pervasiveness of the mineral energy regime is one of the central challenges of creating a sustainable future.[20]

An organic energy regime describes a human society where energy is derived from flows of solar energy entering the ecosystem. Sunlight is the source of nearly all energy on the earth's surface.[21] It warms the planet and, most critically, powers the process of photosynthesis that allows plants to transform solar radiation into chemical energy. Metabolism is the other major process of energy conversion, enabling human and animal bodies to digest plants (or other animals) to provide heat and mechanical energy that can power their muscles. As a result, plants have historically provided the vast majority of human energy needs in the organic energy regime—98 percent or more—through being eaten to power human muscles, fed to animals that can be used for labor or food, or burned to provide warmth and light.[22] The remaining fraction of human energy is harnessed from wind and falling water, also dependent on solar energy. The heat of the sun creates wind currents that can be used by sailing vessels and windmills. Solar energy also evaporates water from the oceans, some of which ends up falling as precipitation in higher elevations, resulting in descending streams that can be used to power mills or float people and goods downstream.

A central feature of the organic energy regime is that the total supply of energy is limited by the availability of land to grow plants. Because plants are the basis of human energy in the organic energy regime, practically all the needs of human existence require the allocation of land. To eat, humans must dedicate land to raising crops, pasturing animals, or hunting and gathering. To clothe themselves, they must set aside land to grow plants like cotton or flax or to raise animals that can provide wool or hides. To build houses, they must cut and shape trees into lumber or burn wood in furnaces to make bricks. To manufacture goods, they need to devote land to produce raw materials such as charcoal, leather, wool, cotton, flax, and straw. Regardless of the type of good, some amount of land is necessary for its production. This results in a zero-sum game. Once all the available land is being used at its capacity, no more can be produced.[23] The size of the pie is fixed, and increasing the amount of one type of good entails sacrificing something else. Expanding manufacturing output, for example, involves dedicating additional land to grow firewood and other raw materials, thereby lowering the supply of food or animals. To gain one thing requires making do with less of another. The carrying capacity of the land presents finite limits to growth.

A second characteristic of the organic energy regime is that population and manufacturing enterprises tend to be decentralized. Not only is their absolute level of production limited, organic energy sources are difficult to transport long distances. Firewood is bulky, heavy, and grown over wide tracts of land, making it expensive to gather large quantities of it in a single place: in nineteenth-century Europe, firewood could only be economically transported overland six or seven hours in any direction since its price doubled every two to four kilometers it was carried.[24] Many crops have a similarly poor weight-to-value ratio, which is why American farmers settling new regions so often transformed their grain into higher-value products like whiskey and pigs that could justify the cost of carriage. And before the advent of electricity, the power of water and wind could barely be transferred at all. Because of limited and decentralized supplies, energy-intensive operations must move to sites of energy abundance, rather than the opposite. Historically, enterprises like glass works, salt manufacturers, and iron smelters were typically located in rural forested areas where they could obtain exclusive access to firewood or falling water. Cities, meanwhile, are energy-scarce locations dependent on the surrounding countryside to supply them with food and fuel. The size of their populations and the amount of production within their borders is limited by the capacity of their hinterlands. In organic energy regimes, population densities typically remain low and communities settle at sites of energy abundance.

Third, in the organic regime, energy is synonymous with personal labor. People use their muscles to wield tools, chop wood, harvest fields, or direct animals. Even when waterpower is available for a flour mill, for example, humans need to unload and hoist grain, sort it after milling, load it into bags, and maintain mill stones. Energy, by and large, is correlated with sweat. Any gains in energy consumption have to be measured against the personal costs of producing it. If one wants a warmer house, one has to chop more wood. If one wants to manufacture more goods, one has to devote energy to working harder or managing draft animals. As a result, in an organic energy regime people have an incentive to limit their overall energy needs.

In essence, an organic energy regime is a Malthusian world of direct linkages between land, population, and production. Although Thomas

Malthus is perhaps best known as a pessimist for his views on the limits of population growth, it is more useful to see him, along with his fellow classical economists Adam Smith and David Ricardo, as an observer of the possibilities and limitations of an organic energy regime.[25] Malthus, Smith, and Ricardo believed there were three primary factors of production: land, capital, and labor. Since land could not be expanded, one could only increase output through adding more capital or labor. These investments, however, were subject to the law of diminishing marginal returns. If one added an extra worker to a field already worked by one laborer, for example, its output would likely increase—perhaps by 50 percent. Adding a second extra worker would increase overall output, but by a smaller amount— perhaps an additional 30 percent. Each additional worker would produce declining returns until growth would be entirely halted. In other words, some growth was possible, but the law of diminishing marginal returns ultimately meant the economy would reach a stationary state. The finite supply of land acted as a negative feedback loop that limited the total production of goods and services.

A mineral energy regime emerges when a society begins to supplement and replace renewable flows of solar energy with centralized stocks such as fossil fuels. Coal and oil are also products of solar energy, but they are formed and used in very different ways. Over a period of millions of years, plants and animals captured the sun's energy, much as they do today. When these organisms died, many of them came to rest underwater where there was little oxygen to break down their organic matter. The slow pressure of gravity from above and heat from the earth's core drove water and gases out of these thick layers of organic matter, eventually producing dense stocks of energy-rich material. Using coal and oil, then, is akin to opening a time warp that unlocks the slowly accumulated energy surplus of eons in instantaneous moments of combustion. Because most electricity has been produced through the burning of fossil fuels or large-scale dams that exceed the capacities of societies in an organic energy regime, it fits the patterns of the mineral energy regime as well. Hydroelectricity from dams on the lower Susquehanna River, for example, was transported long distances, integrated into networks with coal-fired plants, and consumed in ever-increasing quantities. The key distinction is that in an organic energy regime, solar energy must be captured as it flows through the ecosystem via photosynthesis and metabolism; in a mineral energy regime, accumulated stocks of centralized energy can suddenly be accessed at once.

This shift from flows to stocks allows for new patterns of human activity to emerge. Most critically, it transforms the nature of limits. In a mineral energy regime, the total supply of energy is no longer constrained by the carrying capacity of land or the power of muscles. As long as humans can access ever-larger stocks of accumulated abundance, rapid growth can be maintained indefinitely. The zero-sum game of the organic energy regime is eclipsed by the positive feedback loops of the mineral energy regime.

The density and abundance of mineral energy sources also creates the possibility to locate large numbers of people and manufacturing establishments in one place. As concentrated forms of energy, coal, oil, and electricity can justify the construction of elaborate transport systems. If the amount of wood that could be sustainably harvested each year was distributed in an even layer on the ground, for instance, it would be less than four inches thick. By contrast, coal seams are often found in deposits several feet thick with dozens of layers on top of one another, meaning that the energy yield from a single place is hundreds, if not thousands, of times greater.[26] This concentration provides a much larger incentive for capital investment in transport infrastructure because costs can be recouped through the high volume of product shipped.

This density shifts the opportunities for urban growth and the geographic logic of manufacturing. The transport of coal, oil, and electricity to cities transforms them from energy-scarce sites into locations of energy superabundance as the agricultural capacity of their hinterlands ceases to act as a limit to growth. Second, energy-intensive enterprises no longer need to be sited in remote areas. With cheap and abundant energy available in cities, manufacturing establishments can move to urban locations where they can obtain easier access to workers, supplies, and customers. Cities with millions of people and thousands of industrial factories are only possible in the context of the mineral energy regime.

The development of a mineral energy regime creates a different set of incentives for human behaviors. Instead of producing energy, consumers can buy it in a market. As a result, energy is correlated with cost, not sweat. And since investments in large infrastructure systems render coal, oil, and electricity progressively cheaper through economies of scale, low costs encourage users to increase their energy consumption rather than reduce it. Steam engines and electric motors displace much of the effort of human muscles in producing goods. Railroads, electric streetcars and automobiles allow passengers to travel long distances without using their own muscles. Electric power embodies these changes because people rarely know how much energy they are using. Flicking an on/off switch might draw ten, fifty, or several hundred watts of power, but users rarely know the difference. Cheap energy creates the potential for warmer and better-lit houses, access to many more goods, and swift travel without greater personal labor. Energy-consuming behaviors are rewarded in a mineral energy regime in ways that make little sense in an organic energy regime. Actions that appear rational in one regime seem absurd from the perspective of the other.[27]

The constant growth of mineral energy consumption is subject to limits, of course. In the long term, fossil fuels are an exhaustible resource. Coal taken out of a mine or oil pumped from the ground cannot be replaced, except through millions of years of biological and geological processes. Though renewable, hydroelectric dams often trap river silt that shortens their useful life, and dams cannot be expanded indefinitely. Eventually, we will need to return to a system where our energy supply is derived from flows of solar energy, not stocks. In the short term, however—and for our hydrocarbon age the "short term" is likely to be a matter of several centuries—supplies of energy are practically infinite: their use can be expanded to suit human needs without the zero-sum trade-offs of the organic energy regime.

The rise of a mineral energy regime also does not mean that organic energy sources go away. Human beings cannot literally eat fossil fuels, even if the transformation of hydrocarbons into fertilizer has greatly increased agricultural output in many parts of the world. In fact, the development of a mineral energy regime has often been accompanied by a rise in demand for organic energy.[28] However, a key distinction between the growth of the organic and mineral energy regimes, to use the distinction made famous by Malthus, is that the former might grow arithmetically while the latter could grow geometrically.

Tracing the shift from an organic to a mineral energy regime is useful because it connects energy transitions to their broader social ramifications,

both then and now.[29] Life in the mid-Atlantic changed greatly between
1820 and 1930, and new energy practices were at the heart of these developments. In 1820, most people lived in rural areas and worked on farms.
Philadelphia and New York, the region's leading cities, were commercial
trade centers with tens of thousands of residents. Agriculture and trade
were the main economic activities. Manufacturing played a much smaller
role and it was concentrated in rural areas. When people traveled overland,
they used their legs or the muscles of animals. On water, they followed nature's distributions of rivers or plied sea and ocean routes with regular wind
patterns. Prevailing political ideas even shared a remarkable resonance with
the conditions of the organic energy regime. Republicanism celebrated agriculture, decentralized power, and local authority. It was a fitting ideology
in a world where energy was produced locally and derived from the land.

By 1930, most people in the mid-Atlantic lived in cities and many worked
in factories. Industry had become the most dynamic and rapidly growing sector of the economy, eclipsing agriculture and commerce. The geography of
industry had shifted as well; most factories were now located in large cities.
Philadelphia and New York had grown into metropolitan centers with millions of residents and thousands of factories. People traveled at high speeds in
railroads, steamboats, streetcars, and automobiles along routes that were determined by human convenience, not natural landscapes. When not working, abundant energy made new leisure practices possible including listening
to radio, going to the cinema, or driving through the countryside. The nation's politics had also shifted. In a world of centralized power, large corporations, and sprawling cities, the local and limited governance advocated by
republicans no longer seemed appropriate. Many citizens believed the central
government needed to play a much more active role in governing society, as
illustrated by the reforms of the Progressive Era and the New Deal.

Changes in energy practices, therefore, are not simply changes in how
people obtain heat, light, and power. They are reorientations of how people
live, work, and play. Coal, oil, and electricity have enabled previously unimaginable expansions of cities, industrial output, and transport systems.
They have allowed average citizens to access quantities of energy previously
only accessible to ruling elites. Yet due to global warming, current energy
practices are also one of our contemporary world's gravest threats. Our
trade-offs are no longer about alternative land uses; they are about whether

we can maintain our lifestyles without radically altering the ecosystems that we have come to depend on for our survival. In an era of climate change, continuing the patterns of the mineral energy regime is foolish. We must pioneer a new set of human-environment relationships that strike a better balance between short-term self-interest and long-term sustainability. Remembering that we did not always use energy as we do today is a helpful start.

1

Coal's Liquid Pathways

SOMETIME IN THE FALL of 1820, a group of men piloting crude wooden rafts piled with coal pulled into a wharf on the eastern side of Philadelphia. In one sense, there was nothing remarkable about their journey: farmers, traders, and lumbermen had been rafting goods down the Delaware River to the region's main trading center for decades. Upon closer inspection, however, two things were unusual. First, the boatmen had begun their expedition on the recently improved Lehigh River, a waterway whose steep falls, shallow pools, and jutting rocks had previously frustrated attempts to deliver goods from the Lehigh Valley. Several hundred workers had spent much of the previous two years creating dams, stone walls, and hydrostatic gates that funneled, constrained, and directed the flows of the Lehigh River. Their efforts had altered and regulated the river to suit the needs of human commerce. The second distinctive fact about this group was the cargo: anthracite coal. Although Philadelphia craftsmen were accustomed to using bituminous coal from Britain, Nova Scotia, and Virginia, there was no active trade in what many called "stone coal." The city's coal market was small and well stocked; there was no pent-up demand for anthracite. In fact, the men had great trouble finding customers. It was much easier to break up their wooden rafts to sell as used lumber than it was to convince Philadelphians to pay for stone coal.

The names of these boatmen have been lost, and their arrival does not seem to have merited attention from local newspapers. But with the advantage of historical hindsight, the revolutionary nature of their journey is clearer. Over the next forty years, anthracite coal would trigger profound changes in the economy, environment, and society of the mid-Atlantic. Stone coal would be used to forge iron, build railroads, power steam engines, propel boats, and warm the homes of burgeoning urban populations. It would create great wealth, support the growth of eastern seaboard cities, and enable the development of an industrial economy. As residents of the mid-Atlantic became accustomed to using coal, their appetites for fossil fuel energy grew at a dramatic rate. While in 1820 the beleaguered men from the Lehigh Valley had difficulty selling a few hundred tons of coal, by the dawn of the Civil War consumers required annual deliveries of several million tons to maintain their way of life.

How did this happen? The advent of new production techniques, a common explanation for energy transitions, is not sufficient to explain the adoption of anthracite coal. People had been bringing anthracite coal out of the ground for many decades before 1820 without creating a substantial market. Moreover, there were few innovations in coal mining during this time that explain the industry's rapid expansion. We get a better answer when we focus our attention on the anonymous boatmen, for they signify the critical importance of transport networks. Anthracite was found in rural regions distant from the urban markets of the eastern seaboard. Hauling coal in wagons overland was time-consuming, difficult, and expensive. Under such conditions, only small quantities of anthracite could be shipped, and buyers had few incentives to change their energy consumption practices.

The improvements on the Lehigh River pioneered a landscape of intensification linking transport systems, boosters, and consumers. In conjunction with alterations of the Schuylkill, Delaware, Lackawaxen, and Susquehanna Rivers, canals made it possible for anthracite coal to be shipped cheaply, abundantly, and reliably to eastern seaboard cities. Once in markets, boosters encouraged consumer demand by creating new applications for anthracite, teaching users how to burn it in homes and factories, and advertising its benefits. Over time, consumers responded favorably to these encouragements and demand grew rapidly. These forces operated in a synergistic feedback cycle whereby canals increased supply, boosters found new applications for coal, and consumer demand encouraged the expansion of transport networks to further increase supply. The limits and negative feedback loops of the organic energy regime were soon replaced by the mineral energy regime's pattern of continual growth.

Envisioning Canals

The history of Pennsylvania's anthracite coal trade begins over 250 million years ago when the land was flat and marshy. Tall trees and large ferns dominated the landscape. As plants and animals died, many fell into the swamps and decayed in an oxygen-poor environment. With the passage of time, this mass of plant and animal debris formed a brown spongy matter known as peat. This process repeated itself countless times, occasionally interrupted by deposits of mud and sand that formed layers between the peat formations. Then geological forces went to work. Over millions of years, a combination of pressure from the layers above and heat emanating from the earth's core drove moisture and gases out of the peat, turning it into coal; at the same time, the layers of sand and mud were solidified into sedimentary rocks. Most of the world's coal was formed in a similar manner. Depending on the amount of time and strength of the geological forces, more gas and water was removed from the peat, leaving behind deposits of concentrated carbon. Peat first became lignite, then semi-bituminous, and eventually bituminous coal, categories that refer to the relative percentage of carbon left in the material.

In northeast Pennsylvania, however, one additional step occurred. The clash of tectonic plates raised the flat land into mountains, creating additional pressure as the earth was folded over itself. This drove additional amounts of volatile material out of the coal, leaving deposits of nearly pure carbon, known to us as anthracite coal. Such geological activity is relatively rare: most of the world's coal reserves are variations of lignite or bituminous. The many layers of coal in a single place combined to provide northeast

Pennsylvania with a unique underworld: three-quarters of the earth's an-thracite reserves were squeezed into an area spanning less than 500 square miles. The high percentage of carbon in anthracite has several implications. It gives it a hard, shiny appearance like obsidian, and it is difficult to ignite because of the lack of impurities. But once lit, anthracite burns hotter and cleaner than other coal varieties, making it a particularly effective fuel for homes and factories.[1]

In the early nineteenth century, coal played a minor role in American life; organic energy sources provided the vast majority of the mid-Atlantic's needs. Much like the rest of the United States—and indeed, as in most of the rest of the world except certain parts of Britain, Germany, and Belgium— human muscles, animals, falling water, and firewood provided the energy for farming, producing goods, heating homes, and cooking food. Craftsmen in early American cities, including Philadelphia and New York, consumed small amounts of coal, as did a few homeowners. Some who lived in north-eastern Pennsylvania near outcrops of anthracite also burned it in homes and workshops. These uses of coal, however, were the exception rather than the rule. Most entrepreneurs built manufacturing enterprises along the falls of rivers or in rural areas where firewood was abundant. The large majority of the population was engaged in agriculture and relied almost wholly on or-ganic energy sources in their daily lives. The mid-Atlantic was an organic energy regime—a world in which nearly all energy and goods were derived from the land.

Muscles, water, and wood were not limiting factors for mid-Atlantic resi-dents at the time. As European observers had noted since arriving in the New World, the abundance of forests and land offered what seemed to be limitless possibilities. The region included several rivers with falls that could be used to power mills, and large amounts of unsettled land that could feed plenty of draft animals. Given the low population density and small energy demands of the region's farmers, merchants, and craftsmen, shortages were not a chronic condition for most of the mid-Atlantic. Compared with their European counterparts, mid-Atlantic residents lived in a world of energy abundance where "poor American farmers could boast of burning bigger fires than could most European nobles."[2]

Despite the abundance of organic energy sources, in the early 1800s a heterogeneous group of Philadelphia merchants, scientists, industrialists, politicians, and citizens became interested in anthracite coal. Many people had known for several decades that there was coal in the mountains of northeastern Pennsylvania. As early as the 1770s, farmers and craftsmen in Wilkes-Barre and the Wyoming Valley were regularly using anthracite. By the 1790s, large deposits had been identified in the Lehigh Valley, and small amounts of anthracite from the Schuylkill region were being marketed in Philadelphia in the 1810s. Moreover, Philadelphia blacksmiths, nail smiths, distillers, and the Water Works were already using bituminous coal imported from Britain, Nova Scotia, and Virginia. While the trade was small—in 1784, Philadelphia imported around 500 tons of coal, just over 1,000 tons by the early 1790s, and merely 3,000 tons per year by the 1810s—boosters were enticed by the potential profits in replacing foreign imports with domestic supplies.[3]

Philadelphia's anthracite boosters were not deterred by the modest scale of the existing coal trade. Booster logic is future-oriented; the present matters far less. And Philadelphia's anthracite boosters had a clear imagination for the future, derived from observing events across the Atlantic Ocean. Over the previous century, Britain had entered a remarkable period of economic and industrial growth fueled by coal. British industrialists used coal to power large textile mills that enabled the nation to leapfrog all its economic competitors. Coal had led to financial gain, industrial growth, and military strength. Several Americans hoped the young republic would follow a similar path. Thomas Cooper, for example, a professor of chemistry at several American colleges, observed in the early nineteenth century: "In this country every suggestion that brings forward the importance of coal to the public view is of moment: we know little of its value in Pennsylvania as yet. All, all the superior wealth, power and energy of Great Britain, is founded on her coal mining."[4]

But how to develop Pennsylvania's anthracite resources? As contemporary observers knew, mining anthracite was not a major challenge. The erosion of the Appalachian Mountains over millions of years had left coal seams exposed to the surface in many places: at those sites, a pickax, shovel, and brute strength sufficed to gather anthracite. Transport was another story. The mountainous terrain and lack of good roads meant that the Lehigh, Schuylkill, and Wyoming Valleys were poorly connected with the urban centers where potential consumers lived. Moving coal by wagons was expensive, and only small amounts could be transported overland. The reality in the early nineteenth century was that it cost more to ship coal eighty miles overland than it did to import it three thousand miles from Britain.[5] Simply put, the places where American coal could be found were not part of the trade hinterlands of cities like New York and Philadelphia.

When pondering the transport options for the fuel that would eventually pioneer the transition to a mineral energy regime, anthracite boosters turned to the shipping medium most characteristic of the organic energy regime they lived in: water. The buoyancy of water reduced friction, thereby lowering the amount of labor required to move goods. For example, one heavy horse could pull a canal boat carrying between thirty to fifty tons while two draft horses were needed to pull a four-ton wagon overland. Mules provided most of the power for American canals, and three of them could pull a boat loaded with more than a hundred tons of coal.[6] In short, water was desirable because it was an energy-saving device for those who lived in a world where energy was correlated with personal exertion. But these benefits were not always available. Rivers could freeze in the winter, be reduced to a small trickle in the summer, and flood during the spring snowmelt. Rapids could wreck boats in some seasons while exposed rocks along the river bottom could grind trade to a halt in other seasons.

Boosters knew that the Schuylkill and Lehigh Rivers offered a more promising outlet for coal than overland routes, but these waterways could not be used reliably in their natural state. They had variable water levels, steep falls, and jutting rocks that made it difficult for boats to travel downstream. If these rivers could be improved, though, a profitable trade could result. An anonymous analysis from 1821, for example, argued for the virtues of canals: "[Coal] is an article of too much weight in proportion to its value, to bear a transportation by land . . . The immense mines of it in this state, are therefore of no value at present; but make the water communication, and they at once become a source of employment and wealth."[7] Josiah White, pioneer of the Lehigh Canal, made a case for the links between coal, canals, and economic growth explicitly: "The steam engines spread all over England are said to perform many times over the labor of the entire population of that country. The coal for those engines comes on their canals . . . Canals are the foundation of their wealth."[8]

Natural limitations did not dissuade anthracite's boosters. Given the potential advantages of water transport in an organic energy regime, they believed they could follow the lead of many other societies that had altered waterways to fit their needs.[9] They knew that water improvements could take several forms. If a river had a bottleneck at a particular place, they could remove dangerous rocks, build a dam to submerge a set of rapids, or create a short canal around a waterfall. Another option was to create temporary dams, called pond freshets, to build up a pool of water: when a dam was opened, it would release a long wave of high water that could transport goods even during the dry season. Finally, boosters could choose to build a canal, which involved creating a separate channel for the water on one edge of the river, constructing dams and locks at points where the river fell, and establishing a tow path along the entire length so that mules could pull boats.

Which type of river improvement was appropriate depended on who was using the river for what purpose. For example, a farmer who needed to ship goods to market would care about the navigability of the river at harvest time but might have little concern for the river's depth since the total amount of goods being shipped was relatively small. A merchant in a city at the mouth of the river would care about the difficulty of shipping goods upriver to prospective customers. Lumbermen cared primarily about the ability to ship lumber throughout the year, but this task could be accomplished with relatively shallow water levels; they were, correspondingly, common users of pond freshets. Coal transporters, because they envisioned shipping large quantities of a heavy commodity, demanded river improvements that exceeded the needs of previous users. They required deep canals that would allow large boats to travel up and down rivers for as much of the year as possible.

When boosters such as Josiah White turned their attention to improving the mid-Atlantic's rivers, they could draw on a long history of popular support for "internal improvements," as investments in canals, roads, and banks were called at the time. In 1762, Philadelphia merchants were already petitioning the provincial Assembly to investigate the west branch of the Susquehanna River to see if a connection could be established with the Ohio River. The American Philosophical Society recommended a canal linking the Schuylkill and Susquehanna Rivers as early as 1771. In 1789,

[handwritten note: emphasis on canals began, varied by state, fed. gov. didn't have much say]

prominent I *[handwritten: & at this time, cheaper to get coal shipped from Britain than transport it less than 100 mi. on land]* orris and David Rittenhouse formed the nland Navigation to encourage the imp re. Philadelphia printer, lawyer, and politician William Duane urged Pennsylvanians to demand that their elected representatives support internal improvements in a series of letters in his *Aurora* newspaper in 1810. These efforts bore fruit, as by 1810 Pennsylvania had invested more capital in internal improvements than any government other than France.[10]

New Yorkers were also active proponents of internal improvements. The Empire State had more miles of turnpike in 1808 than any other state. In 1815 the State Assembly authorized construction of the Erie Canal and petitioned Congress for financial support and land rights.[11] But not all Americans believed large expenditures for internal improvements were justified. Despite the attempts of some Virginia boosters to receive state assistance for the improvement of the James River, their projects were consistently rejected by the state government, which was controlled by eastern farming interests who saw little benefit in the project. Without a canal, the once-promising bituminous coalfields near Richmond languished. Differences in state policy meant that Pennsylvania anthracite would fuel America's early industrialization, not Virginia bituminous.[12]

The role of the federal government in stimulating transport infrastructure was relatively minor during this period. As evidenced in the heated debates between Federalists and Republicans over the charter of the First and Second Bank of the United States, many feared the expansion of centralized power. Projects that were sponsored by state and local governments generally received wider support than national endeavors. The federal government, therefore, was often limited to approving projects, commissioning reports, and constructing postal roads.[13]

What animated these early boosters? While many of them were merchants and businessmen who stood to profit from increased commercial activity, it would be too simplistic to see them as solely driven by the pursuit of profit. Political values mattered greatly. Many transport boosters hoped to create a strong and integrated nation out of a collection of young states, a particularly pressing task during the early years of the republic. They believed that improved infrastructure would allow for greater trade and communication among the young nation's scattered citizens, thereby binding them together. In seeking aid for the Erie Canal, New York commissioners noted: "[Canals] constitute improvements peculiarly fit for a republic. They contribute equally to the safety and opulence of the people, and the reputation and resources of the government. They are equally desirable in reference to the employments of peace, and the operations of war. In whatever light they are viewed, they seem to combine the substantial glories of the most splendid and permanent utility."[14] Internal improvements were not just a commercial activity for early boosters, they were nation-building.[15]

Early Efforts to Improve the Lehigh River

Giving speeches about the benefits of canals proved far easier than actually constructing them. The first decades after the nation's independence were littered with failed endeavors. The amount of labor and capital necessary to improve rivers was often significantly greater than boosters had anticipated. Benjamin Franklin, for example, was part of a group that led an eighteenth-century effort to improve navigation along the Schuylkill River, but financial limitations restricted their activities to removing a few particularly large rocks from the middle of the river. Nor is building a canal a straightforward task: it is not simply a ditch that can be dug once and used forever. Canals are complex technological systems requiring the creation of feeder reservoirs, locks, and dams, knowledge of underwater adhesives, and regular maintenance.[16]

After numerous false starts, rhetoric began to meet reality on the Lehigh and Schuylkill Rivers in the late 1810s. The two projects were conceived very differently. The Lehigh River was developed by a small group of men with only the coal trade in mind. As a result, they began with a cost-effective descending-only navigation scheme. The Schuylkill River's developers, by contrast, originally envisioned a conduit for agricultural and manufactured goods. They began with a full canal system, and their elaborate plans eventually cost more than four times the initial estimates. Despite their differences, both navigation systems served a similar end: creating a landscape of intensification in the mid-Atlantic that stimulated America's first fossil fuel energy transition.

The process of turning the Lehigh River into a coal highway took nearly thirty years. The anthracite resources of the Lehigh Valley had been identified as early as 1791. Philip Ginder, described in various accounts as either a farmer or a hunter, allegedly tripped over a black stone while walking on Sharp Mountain. Suspecting that it might be coal, Ginder took a sample to Jacob Weiss, an area merchant familiar with anthracite from the Wyoming Valley northwest of the Lehigh Valley. Weiss confirmed Ginder's guess and began to contact his wealthy friends in Philadelphia to mine and market the coal. Together with his cousin Michael Hillegas (former Treasurer of the United States), his brother-in-law Charles Cist (a publisher), his colleague John Nicholson (Comptroller-General of Pennsylvania and a land speculator), and others, Weiss created the Lehigh Coal Mine Company. The company bought 10,000 acres of land surrounding the discovery site and attempted to develop a coal trade.[17]

It turned out that while anthracite could be found in many places in the Lehigh Valley, Ginder had stumbled upon a particularly fortuitous site. At Sharp Mountain (soon renamed Summit Hill), the Mammoth Vein, a belt of anthracite coal fifty to a hundred feet thick, rose to the surface. To extract the coal, miners only needed to clear the top level of dirt and then break off pieces of coal with picks and shovels. Because the site was above water level, drainage was not an issue. As a result, coal could be extracted without expensive shafts, tunnels, or water pumping systems. Moreover, the vein clustered massive quantities of coal in one place. Even as late as 1983, the area was still being mined by a subsidiary of Bethlehem Steel: over its history, an estimated 250 million tons were removed from the site.[18] To put this extraordinary energy density into context, the Summit Hill mine contained the energy equivalent of all the wood in a forest twice the size of New Jersey.[19]

Mining coal at Summit Hill required little more than personal exertion, but getting that coal to market presented a much greater challenge. The mine was located nine miles from the Lehigh River, forcing the company to build a road between Summit Hill and Lausanne, the closest point on the river. The road allowed horse-drawn wagons to carry coal, but drivers charged as much as $4 per ton to work in such a remote location, and the steep grade prevented it from being used in icy weather.[20] The company also had to deal with the limitations of the Lehigh River. From Lausanne, the river fell more than 300 feet over the course of its 46-mile journey to Easton. Sharp rocks filled the river bed; ledges of slate hampered navigation at other points. Oftentimes, the river was so shallow that boats would scrape along the bottom. During times of high river flow, it was possible to ship goods on arks—simple flat wooden boats that would be dismantled and sold as lumber with the rest of the goods at the end of the journey—although this process always involved a risk of the primitive vessels sinking. At Easton, the Lehigh met the Delaware River, which flowed on to Philadelphia. Compared with the Lehigh, the Delaware was much easier to navigate, though it was also subject to flooding, droughts, and winter ice.

The crude road and unimproved river enabled the Lehigh Coal Mine Company to deliver small quantities of coal to Philadelphia, but not on a competitive basis. By 1800, the company was essentially moribund, unable to match the price and convenience of wood and imported coal. The company also lost much of its vitality after the 1793 yellow fever epidemic killed as much as 20 percent of Philadelphia's population. Combined with the generally poor business prospects for Philadelphia merchants as New York became the nation's premier port, the principals of the company lacked the resources to make further investments in coal. Several of the Lehigh Coal Mine Company's founders went bankrupt and died poor, including Cist, Hillegas, Morris, and Nicholson.[21]

Over the next two decades, a few other parties attempted to develop the Lehigh Valley's coal trade. In 1807, two men named Rowland and Butland obtained a lease from the dormant Lehigh Coal Mine Company to mine coal at Summit Hill but shipped only small quantities. The terms of the lease—a single ear of corn per year—reflected the low value of land in a remote location and the general lack of interest in anthracite. In 1813, Jacob Cist, son of Charles Cist and nephew of Jacob Weiss, led a renewed effort to introduce Lehigh coal to Philadelphia markets. During the War of 1812, Britain cut off coal shipments to American ports. Coal that had previously sold for thirty cents a bushel suddenly cost more than a dollar. The sense of crisis was so strong that a group of Philadelphia craftsmen worried about fuel shortages formed The Mutual Assistance Coal Company of Philadelphia for the Promotion of Manufactures to establish a more reliable coal supply. Cist, along with his partners Isaac Chapman, Charles Miner, and John Robinson, took advantage of this fuel crisis to seek to develop a permanent market in the Quaker City.[22]

Cist and his colleagues did relatively little to improve the transport infrastructure, and as a result, their efforts did not initiate an energy transition. In 1813, Cist sent coal in wagons from the Wyoming Valley to Philadelphia where it sold for a dollar a bushel. His shipment costs of twenty
dollars per ton, however, left little room for profit (a ton is equivalent to approximately twenty-eight bushels). In the following years, the partners used
the Lehigh Coal Mine Company's old road to send coal from the Summit
Hill mine to the banks of the Lehigh River, where it was shipped to market
via arks. Water-based transport cut their costs in half, but still gave them
little room to make money. While coal could be mined for a dollar a ton,
shipping expenditures were nearly ten times that amount at $9.50 a ton.[23]
In comparison, an 1816 report from the U.S. Senate noted that goods could
be delivered 3,000 miles from Europe for nine dollars a ton.[24] Only the ar-
tificially inflated prices of coal during the War of 1812 allowed Cist and his
partners to stay in business for a few years. Once the war ended and bituminous imports resumed, the market for anthracite collapsed.

Notwithstanding his business failures, Cist became anthracite's most
notable early booster. While he did not address the issue of transport, he
recognized the other major challenge facing anthracite boosters: the difficulty of lighting stone coal. Unlike bituminous coal, anthracite will not
ignite if simply tossed into a fire because it has relatively few volatile elements. To burn anthracite effectively, users needed to know how to kindle
the fire properly, arrange the stove or furnace to achieve the correct airflow,
choose the right-size pieces, and avoid overpoking. Consumers' lack of
experience using anthracite had led to some notable market failures in the
past. In 1806, for example, William Turnbull shipped a few arks of coal
down the Lehigh in an attempt to supply the coal needs of the Philadelphia
Water Works. When the Water Works could not get the coal to burn, they
dumped the remaining coal in the street to be used for gravel. Frederick
Fraily, a state senator from a district along the Schuylkill River, denied the
presence of coal in his region, stating that there was just a black rock that
would not burn.[25] To overcome these prejudices, Cist drew on the knowledge of farmers and craftsmen in the Wyoming Valley who had successfully
used anthracite for several decades and pursued a multipronged strategy to
spread these practices to Philadelphians. He hired Peter Yarrington, a Wyoming Valley blacksmith, to visit Philadelphia craftsmen and demonstrate

how to use anthracite. He published circulars in the city's newspapers describing the benefits of anthracite. He also engaged in scientific studies expanding the base of knowledge about stone coal, for example, by mapping coal seams and providing estimates of the available reserves. These efforts bore only minimal fruit for Cist's enterprises, in large part because high transport costs rendered anthracite more expensive than wood or imported coal. His labors nevertheless laid the groundwork for the future growth of anthracite consumption.[26]

Cist's most significant contribution, ironically, may have been introducing Josiah White to stone coal. White soon became one of the most significant figures in the development of the anthracite coal industry. He spearheaded the effort to improve the Lehigh River and took up the task of developing consumer markets. More than any other individual, White shaped the timing and patterns of the early anthracite coal trade.

Josiah White was born in Mount Holly, New Jersey, in 1781 to a devoutly Quaker family of moderate means. He received only a rudimentary education but possessed a remarkable degree of practical ability. After beginning an apprenticeship with a Philadelphia hardware store owner at the age of fifteen, he was running the store by himself two years later. Soon after, he opened his own store and had amassed a small fortune of $40,000 by the age of twenty-eight. He planned to retire as a gentleman farmer, but reconsidered after his young wife died. Grief-stricken, White spent the next two years traveling before returning to Philadelphia in 1809 and remarrying.

In 1810, White decided to enter the business world once again and purchased property rights along the Schuylkill River on the outskirts of Philadelphia. He demonstrated his considerable mechanical aptitude by designing the first dam for a river that size in America. His angled dam allowed him to generate power from the river and charge tolls for passage.[27] Like many of his countrymen, White was motivated both by financial opportunity and civic responsibility with his river improvements: "If I succeeded," he wrote in his memoirs, "it would lead to a similar improvement in the interior of Pennsylvania which would be of great public good. While the water power & the Falls would make it a profitable investment to me & fully as well as to invest my capital elsewhere."[28]

White established two factories on the property to manufacture iron nails and wire. His innovative manufacturing practices soon drew the interest of

Josiah White. (Hagley Museum and Library)

Erskine Hazard, who became his partner in 1811.[29] It was at the factories that White and Hazard first encountered anthracite coal, and their experience reflects the general difficulty most people found during their initial attempts to use the fuel. After purchasing a small quantity of anthracite, White and his workmen tried to ignite the coal for several hours before giving up in frustration. They shut the furnace door and left the factory. A worker who forgot his coat returned thirty minutes later and was shocked to find the furnace door glowing with heat. They had accidentally discovered the secret to burning anthracite—the air had to flow through the coal rather than over it. With the anthracite lit, the men rushed back to the factory and were able to make four runs of iron wire from the single batch of coal. From this point forward, Josiah White became a committed advocate of anthracite; he estimated that using it instead of bituminous cut his production costs by two-thirds because the higher heat levels required only a quarter of the fuel and half the labor.[30]

Improving the Lehigh River

Yet White and Hazard's future was not to be in iron. In April 1815, a fire destroyed their factories. Deep in debt, the men turned their attention from using coal to supplying it. Unlike earlier anthracite pioneers, they focused immediately on transport. They looked first to the Schuylkill River, where White's dam had already demonstrated his ability to transform a natural waterway. At the time, several other parties were interested in improving the Schuylkill River, inspired by the potential of a lucrative trade between Philadelphia and the rich agricultural lands northwest of the city. White and Hazard, however, fixated on the Schuylkill Valley's outcroppings of coal. Though the existing coal trade was negligible, they believed it could be increased dramatically.

White and Hazard were not able to gain control over the development of the Schuylkill River. Despite their repeated petitions to the Pennsylvania legislature requesting a corporate charter to improve the river, boatmen reacted negatively to their proposals. They pointed out that White charged the maximum allowable toll at his dam and feared that he would do the same along the entire length of the river. When the legislature authorized a private company to build a canal along the length of the Schuylkill River in 1815, White was denied active management of the company. Even though he purchased the maximum allowable number of shares, he was relegated to an oversight role at the first meeting of the board of directors. He offered several proposals to the directors about designing the canal to be an effective conduit for coal, emphasizing the importance of immediate steps to improve downward navigation, but his ideas were rejected. The directors opted for a smaller canal supporting boats traveling in both directions that would favor farmers and manufacturers. The Schuylkill Canal was expected to be a conduit for the organic energy regime.[31]

Shut out of active management of the Schuylkill Canal, White is reported to have exclaimed in a rage: "This ends our using the Schuylkill! I'll go to another region! The . . . Lehigh . . . I'll make the Lehigh a rival to the Schuylkill."[32] Perhaps apocryphal, the quotation nevertheless captures a decisive switch in White and Hazard's strategy. Still in dire financial straits in December 1817, White rented a horse and borrowed surveying equipment so that he could investigate the Lehigh River and the region's coal resources. George Hauto, a flamboyant man who often visited White and Hazard to discuss engineering matters, joined him. White returned convinced that he could make the necessary improvements, and he formed a partnership with Hazard and Hauto.

Few people shared White's confidence, a fact that worked both for and against the partners. Widespread skepticism made obtaining a corporate charter much easier. At the time, corporate charters had to be approved by a vote of the state legislature, making them rare and valuable. Hauto went before the legislature asking for extensive rights to the river including the authority to ship and mine coal, charge tolls, and obtain triple indemnities against any party that damaged the canal. The charter was granted without much debate, largely because everyone expected the partners to fail. According to White's recollection, there had been at least seven charters granted to improve the Lehigh over the last half-century, and none had succeeded. One legislator reportedly exclaimed that the men had been "given permission to ruin themselves." Though the broad corporate privileges, in particular the right to ship and mine coal, would later be hotly contested, the enterprise appeared so dubious at the time that it hardly seemed worth debating. The partners were also able to lease the old Lehigh Coal Mine

Company's properties easily as no other parties were interested in developing them.[33]

Low expectations may have been a political asset, but they were also a financial liability. The lack of faith in White's endeavor made it much more difficult to raise capital. In his memoirs, he described how prominent Philadelphians received his proposal: some politely refused while others rudely picked up a newspaper to signal the end of the discussion. To make their project more attractive, the partners pursued several strategies, including hiring independent engineers to survey the lands and evaluate the proposal, splitting the company into coal mining and transportation branches, and agreeing that investors would receive dividends before the partners. White and Hazard had also expected Hauto to help them raise money from his wealthy friends in New York and Baltimore. Their faith was not rewarded; the two eventually forced him out of the partnership after learning that Hauto was widely considered a confidence man.[34]

White and Hazard's struggle to attract investors was not a symptom of a broader social resistance to transport infrastructure. Just two years earlier, the Schuylkill Navigation Company had quickly raised $500,000. Instead, potential investors worried about the challenge of improving the Lehigh River and doubted the market for anthracite. The sparsely populated Lehigh Valley also offered fewer local investors compared with the more densely settled Schuylkill region. After many weeks of promoting the project, White and Hazard got financial backing from John Stoddart, a successful land speculator and an owner of lumber lands in the Lehigh Valley. Stoddart was widely respected in Philadelphia financial circles, and his outlay convinced several others to join in, thereby providing the necessary capital for what would become the Lehigh Coal & Navigation Company.[35]

With capital, a corporate charter, and the rights to coal properties in the Lehigh Valley, White and Hazard turned their attention to improving the river and road from Summit Hill. At this point, White's practical mind proved to be a great advantage. Because there was little incentive to ship goods upriver to the relatively few residents of the upper Lehigh Valley, they devoted their attention to creating a descending-only navigation system. Their primary engineering strategy was to create a navigable channel in the middle of the river for wooden arks that would carry coal. In 1818, White and thirteen workers started removing protruding rocks from the middle of the river near Lausanne and building stone walls at shallow points. By the end of the year, there were over three hundred men working on the river, a group that White estimated to be the largest force engaged in a public improvement project in Pennsylvania at the time.[36]

When surveying the Lehigh River, local residents told White that the water never dropped below a certain level. He quickly discovered the river was more variable than expected: a drought the next year lowered the water level a foot below this line. In response, White turned to the system of pond freshets to ensure adequate water depth for shipping. But while the artificial dams used by lumbermen were often temporary, White needed a more permanent system that could be used again and again. To this end, he developed an innovative lock mechanism that made it simple to trap and release water. Using hydrostatic pressure, a gate could be opened by pressing a lever that released a wave of high water capable of carrying several arks to the next lock. When the last boatman passed, he could press the lever again to close the gate and build up a new pool of water. If a curious passerby asked what the men were building, they responded that the gates were "bear traps," an early form of trade secrecy. The name stuck, and White filed for a patent on his design in December of 1819. By the next year, enough bear trap locks were complete that the company could begin to make regular coal shipments to Philadelphia.[37]

The partners also found it essential to improve the road from Summit Hill to Lausanne. White re-graded the road so that it descended its entire length without a single rise, claiming that this was the longest such road in America at the time.[38] In addition, he redesigned the wheels of the wagons used to carry the coal, giving them varied widths and coating them with iron. Thus equipped, the wagon wheels flattened and improved the road over time rather than creating ruts. These changes to the road allowed White to lower the cost of transporting coal from the mines to the river from Cist and Chapman's four dollars per ton to 62.5 cents by the early 1820s.[39] In addition, White and Hazard turned the fledgling community of Mauch Chunk, just north of Lausanne, into a company town and the center of the Lehigh Valley's coal trade.

Josiah White's vision and management were essential to the success of the enterprise, but he did not transform the Lehigh Valley himself. Hundreds of hard-working men gave their sweat, blood, and on occasion, lives

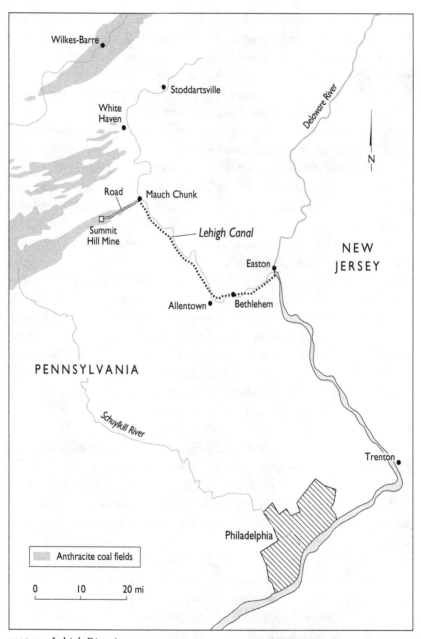

MAP 1.1. Lehigh River improvements.

...ams a reality. And while their efforts would help pio-
...energy regime, their energy was drawn from organic
...ools were shovels, picks, wheelbarrows, and most important, human muscle. To create the bear trap locks, the men spent several hours a day up to their waists in water, with a hole cut in the toe of their boots so that the water would drain out when they stepped out of the river. The river banks were largely unsettled, so White constructed a series of flat boats that served as a floating camp for the workers. After completing a given section of the river, they floated the boats down river a little way, anchored, and began working again. When primitive mattresses were purchased a few years later, workers considered it a major upgrade in living conditions.[40]

Work relations seem to have been relatively smooth, as there were no reported strikes. White adopted the dress of the workers (red flannel shirt, buckskin coated pants, boots with holes in the toe) and worked in the river with the men. The managers nevertheless took several precautions that indicate separations between themselves and the workers. They made clear, for example, that all wage checks had to be signed by at least two of them, so that a group of workers could not accost one of the managers in the forest and force him to sign a check. In addition, the managers instilled "cob" laws borrowed from sailing culture. Workers who took more food than they could eat, ran "in any way uncivel" to their meals, or misbehaved in other ways, were to be cobed, or spanked with a paddle.[41]

We do not know much about the laborers themselves. Commentators at the time were quick to distinguish the thrifty, hard-working Yankee or German laborers from the dirty, drinking Irish hands, a common trope of the mid-nineteenth century. For instance, Anne Royall, a traveler who recorded her journeys, wrote: "But the Teagues, poor fellows, they are strung along the canal, scarcely alive, stupid from drink . . . I have been informed that they generally live about 18 months after coming to this country, and work and drink most of the time. They care little about eating, provided they get whiskey."[42] Without doubt these sentiments say more about nineteenth-century attitudes than they do about the workers themselves, who labored under difficult circumstances and faced continual danger from accidents, the elements, and disease. Canal work was known at the time as the "roughest of rough labour" and was therefore "performed by the lowest of the low."

Its characteristics were "strenuous, body-sapping work, crude, deleterious conditions, ubiquitous disease, the lurking spectre of death."[43] The demands for personal exertion in the organic energy regime could come at great cost to the bodies of workers.

By the fall of 1820, the river was sufficiently improved that the company could send its first 365 tons of coal to market. Eight of eleven bear trap locks had been completed along with several wing-dams and miles of stone walls enabling boatmen to pilot rough wooden arks piled with coal down the river. A few arks were joined together with chains and steered down the river with long wooden oars. Once the boatmen arrived in Philadelphia, they broke up the arks to be sold as lumber. They kept the iron nails and walked back up to the Lehigh Valley to repeat the journey. As the practice became more established, local inns began to offer free use of their wagons to transport the men in exchange for their patronage.

The accomplishment of White, Hazard, and their workers during these years is quite extraordinary, especially in comparison with the history of other canal projects during this era. By creating a descending-only navigation system, they were able to begin shipping coal at competitive prices within a couple years and for less than $200,000 in sunk costs. The full canal system along the Schuylkill River, by contrast, would take ten years and more than two million dollars to complete. White's practical mind, technical innovation, and determination made the Lehigh River the nation's first coal highway.

Organic Dreams and Mineral Realities on the Schuylkill River

Improvements on the Schuylkill River were driven by a different set of goals than White's vision of a descending-only navigation system on the Lehigh. The Schuylkill Navigation Company was chartered with the aim of establishing trade relationships between Philadelphia and the rich agricultural regions of central Pennsylvania: it was designed to serve the needs of those living in an organic energy regime. Much of its initial funding came from local farmers buying shares in the company, and it was planned from the beginning as a two-way navigation system. A brief history of the Schuylkill

Canal highlights a number of similarities and differences in the ways early-nineteenth-century Americans approached river improvements.

The development of closer trade relationships with central Pennsylvania was particularly important to Philadelphia merchants because many feared losing the state's lucrative grain trade to Baltimore. Philadelphians were right to worry; Baltimore had grown from a small port to a major wheat exporter in the decades surrounding the turn of the nineteenth century. Much of this wheat was grown in central Pennsylvania and then shipped over roads or down the Susquehanna River to the Chesapeake Bay. Philadelphia merchants felt entitled to the benefits of this wheat trade, but for many central Pennsylvania farmers, cheap transport outweighed state loyalty. Improving the Schuylkill River, therefore, offered a mechanism for Philadelphia boosters to bind central Pennsylvania to what they considered its "natural" metropole.[44] Of course, there was very little natural about where wheat was transported. Commodity flows reflect human decisions about political boundaries, trade policies, and infrastructure investments.[45]

The charter of the Schuylkill Navigation Company also reflected the influence of republican values and the desire of many politicians to balance public and private interests. Whereas White and his partners were able to get a very generous corporate charter because they were expected to fail, politicians debated the charter for the Schuylkill Canal much more vigorously because success seemed likely. Each share in the company cost fifty dollars but could be purchased with a deposit of only five dollars, making it accessible to many farmers. Investors were limited to a maximum of twenty shares per person, preventing any single individual from gaining disproportionate control. Moreover, each region along the canal was given the right to purchase a set number shares, ensuring a geographic spread of ownership. This careful balance between corporate privilege and the broader public good meant that the first third of the nineteenth century saw the most widespread patterns of stock ownership seen in the antebellum era.[46] The company was able to quickly raise $500,000 in 1815, the route was surveyed in 1816, and construction began that year on a canal three feet deep intended to support boats carrying twenty-five tons of goods.[47]

With the exception of White and Hazard's petitions before they turned to the Lehigh Valley, the coal trade was an afterthought during the initial stages of the Schuylkill Canal: in 1817, the company's directors thought it optimistic that there could be ten thousand tons of coal shipments per year.[48] Agricultural goods, lumber, and manufactured products were the imagined objects of trade. But within a few short years, the company's directors began to realize that coal would be a much more important part of the trade than they had originally planned. They also discovered that construction was far more expensive than their initial estimates. By 1821, the company was facing bankruptcy. It was rescued by a loan of several hundred thousand dollars from Stephen Girard, a Philadelphia land speculator who was widely believed to be America's richest man. Reflecting the view that canals were intended to achieve the general good, Girard eventually donated most of his estate, including his holdings in the Schuylkill Navigation Company, to the city of Philadelphia.[49]

Raising more money to keep the project going, however, required the directors of the canal company to gain approval from the state legislature to amend their charter to authorize the sale of additional shares. Because it was now recognized that coal would be an important article of trade along the canal, the Pennsylvania Assembly insisted that in return for the privilege of raising more money, the canal company cede its right to mine coal. This decision further reflected the attempt to make compromises between those who wished to expand the economy and those who feared the spread of corporate power. It would also have important implications for the development of the Schuylkill Valley: a single large corporation did not dominate the mining of coal in the region during the antebellum period. In the Lehigh Valley, by contrast, the Lehigh Coal & Navigation Company controlled both the production and the transport of anthracite because its charter gave it the right to perform both functions. By limiting corporate privileges, the Pennsylvania Assembly reduced the influence of monopoly power in the Schuylkill Valley.

The canal was finally completed in 1825, after nearly a decade of construction and at a cost of more than two million dollars. This was an incredible sum of money, making the company one of the most heavily capitalized enterprises in America at the time.[50] It immediately became a widely used transport network. While large quantities of agricultural goods were shipped along its length, anthracite quickly became the main article of trade. In 1830, farmers sent roughly 12,000 tons of grain and flour but boatmen delivered nearly 90,000 tons of coal to market. By 1840, over 450,000 tons of coal were transported, comprising three-quarters of the total tonnage hauled along the river that year.[51] The organic energy flows imagined at the time of incorporation became a sideline to the main activity of shipping mineral energy. The Schuylkill had joined the Lehigh as a coal highway.

Creating a Market for Anthracite Coal

The ability to transport coal, first along the Lehigh and then along the Schuylkill, created a new problem for boosters: convincing users to buy it. Residents of Philadelphia and New York were already well supplied with organic energy sources and small amounts of imported bituminous coal. Despite occasional shortages of coal imports or firewood, there was little demand for anthracite coal. White and Hazard learned this the hard way: their corporate history notes that the first 365 tons of anthracite coal delivered in 1820 were sold "with difficulty."[52] The next year they shipped 1073 tons, but "still the consumption of families . . . was insufficient to take this small quantity [and] the balance [was] sold to factories."[53] Yet boosters who had invested large sums in canals could not afford to sit by and let meager demand undermine their efforts. They needed to build demand if they were to pay off debts and return dividends to investors. The sunk costs of transport systems encouraged human agents to intensify demand for mineral energy.

Most consumers in 1820 disregarded anthracite coal because it was more expensive and difficult to use than its alternatives. The construction of canals addressed the first problem. By lowering the transport costs, improved waterways allowed merchants to sell anthracite at ever-decreasing prices: one ton of Lehigh coal purchased wholesale in Philadelphia decreased from $8.40 in 1820 to $6.50 in 1830, a price that rendered it cheaper than imported bituminous coal or firewood.[54] However, boosters still needed to address the second challenge: the inconvenience of its use. Converting to any new fuel is a challenge, requiring consumers to invest in new technologies, develop relationships with new suppliers, and learn new techniques. These challenges were particularly acute for anthracite coal because it was so hard to ignite.

Craftsmen were the first to use anthracite coal in Philadelphia, particularly during the War of 1812, but they were not the primary target for anthracite boosters in the 1820s. A market with much more potential for growth existed: homes. Urban residents required massive quantities of firewood each year to meet their heating and cooking needs. Contemporaries reported widely varying consumption levels at the time: a poor family in Philadelphia needed at least two and a half cords of wood each winter according to a philanthropic organization in 1831 (a cord is a stack of wood eight feet long, four feet high, and four feet wide). Families with larger households and greater means used much more. One wealthy writer in the early 1830s reported burning twenty-four cords of wood a winter. On average, eight cords of wood for the year likely represented a reasonable expectation for a family's needs. As the typical Philadelphia household held roughly six people, this works out to a little more than a cord of wood per person per year.[55]

If we extrapolate these fuel requirements to the population of Philadelphia and its surrounding county (137,097 in 1820), we can estimate that residents consumed 175,000 cords of wood in 1820 alone to heat their homes and cook their food. An 1821 analysis claimed that Philadelphia and New York City together burned 600,000 cords of wood; assuming slightly more than half of this total was consumed in New York City, approximately 100,000 additional cords of wood were used by Philadelphia's Industries.[56] By this time, many of the trees immediately surrounding Philadelphia had been felled, and the supply was coming from forests along the Delaware, Schuylkill, and Lehigh Rivers. As a result, the cost of firewood nearly tripled over the latter half of the eighteenth century, rising at a greater rate than food, clothing, or housing. Commentators began to wonder whether the cost of firewood would limit the growth of eastern seaboard cities.[57] The mid-Atlantic's reliance on wood for home heating was subject to the negative feedbacks of an organic energy regime.

The huge size of the market for firewood attracted the interest of anthracite boosters for obvious reasons. If they could convince a sizable percentage of the population to use anthracite in their homes, their challenge would not be in selling 365 tons, but rather in supplying enough coal to meet the needs of hundreds of thousands of urban residents. Articles promoting the use of anthracite argued that it would take about one ton of coal per month during the six cold months of the year to keep a family warm, or roughly one ton per person per winter. Here was a sizable market: one investor's pamphlet noted that if a quarter of the wood consumption of the eastern seaboard were displaced by anthracite, the company could generate profits of $250,000 annually.[58]

Of course, the difficulty of burning anthracite stood in the way of boosters' ambitions. The challenge is well documented by an 1827 guide for servants. The author devoted fifteen pages to the process of using anthracite for home heating, covering everything from buying coal, breaking it, starting a fire, and keeping it going. As the author prefaced his instructions: "Very few servants at first understand the method of kindling and continuing a fire of Lehigh coal, many will never learn, and many more . . . make but a bungling piece of work of it . . . it must be granted that a knowledge of how to make a Lehigh coal fire, when it is becoming so common in this country, is quite an acquisition." The text includes such advice as breaking the coal into the right-size pieces ("about as large as your fist, if your hand is rather a small one"), using the right kindling ("charcoal, unless dry hickory be preferred"), keeping the fire going ("judicious use of the poker is essential to the well-being of an anthracite fire"), as well as an analysis of the relative merits of anthracite ("I place *cleanliness* at the top of its virtues,—cleanliness as to smoke, dust, and smell").[59] In addition to the challenge of igniting anthracite, consumers also had to invest in specially designed stoves or grates, a significant upfront cost investment. An anthracite fire also meant abandoning the pleasant flame of an open hearth, thereby causing many to object on aesthetic grounds.

Anthracite boosters, particularly the owners and operators of transport companies, adopted several strategies to counter these objections. While Josiah White was directing the company's operations in the Lehigh Valley from Mauch Chunk, he had his wife keep an anthracite fire constantly burning in their Philadelphia home to demonstrate the proper techniques to prospective customers.[60] Other boosters joined the effort as well. Scientists performed experiments detailing the superior heating qualities of anthracite.[61] The Fuel Savings Society, a philanthropic organization concerned with the high cost of heating in Philadelphia, contracted with the Steinhaur & Kisterbock company to build stoves cheap enough that poor families could adopt anthracite.[62] This period saw extensive experiments with stove design, many of which were constructed to burn anthracite. Between 1815 and 1839, there were 329 patents issued for new stove models, representing nearly 4 percent of the Patent Office's awards.[63]

Though it is common to think of anthracite as an undifferentiated product, not all coal was the same. Just as American capitalists took natural products with widely varying characteristics—like cotton, wheat, and animals—and created simplifying classification systems to facilitate their sale in impersonal markets, anthracite boosters sought to provide consumers with a regularized product.[64] Each layer of coal was slightly different due to a combination of distinct geological forces and erosion patterns. The particular folding patterns of the mountains meant that the southeast edges of a coalfield typically produced softer coal with less carbon than the northwest edges. Coal mined at various locations and depths burned slightly differently, and merchants soon began to distinguish between "red ash" and "white ash" coals based on the residue each left after burning. Red ash coals generally ignited more easily than white ash coals and were often preferred for home heating. The preparation of coal also mattered. Anthracite coal burns much more readily when placed in a stove or furnace with similar-size chunks—egg-size pieces being optimal for home use. If the pieces of slate often found mixed with anthracite were not removed, consumers would have a harder time burning the coal. And if coal was stored for long periods of time exposed to the rain, its quality might diminish as well. Rendering the complexities of the natural world into a few standardized grades was a challenge for the fossil fuel industry as well as farmers. Anthracite merchants simplified coal's complexity by selling it in a few standard sizes—pea, stove, chestnut, egg, and lump—and categories—such as Schuylkill red-ash or Lehigh white-ash.[65] By teaching consumers to manage an anthracite fire, performing research to demonstrate its superiority, designing stoves, and creating standardized products, boosters manufactured demand for a product most mid-Atlantic residents initially ignored.

Early Steps into the Mineral Energy Regime

By the early 1830s, anthracite boosters had begun to initiate an energy transition in Philadelphia and New York City. Coal shipments along all canals grew from just under 35,000 tons in 1825 to nearly 175,000 tons in 1830 to over half a million by 1835.[66] Although reliable data on consumption at a household level are notoriously rare for this period, available evidence reveals that the use of anthracite in home heating increased rapidly and absorbed a large share of this total. In 1830, Philadelphians spent $308,400 for coal, a figure that indicates the purchase of approximately 35,000 tons of anthracite. If a little more than half of this anthracite was for home heating, it suggests that roughly 10 percent of the population had converted to anthracite over the previous decade.[67] Residents of New York City showed a similar pattern. The city was sufficiently dependent on anthracite for home heating that market shortages during the particularly cold winter of 1831–1832 led to widespread panic.[68] In 1832, New Yorkers imported over fifty thousand tons of anthracite coal. Assuming that it was used by both homeowners and business enterprises, about 10 percent of New York's population was using anthracite for home heating.[69] In addition, eastern seaboard cities like Boston and Providence were importing anthracite for home heating purposes by the 1830s.[70]

Boosters also turned their attention to the use of anthracite by businesses, both as a direct source of heat and to power steam engines. Many enterprises required a source of heat, if only to keep their work environments warm. Even the Lowell textile mills, the quintessential industry based on waterpower, were importing over seven thousand tons of anthracite a year by 1833 for heating purposes.[71] Other factories required large amounts of direct heat for their operations. Bakers, brewers, distillers, brick-makers, sugar refiners, tanners, bleachers, salt-makers, metal-workers, and more all required heat to make a finished product. Boosters worked with these enterprises to modify equipment to withstand the heat of an anthracite fire and to separate the gas emissions from edible goods to ensure they did not taste of sulfur or soot. Even hat-makers were using anthracite to heat the pots of water necessary for shaping materials in the early 1830s, according to news reports.[72] As anthracite coal was the cheapest heating fuel available in Philadelphia and New York by the 1830s, it was likely that many of these businesses had converted to coal for their heating needs.

The other major use of anthracite by manufacturing enterprises was in steam engines that could supply power on shop floors. In 1820, few steam engines were operating in America: it has been estimated that there were as many as one hundred water wheels for each steam engine at the time.[73] Anthracite did not work immediately for the small number that were in operation: the coal burned with a high heat and a low flame that often melted the walls of the boiler. After numerous experiments, the first reported successful application of anthracite in a steam engine in the United States occurred in 1825 at the Phoenix Nail Works of Jonah and George Thompson, about twenty miles outside Philadelphia, near the Schuylkill River.[74]

With many of the technical problems addressed, Philadelphia soon became the nation's leading site of steam engine use. In 1831, a newspaper reported between sixty and eighty steam engines in Philadelphia were burning anthracite, with more operating in New York City and on steamboats.[75] According to trade journals, nearly all of the steam engines in Philadelphia were fueled with anthracite.[76] By 1838, Philadelphia County led the nation in the use of steam engines and the various applications to which they were applied. According to a report prepared by U.S. Treasury Secretary Levi Woodbury, almost 10 percent of the stationary steam engines in the United States (178 of 1,860) were located in Philadelphia.[77]

Urban consumers benefited from a new source of cheaper energy, particularly one that burned cleanly; the environment of the rural sites of production did not. Many of the first coal deposits to be exploited were located in river valleys where thousands of years of erosion had exposed anthracite seams to the surface. At these sites, miners could use pickaxes and shovels to gather anthracite. But when they removed the coal, they also removed large quantities of rocks and dirt, along with noxious pollutants that had previously been trapped underground. Rain and the force of gravity swept much of this debris into the region's rivers, thereby introducing new chemicals into the ecosystems and polluting sources of drinking water. A pattern had begun that would be repeated throughout history: the gains of urban consumers came at the expense of environments in which energy resources were produced.[78]

The initial consumption of anthracite during the 1820s marked a beginning foray into a mineral energy regime. It should be clear, however, that organic energy sources still predominated. If one in ten homes were heated with anthracite, the other nine relied on firewood. Anthracite boosters considered winning a quarter of the share of the wood heating market to be an ambitious goal.[79] For every enterprise using a steam engine or anthracite stoves, many more relied on falling water and wood. But anthracite consumption was growing quickly, and the mineral energy regime had begun to take root in the mid-Atlantic.

Expanding the Canal Network

Consumers' increasing demand for anthracite encouraged investors to expand the fuel's transport network. Buoyed by the success of Josiah White and others in establishing new markets for anthracite, boosters enlarged existing systems and built several new canals in the 1820s and 1830s to bring anthracite to eastern seaboard markets. Supply began to respond to demand in a synergistic cycle.

The Lehigh Coal & Navigation Company quickly found that its road and descending-only navigation system could not handle the rising pace of anthracite shipments. Only five years after its initial deliveries to Philadelphia, the company had already crossed the threshold of 28,000 tons a year. In 1827, to facilitate bringing coal from the Summit Hill mine to the Lehigh River, White installed railroad tracks along the nine-mile road. Because the road descended with no elevation gains, these tracks allowed railroad cars filled with coal to travel using the free energy of gravity. Once the coal was unloaded at Mauch Chunk, mules hauled the empty wagons back to the mines, completing two trips in a typical day. This was the longest railroad in America at the time, and it saved two-thirds of the cost of shipping coal from mine to river. The railroad also became a tourist attraction and an early inspiration for roller coasters: open-top cars designed for passengers achieved speeds up to thirty miles an hour on the twenty-minute descent, an exhilarating experience for those who rarely experienced movement faster than a horse's gallop.[80]

The same year, the company also decided to replace its descending-only navigation system of bear trap locks with a full canal system. Wood limitations shaped this decision. At first, disposable arks were a convenient way of shipping both coal and lumber to Philadelphia and achieving dual profits. But increased shipments strained the lumber capacity of the Lehigh Valley. In 1827, the company estimated that the total number of arks needed to transport its coal would have measured over fifteen miles if they were laid end-to-end, and the forests above Mauch Chunk were being rapidly depleted. The output of the organic energy regime could not keep pace with the exponential expansion of the mineral energy regime. Though the company likely did not know it at the time, this deforestation also reduced the ability of the valley's soils to retain water, thereby exacerbating the damage of floods in future years.[81] What the company did realize was that a canal system would allow the use of boats that were not disposable and relieve the bottleneck. As White was always a strong booster for growth, he insisted on an extremely ambitious plan. He opted for a canal wide and deep enough to allow ocean-going steam vessels to travel to Mauch Chunk and designed locks big enough to allow two boats to enter at a single time. The system, initiated in 1827 and completed in 1829, had the capacity to ship more than two and a half million tons of coal a year.[82] At the time, this seemed like an impossibly high number, although within another four decades, the anthracite shipments from the Lehigh Valley exceeded this amount.[83]

The 1820s and 1830s also witnessed a flurry of new canal developments. The Wurtz brothers of Philadelphia pioneered the third major canal from the coal regions to the eastern seaboard: the Delaware & Hudson Canal. This system connected the northern coalfields of the Wyoming Valley with the Hudson River north of New York City via a 60-mile canal along the Lackawaxen River. When the company's shares first went on the market in 1825, it was considered a hot investment opportunity: the entire $1.5 million capitalization was sold out by two in the afternoon.[84] Work began on the canal that summer; the first canal boats crossed it in February of 1829.[85] Once the canal boats reached the Hudson River near Kingston, they could easily float the remaining distance to New York City, giving the city its first direct outlet to the coal regions.

The New York market in the 1830s was also served by two canals traversing New Jersey. In 1824, the Morris Canal Company was chartered to cross the mountainous northern part of the state, thereby connecting Easton with the New York harbor at Jersey City. As with the Delaware & Hudson Canal, the shares sold immediately in a speculative craze. But construction did not proceed smoothly. The company had trouble installing inclined planes and steel hoisting ropes at the western end of the canal. In addition, the small capacity of the boats limited the amount of traffic along the line when it was opened in 1831. But even though the company never

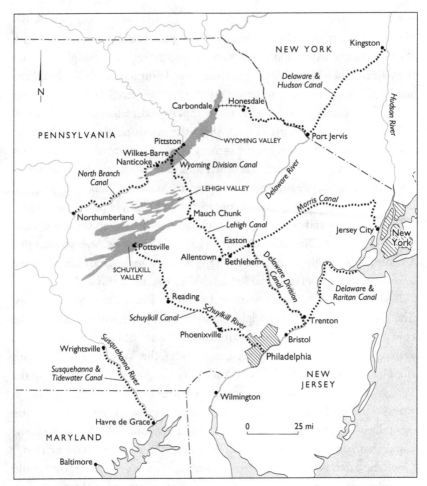

MAP 1.2. Anthracite canal network, ca. 1843.

achieved the financial results its investors had anticipated, it stimulated
the development of local industries in the mineral-rich regions along its
path by bringing coal to manufacturers and providing cheap transport
for their products.[86] The Delaware & Raritan, New Jersey's second coal
canal, was far more successful. Begun in 1830 and completed in 1834,
the canal allowed coal boats to travel from Trenton, New Jersey, to New
Brunswick, where the Raritan River led to the New York harbor. Due

to the relatively flat terrain, few locks were needed and large quantities of coal were soon being shipped along its length. In some cases, coal from the Lehigh or Schuylkill Valleys was sent directly to New York along the Delaware & Raritan Canal, bypassing Philadelphia's wharves altogether. By 1860, this route shipped more than a million tons of coal annually.[87]

Three other Pennsylvania canals contributed to the coal trade. In 1827, the state authorized the construction of the Delaware Division Canal between Easton and Bristol. Though the Delaware River was often navigable in its natural state, it did not always have sufficient water depth for heavy boats. Completed in 1833, the canal extended the shipping season and permitted larger boats to travel the river. Improvements to the upper Susquehanna River connected the Wyoming Valley to Harrisburg and Baltimore. As part of its grand effort to bind the commonwealth together with a network of canals, the state of Pennsylvania authorized the construction of the North Branch Canal in 1828; it was completed in 1831 between Northumberland and the Nanticoke Dam, fifty-five miles upriver. The Wyoming Division extended this canal for another seventeen miles above this point upon its completion in 1834. Finally, the Susquehanna & Tidewater Canal was opened in 1840, making it easier for boats to travel along the rapidly descending lower Susquehanna River.[88]

All these canals were built with the coal trade in mind. Their pioneers also shared geographic assumptions about where coal would travel. Each line made it possible for coal to flow out of the anthracite regions to cities near the eastern seaboard. Philadelphia and New York City, and to a lesser extent Baltimore, Trenton, Wilmington, Easton, Albany, Providence, and Boston were the intended markets. The choice of eastern seaboard cities as termini for the canals made sense at the time—after all, they were the sites where consumers were concentrated. But over time, the flow of coal to these points created further divisions between city and country. The mineral abundance of the anthracite regions helped revolutionize urban life by supporting large populations and extensive industrial growth. The one-directional nature of these energy flows was matched by a corresponding imbalance in the benefits accrued from the anthracite trade. Eastern seaboard cities would eventually receive the lion's share of benefits resulting from the anthracite

Coal boats being weighed on the Lehigh Canal. (*Harper's Weekly* 17, no. 6 [1873], Harvard University, Widener Library, P 207.6 F)

trade while the towns and environment of the anthracite regions bore most of the costs. Canals facilitated the sacrifice of the anthracite regions to supply the desires of distant consumers.

Canals supplied the mid-Atlantic with mineral energy, but as with mining coal, their success relied on the powers of the organic energy regime. Humans and animals labored long and hard to haul boats up and down the region's improved waterways. Because of the multiple jobs involved in operating a canal boat—loading and unloading coal, tending mules, preparing meals, steering the boat—the labor of an entire family was often required. A typical journey started near the mines with the boat filled to capacity. Each day's work began as early as four in the morning, when the mule driver, often a boy as young as ten, prepared the animals for the day's walk. After breakfast, the mules were hitched to the boat and driven along the canal's towpath while the boatman steered. They traveled until arriving at a lock, where they paid a toll to the lock attendant and continued their journey until sunset, before rising early the next morning to set off again. Once they reached their terminus—often a wharf in Philadelphia or the New York harbor—they unloaded their coal. After taking on more food for humans and animals, the journey was repeated in reverse. If lucky, they picked up cargo, such as manufactured or imported goods, to deliver to a point upriver. Otherwise, they hauled their empty boats back to the mines. Under good conditions, a canal boat might travel between twenty and thirty miles in a day.[89]

The millions of dollars spent on coal canals and the countless days of hard labor shipping anthracite demonstrate the critical nature of transport infrastructure in the development of America's first fossil fuel energy transition. Financially, the investments in the transport of coal far exceeded the investments in coal mining. By 1834, for example, over $9,750,000 was invested in transport infrastructure in the anthracite regions while only $1,270,280 was devoted to the mines themselves (and much of this capital was spent on boats and wagons).[90] Mining coal was physically demanding labor, but there were few barriers to extracting it from the ground, particularly in the early years of surface mining. Getting coal to market, in contrast, was difficult and expensive. Transport improvements drove the energy transition to anthracite.

By the middle of the 1830s, canals had dramatically altered the rivers of the mid-Atlantic. Artificial waterways funneled, regulated, and augmented the flow of the region's rivers to suit the needs of human commerce. Storage reservoirs minimized seasonal differences in water flow; dams turned dangerous rapids into smooth stretches of water punctuated by controlled descents in locks; and towpaths traversed by mules and boys replaced currents as the main source of forward motion. While nature was not controlled—years of drought could lower total shipments and heavy rains could produce devastating floods—these transformations of the landscape were sufficient to create new patterns of commodity flows. The mineral resources of the Schuylkill, Lehigh, and Wyoming Valleys, long considered too inconvenient or expensive to use outside of the region, now kept the residents of eastern seaboard cities warm and powered their factories. The mid-Atlantic's rivers had been turned into coal highways. Crucially, these transport networks were not passive conduits. The sunk costs invested in these systems exerted a steady pressure on their operators to increase demand for anthracite. Canals created a landscape in which the intensive consumption of mineral energy sources became a logical outcome.

If in 1820 the arrival of coal arks at the Philadelphia port drew little notice, the same was true two decades later, albeit for a different reason: anthracite coal had become routine. Between April and December, a steady stream of canal boats arrived six days a week at Philadelphia's coal wharves. Large blocks of the city's northern edge along the Delaware River were turned into giant coal stockyards where consumers could purchase it wholesale or have it delivered to their homes on horse-drawn wagons. There was nothing remarkable about the delivery of anthracite coal because it had become an established part of the Quaker City's daily patterns.

2

The Anthracite Energy Transition

In 1851, PRINCE ALBERT and the British Royal Society of Arts invited manufacturers from around the world to display their crafts in England at The Great Exhibition of The Works of Industry of All Nations. Soon known as the Crystal Palace Exhibition, in reference to the giant iron and glass structure created by Joseph Paxton to house the exhibits, the event was a tremendous sensation. Millions of people visited the fair between May and October to see manufactured goods, scientific instruments, and cultural displays; it was so well attended that its profits endowed educational funds and museums. Moreover, as the organizers hoped, the fair highlighted the leading role of British firms. The event was such a success that its model was repeatedly replicated. For more than a century after the Crystal Palace Exhibition, various nations have jockeyed to host world's fairs that would demonstrate the innovativeness of their industries.

For American manufacturers, however, the Crystal Palace Exhibition began on a sour note. American organizers had reserved a large number of booths, but when the fair opened in May, few of the exhibits had arrived and international observers scoffed at the empty spaces. Over the next couple months, however, popular opinion began to shift. Once the exhibit room was filled, American manufacturers won acclaim for the quality and affordability of their goods. Whereas many European products were ornately decorated and expensive, the simple and affordable American designs were praised for their functionality. American agricultural implements, textile machines, and guns drew particular note, and Americans won a greater percentage of prizes per entry than any other nation. By the end of the fair, the British were so impressed that the government formed a committee to travel to the United States and report on the "American system" of production.[1]

The Crystal Palace Exhibition was a symbolic turning point for American manufacturing. For many European observers, it seemed that American industry had taken a sudden step forward. The former mercantile outpost was no longer simply a site for the extraction of raw materials—it was now an economic competitor. The success of American exhibitors, however, was a process several decades in the making. Over the previous thirty years, industrial growth and factory production had grown tremendously in the young republic, supported, in great measure, by the anthracite canal network and the abundant mineral energy of coal. Americans had not just learned to manufacture high-quality goods, they had begun to create new relationships between energy and society that were facilitating the sustained growth of an urban and industrial economy.

The energy transition to anthracite was driven by the synergistic feedback loops pioneered by coal canals. As boosters deepened the market for anthracite in homes, factories, steam engines, and iron production, the mid-Atlantic began to take on several characteristics of a mineral energy regime. Anthracite coal supported levels of urban and industrial growth impossible in a world powered by water, wind, and wood. It led to new patterns of transport and experiences of space and time. But the benefits and costs of these changes were not distributed equally. Canals shipped coal to certain points but not others. For many, increasing their consumption of anthracite led to warmer homes, cost savings, and higher levels of production. For others, these practices led to local environmental degradation and comparative economic disadvantage as they were bypassed by those with more favorable access to coal. The nation's first fossil fuel energy transition was not egalitarian.

Consuming Anthracite, Shaping the Mineral Energy Regime

The improvements to the Lehigh River in 1820 established a landscape of intensification that stimulated the intensive growth of the anthracite industry. Coal shipments and consumption grew at a rapid rate, nearly doubling every five years and far exceeding population growth: over 800,000 tons delivered in 1840, more than three million in 1850, and over eight million by 1860.[2] Remarkable as these numbers are, these totals understate how much anthracite was actually consumed, as they do not include coal used in the anthracite regions themselves. This vast increase in energy consumption laid the roots for the emergence of a mineral energy regime. Exploring the growth and consequences of increased coal consumption in homes, steam engines, and ironworks reveals the ways in which mineral energy began to reshape life in the mid-Atlantic during the antebellum period.

Homes constituted the first large market for anthracite coal. Even though fossil fuels are often associated with industrial consumers in the popular imagination, residential markets have played pioneering roles in driving energy transitions.[3] This was particularly true in the case of anthracite. By the early 1830s, boosters had already convinced several thousand residents of Philadelphia and New York to adopt coal in their homes. Over the next several decades, anthracite steadily gained market share until it was the dominant home heating fuel in eastern seaboard cities. This growth was facilitated by steadily lowering prices as larger transport networks decreased per-unit costs. The price of one ton of Lehigh coal purchased wholesale in Philadelphia decreased from $6.50 in 1830 to $5.50 in 1840 and to $4.50 in 1850.[4] By contrast, a cord of wood in the 1830s cost between four and seven dollars in Philadelphia and offered at most three-quarters of the heating value of a ton of anthracite. Moreover wood, as part of the organic energy regime, was not subject to the same positive feedback loops that characterized anthracite: as its supply became scarcer along the Schuylkill, Delaware, and Hudson Rivers, its price increased. Anthracite, therefore, soon became the cheapest heating fuel available to residents of Philadelphia and New York City.[5]

The wider distribution of stoves also facilitated the spread of anthracite into home heating markets. At the beginning of the nineteenth century, most households were heated with open hearth fires. This was not suitable for anthracite because in order for it to burn properly, air needed to flow through the coal and the ashes had to be able to fall away so they would not smother the flame. Over the 1830s and 1840s, inventors filed a proliferation of patents for new stove designs, many of which were designed to burn anthracite. With improvements in production—including efficiencies gained through using anthracite coal in the manufacture of iron—the cost of stoves fell to a point where even working-class families could afford them. By the 1830s, low-end stoves cost between ten and twenty dollars and philanthropic organizations offered models to poor consumers for less than six dollars. At mid-century, roughly 90 percent of houses in the northern states used stoves for home heating. While we do not know for certain what fuel was used in these stoves, the widespread expansion in stove use likely reflected a significant transition from wood to anthracite coal by residential consumers.[6]

By 1860, the vast majority of homes in large eastern seaboard cities were being heated by anthracite. Even in Boston, a physician reported in 1868 that 99 out of 100 homes in that city were heated by anthracite; as anthracite was cheaper in Philadelphia and New York City, it is likely that at least nine of ten homes in these cities were warmed mainly by coal at the dawn of the Civil War.[7] With a population of 565,529 in 1860, citizens of Philadelphia City and County likely burned between 500,000 and 600,000 tons of anthracite that year to keep warm, approximately half of the city's total coal consumption.[8] New York City, with a population of over 800,000 people in 1860, required at least three-quarters of a million tons of coal for home heating purposes. Although it is harder to make estimates for other cities on the eastern seaboard, large percentages of the population of cities including Providence, New Haven, and Albany were also likely using anthracite for home heating based on extensive coal deliveries to these locations.[9]

Shifting from wood to coal for home heating came with several consequences for mid-Atlantic families. The introduction of coal likely made houses warmer and more comfortable for most consumers because of its higher heat output and lower cost.[10] It also altered the gender dynamics of household labor. The gathering, sawing, and stacking of firewood was usually performed by men; women tended, cleaned, and cooked on stoves. An efficient coal stove saved the man's work of gathering fuel but not the woman's work of cooking or cleaning.[11] Substituting coal for wood thereby shifted the relative balance of housework from men to women. In addition, buying coal integrated some families further into the market economy by replacing the collection of wood by personal exertion with cash purchases of anthracite.

Over the long term, the substitution of coal for firewood also helped to push the mid-Atlantic toward a mineral energy regime. This can be seen most clearly by considering the amount of firewood that would have been necessary to support the population of the mid-Atlantic's burgeoning cities in the absence of coal. Since about one and a quarter cords of wood were needed per person per winter for heating purposes and at least another quarter of a cord was consumed for cooking, we can estimate a minimal need of one and a half cords of wood per person. Philadelphia in 1860, therefore, would have required at least 850,000 cords of wood just to support the needs of its residents. Under good forestry practices of the time, one could expect to harvest a cord of wood from two-thirds of an acre in a sustainable manner. As a result, to support their annual heating and cooking needs, Philadelphia's residents would have needed a dedicated forest hinterland of 567,000 acres, an area covering 885 square miles or roughly 2 percent of the state's land.[12]

It would have been possible for Philadelphians in 1860 to meet their heating needs with wood, but it would have required difficult trade-offs. The city could theoretically have established a large wood reserve, but any land sufficiently near the natural waterways necessary for transport would have been more valuable for farming. Another option would have been to tap the vast forests of Maine and North Carolina to fill the gap. However, the additional drain on these forests by residents of eastern seaboard cities would have significantly increased the cost of firewood and the rate of exhaustion. Because most American buildings were made out of wood at the time, it would have also raised the price of lumber and made housing more expensive.[13] As a result, relying on firewood instead of anthracite may have been possible, but it would have forced Philadelphians to preserve land for firewood and contend with the zero-sum trade-offs of the organic energy regime. Moreover, the negative consequences of firewood dependence would have become more acute as Philadelphia's population grew to 675,000 in

1870, 875,000 in 1880, and over a million by 1890.[14] As a cheap and abundant heating fuel requiring minimal land for its production, anthracite enabled the rapid growth of nineteenth-century cities.

We can trace a similar dynamic with the increasing use of anthracite by factories around this time. While the data for consumption by industry are fragmentary, a logic of intensification was clearly present. Factory owners discovered that ever-increasing supplies of anthracite at ever-decreasing prices allowed them to grow those aspects of their business involving heat. By the middle of the century, this led to a discernible pattern of industrial growth in Philadelphia. Whereas abundant waterpower in New England encouraged the growth of textile mills focused on spinning and weaving, Philadelphia manufacturers took a leading role in heat-intensive operations, including bleaching, dyeing, paper making, distilling, and metal-working.[15] Philadelphia soon became a prominent location as well for sugar refineries, glassworks, locomotive works, and foundries—all industries that required enormous amounts of heat.[16] The use of anthracite coal in factories shaped the mineral economy in a manner similar to its use in home heating. At first, the conversion to anthracite was simply a substitution of one fuel source for another. Over time, however, the fact that anthracite coal consumption could be expanded exponentially and concentrated in a single place created a new set of relationships between land and energy consumption. Shipments of anthracite coal transformed cities from energy-scarce places in organic economies into sites of superabundance capable of supporting dense concentrations of people and factories. Simply put, without abundant energy from anthracite, it would have been impossible for Philadelphia to claim the moniker "workshop of the world."

For consumers, cheap and abundant anthracite facilitated a new everyday relationship with energy. Consumers discovered that it was easier to add coal to keep a fire burning overnight than it was to expend the effort of starting a new fire in the morning. One set of craftsmen described their routine as follows: "Our practice is, in the morning when we leave the shop for breakfast, to throw a quantity of coal on the fires which will be fit for working on our return, and will last until we leave it at 9 in the evening, when we again put on a quantity which lasts until the next morning at breakfast time."[17] Such practices were directly encouraged by the operators of the canal companies. The Lehigh Coal & Navigation Company advised consumers to keep fires going all night to save their labor in the morning: "If the coal is suffered to continue in the grate all night, the trouble of making fire is saved at very little additional expense for coal."[18] These practices reflected a shift from the organic to the mineral energy regime. In the former, the use of energy was related to personal exertion through chopping, sawing, splitting, and stacking firewood. Using more fuel required more labor. With anthracite coal, this dynamic was reversed: it was easier to add more coal than to start a new fire. More mineral energy meant less personal labor.

Engines of Power

The use of steam engines in factories, coal mining, and vehicles also shaped the mid-Atlantic's development of an industrial economy. In the 1820s and 1830s, boosters addressed many of the challenges involved in using anthracite to fire steam engines. By 1838, Philadelphia led the nation in the use of steam engines, with many also operating in New Jersey and New York City.[19] There are no reliable data on steam engines from 1850 and 1860, but by 1870, it was reported that there were 1,877 establishments using steam power in Philadelphia with a total capacity of 49,674 horsepower consuming more than a quarter million tons of coal annually.[20] To put this growth into context, the 178 stationary steam engines in Philadelphia in 1838 had a combined capacity of less than two thousand horsepower, meaning that the energy available from steam engines grew more than twenty-five fold in three decades.[21]

The use of steam engines in manufacturing contributed to two shifts from the organic to the mineral energy regime. The first was the exponential increase in energy consumption, shown by the large growth of steam engines and coal demand. The second was geographic. In an organic energy regime, people moved energy-intensive activities to sites of energy abundance. Cities, even if they were founded along waterfalls and near forests, experienced finite limits to growth. Steam engines were not subject to the same limits. As long as more coal could be supplied, industrial energy use could be continually expanded within a small geographic area. With steam engines, factory owners had the means to locate their plants in close proximity to workers, suppliers, and markets. This potential had long appealed to Philadelphia industrialists. At the beginning of the nineteenth century, the inventor Oliver Evans noted the potential superiority of steam engines over organic energy sources: "Water-falls are not at our command in all places, and are liable to be obstructed by frost, drought, and many other accidents. Wind is inconstant and unsteady: animal power, expensive, tedious in the operation, and unprofitable, as well as subject to innumerable accidents. On neither of these can we rely with certainty. But steam at once presents us with a faithful servant, at command in all places, in all seasons; whose power is unlimited."[22]

The shift of heavy manufacturing from rural sites with abundant forests or falling water to large cities altered the geography of America's industrial development. Many of the nation's first factories were centered in small mill towns in the New England countryside alongside falling streams. For many observers, the bucolic nature of these sites was heralded because it could be favorably compared with the dark and satanic mills of Britain. If America was to develop an industrial economy, many hoped that the small size of the enterprises and the pastoral beauty of the locations would be consistent with republican values.[23] While few sites actually achieved these lofty ambitions—mill owners could be autocratic, many enterprises caused extensive local environmental damage, and these factories often led to concentrations of wealth—the New England mill created a powerful mythology within American culture. However, the conjunction of anthracite coal, steam engines, and eastern seaboard cities soon led to the eclipse of the New England mill town. Urban factories powered by coal became the norm: the Philadelphia model replaced the Lowell model. According to the historical geographer D. W. Meinig, by mid-century "the dominant patterns of industrializing . . . America would come to resemble . . . Pennsylvania much more than the model mill towns of New England."[24]

One of the most dramatic expansions in the use of steam engines came from mining anthracite, a process that reveals the positive feedback loops of the mineral energy regime. During the first years of the anthracite industry, coal miners had little need for steam engines because they were able to access large quantities of anthracite near the earth's surface. By removing a top layer of rocks and dirt, laborers could extract anthracite with a pickax and shovel. As demand for coal increased and the surface veins of anthracite were exhausted, however, miners were forced to dig further underground using sunken shafts. Subsurface mining introduced new problems: mines began to fill with water, coal had to be hauled much further to the surface, and ventilation fans were needed to remove noxious gases. Beginning in the late 1830s, miners increasingly turned to steam engines to address these problems. Their decision was not surprising—after all, coal mining gave rise to the development of the steam engine in the first place. The problem of pumping water out of mines in Britain had given Thomas Newcomen the impetus to develop the steam engine in the early eighteenth century.[25]

The use of steam engines in the Schuylkill Valley illustrates these trends. In 1840, there were only a dozen steam engines employed to mine coal. This number multiplied rapidly, increasing to 165 by 1850 and 320 by 1865. As the Schuylkill Valley produced approximately two-fifths of the region's anthracite, there were likely more than 700 steam engines at work in coal mining by 1865. Their combined capacity of more than 40,000 horsepower represented an incredible fifty-fold increase in the amount of mechanical power available to miners in the span of a quarter century.[26] The consumption of coal in order to mine coal introduced aspects of the mineral energy regime to the coal regions. Ironically, while the regions were producing the energy source that would pioneer the mineral energy regime, much of the energy to produce and transport coal came from the organic energy regime. While steam engines assisted these efforts by draining water and hoisting coal, most other aspects of anthracite mining were not intensively mechanized until after the Civil War. The muscles of humans and animals still removed anthracite from underground deposits, loaded it into cars and boats, and then pulled it in boats along canals. Therefore, coal mining was a hybrid of organic and mineral energy regimes.

Marine vessels comprised a third significant market for the use of anthracite in steam engines. Americans were pioneers in the adoption of steam power for marine transport because the nation was so geographically dispersed and waterways offered the potential of much cheaper shipments than land routes. Beginning with Robert Fulton's *Clermont* in 1807, early steam vessels burned wood, which was initially abundant along the paths of the boats (mostly the Delaware and Hudson Rivers and the Atlantic coast). However, steamboats' massive appetites for fuel soon reduced supplies of timber: in 1828, it was reported that the New York City fleet of steamers consumed 200,000 cords of pine per year and that Philadelphia's fleet used

150,000 cords. Deforestation quickly followed. Most of the fuel wood came from New Jersey, though some was imported from North Carolina. As early as 1829, the pine lands of New Jersey, previously considered of low value, were being rapidly depleted by steam vessel operators and charcoal producers. The deforestation along commonly traveled routes in the American mid-Atlantic and northeast revealed that organic energy sources could not support the continued growth of the nation's steamships.[27]

As with other uses of anthracite, the coal transport companies played a critical role in leading an energy transition. The Lehigh Coal & Navigation Company began experimenting with anthracite-powered steamships in 1826; five years later their boat *The Pennsylvania* was towing coal barges up and down the Delaware River. The energy contained in three tons of anthracite allowed the boat to pull four hundred tons more than sixty miles, and the company soon expanded its fleet. The Delaware & Hudson Company also dedicated great effort to introducing anthracite into steam vessels. The company believed that the particular characteristics of coal from the Wyoming Valley (some of it had more volatile gases than Schuylkill or Lehigh coal and was therefore easier to ignite) gave it an advantage for producing steam. In addition, steam navigation was of great importance to the commerce of New York City, which consumed most of the coal delivered by the Delaware & Hudson Canal. The company absorbed the costs of converting fireboxes and grates in New York City ferries, gave free anthracite to steam vessel owners willing to experiment with its use, and supported efforts by entrepreneurs to develop marine boilers designed for anthracite.[28]

The extensive use of anthracite coal in steam vessels gained momentum during the 1830s. Only six vessels in the New York harbor burned anthracite in 1831, but the practice was common by the end of the decade. In 1845, the Coal Mining Association of Schuylkill County determined that there were 35 steamboats based in Philadelphia using 45,000 tons of anthracite annually and twice as many in New York. By the 1850s, over half the steamships in the American coastal trade burned anthracite. Even the U.S. Navy took note of these developments; their engineer-in-chief oversaw a study that determined that anthracite coal provided 66 percent more power than bituminous, leading him to recommend its use.[29]

The other great transportation revolution of the antebellum era was the steam-powered railroad. For the small number of railroad tracks laid in

America during the 1820s, such as the Lehigh Coal & Navigation Company's link between mine and river, animals and gravity usually provided the necessary energy. But if steam power could be substituted for mules or horses, boosters recognized the opportunity for greater speeds and larger loads. Despite initial high expectations for the use of anthracite in railroad locomotives, this market took much longer to develop than boosters had initially hoped. This was a surprising result to many, especially since one of the first successful American locomotives, the "Tom Thumb" of the Baltimore & Ohio Railroad in 1832, burned anthracite.[30] However, in locomotive engines, the intense heat of anthracite was a liability: it melted grates, developed clinkers that impeded combustion, and destroyed boilers. In addition, it was harder to control the flame of an anthracite fire to increase or decrease the power output when the train was starting, stopping, or going up slopes. Even the Reading Railroad, which began operating in the early 1840s with anthracite as its primary cargo, mainly burned wood during its first decade. Only once company engineers undertook an intensive research program to convert their engines to anthracite did the Reading Railroad begin to consume coal as well as to ship it. Each two-hundred-mile round-trip between the anthracite regions and Philadelphia, for example, required the Reading Railroad to burn about nine tons of coal. By the 1850s, many other railroads in the anthracite regions were fueled by anthracite as well. This energetic abundance allowed a massive increase in the size and speed of freight: mineral-powered trains could pull more than seven hundred tons at a rate several times faster than the pace of animals.[31]

Coal-powered boats and railroads helped transform notions of time and space for Americans at the dawn of the Civil War. In the organic energy regime, sailboats were subject to the variations of the winds. They could be stranded in a port until favorable winds arose and the length of a journey could vary immensely; as a result, establishing regular trade schedules was difficult. Moreover, upriver navigation was slow and expensive for sailboats: ascending the Hudson River from New York to Albany, for example, could take more than a week. Steamboats changed this logic. Captains no longer had to wait for the wind, so boats could travel according to schedules determined by merchants and they could compensate for currents by adding more coal to the boilers. With a steamship, the trip from New York to Albany could be completed in less than a day.[32] The spread of railroads gave those in the mid-Atlantic even greater control over the distribution of people and goods. Whereas the vast majority of transport in the organic energy regime occurred along rivers, lakes, and coasts, the iron horse allowed goods to be shipped rapidly and cheaply between overland places for the first time: trade no longer had to follow nature's distribution of waterways. In addition, the speed at which railroads traveled was often so remarkable as to be disorienting to many mid-nineteenth-century Americans: passengers frequently experienced passing landscapes as an unintelligible blur.[33] Coal-powered transport, along with innovations in communications like telegraphy, thereby contributed to a growing sense in mid-nineteenth-century America that time and space were being conquered.

Producing Iron

Iron production was the final major category of anthracite consumption in the antebellum period. It was one of the most important and revolutionary uses of coal and effectively illustrates the growth potential and shifting spatial geography of the mineral energy regime. For decades before the introduction of anthracite, American ironmasters used charcoal to smelt iron. Because of its dependence on vast quantities of trees (charcoal is wood burned in the near absence of oxygen), the charcoal iron industry was decentralized and the output of each operation was modest. A typical early-nineteenth-century establishment producing 600 tons of iron a year required one acre of timber a day to produce charcoal. This meant that for sustainable operations, assuming 300 days of operation a year and 30 years to reforest land, the iron company would need a 9,000-acre plantation.[34] Moreover, because charcoal is a brittle substance, it could not be transported far overland without breaking into small and unusable pieces. This constraint limited the total energy supply that could be gathered at a single location, thereby encouraging decentralized operations with relatively small outputs.[35] As was logical in an organic energy regime, iron plantations moved to places where there were many trees and few competing demands for the land.

Replacing expensive charcoal with cheap anthracite enticed many iron producers. But the task was formidable. Iron smelting is a complex process and the fuel has to supply heat, provide structural support, and remove impurities from the ore. Yet the rewards were large as well. Because iron was an essential input into so many other industries—including steam engines, stoves, and machine tools—a wide range of parties sought to encourage development of techniques that would overcome these challenges. The Franklin Institute, a scientific association in Philadelphia, advertised prestigious gold-medal prizes to anyone who could smelt iron with anthracite. Nicholas Biddle, head of the Second Bank of the United States, gathered with several wealthy men to award $5,000 to the first party able to keep an anthracite smelter running for three months. The state of Pennsylvania passed a law making it easy for companies manufacturing iron with anthracite to obtain a corporate charter. Transport companies were also active boosters. The Lehigh Coal & Navigation Company recruited ironmasters from overseas and offered free waterpower from the canal to any enterprise manufacturing iron with anthracite along the Lehigh River.[36]

Despite the concerted effort of several parties, it took years of experimentation until the technical problems were resolved. Following a common pattern in American industrial development, some of the solutions came from overseas. Welsh ironmasters, who had experience working with hard coals, made key breakthroughs during the 1830s. Men such as David Thomas, a Welsh ironmaster lured to the Lehigh Valley in 1839, helped bring this expertise to America to supplement domestic efforts. By 1840, several parties in America began to achieve success. The immigration of skilled workers from Europe was a great boon for American iron production and coal mining during this period.[37]

The switch from charcoal to anthracite was not simply a change in fuel source: it created new patterns of industrial development. With mineral energy for fuel, iron production could grow rapidly and it could be densely concentrated in massive smelters close to urban centers. In 1847, more than forty enterprises were producing over 150,000 tons of iron with anthracite. By the dawn of the Civil War, the annual total was over a half million tons. While the charcoal iron industry continued to grow as well, the rate was much less dramatic—a roughly 25 percent increase in the same time period.[38] Characteristic of the organic energy regime, the charcoal iron industry grew arithmetically; characteristic of the mineral energy regime, the anthracite iron industry grew geometrically.

This growth in the anthracite iron industry consumed enormous quantities of coal. Producing one ton of iron required at least two tons of anthracite. Another quarter ton of coal was needed to power furnace bellows if waterpower was not available. Processing iron into products such as rails, nails, and plates absorbed even more anthracite: two tons of coal to roll or puddle a ton of iron and as many as eight tons of coal to manufacture a ton of steel.[39] By 1860, the anthracite iron industry was consuming more than a million and a half tons of coal a year, more than a fifth of all anthracite shipments.[40] To put this energy demand into perspective, in the organic energy regime this level of production would have required more than three and a half million acres of land to have been devoted to growing trees for charcoal, a ninth of Pennsylvania's area. By 1886, anthracite iron production exceeded two million tons, a level of production requiring a forest larger than the state itself. Pennsylvania iron production quickly eclipsed the capacities of the organic energy regime.[41]

The anthracite iron industry, by contrast, did not encounter limits to growth. It could also support greater levels of output in a single place. The limited ability to concentrate charcoal at one site meant that the average furnace produced much lower volumes of iron: in 1847, the average anthracite operation produced five times the amount of the average charcoal operation; by 1864, the ratio was ten to one.[42] Moreover, this production occurred in a radically different geography. Because charcoal iron furnaces required large quantities of land, they were disproportionately located in rural areas where there were no competing demands for the forests. By contrast, anthracite iron forges were densely concentrated along the banks of canals. Three-quarters of the nation's anthracite iron furnaces were in eastern Pennsylvania in 1856; in 1873, 99 percent were in the mid-Atlantic. Nearly all of these sites were immediately adjacent to coal transport routes. As a result, anthracite iron was not only cheaper to make, it was also cheaper to transport: shipping iron from inland rural furnaces to Philadelphia or New York typically cost five to eight dollars per ton, whereas canal boats could deliver iron for as little as a dollar per ton.[43]

This geographic concentration did not occur by accident—it was shaped by the landscape of anthracite canals. Canals encouraged the concentration of iron furnaces along their banks because they offered a cheap and abundant source of energy, facilitated the movement of other goods related to the iron industry (including ore, limestone, and finished goods), and frequently provided waterpower that could operate furnace bellows. Therefore, canals did not just shape the flows of coal, they also structured the geographies of energy-intensive industries. If the anthracite canals were the backbone of the mineral energy regime, it is not surprising that the region's most energy-intensive enterprises were attached like ribs.

The production of anthracite iron also embodied the logic of the mineral energy regime because it did not require social trade-offs regarding land use. Coal made it possible to increase iron production without sacrifices in other domains. In 1864, there were thirty furnaces in the Lehigh Valley that used nearly 500,000 tons of coal to produce more than 200,000 tons of iron in an area of only 730 square miles.[44] This density of production was impossible in an organic energy regime: the demand for charcoal would require the entire region to be dedicated to forests. Characteristic of a mineral energy regime, however, the Lehigh Valley's agricultural output increased at the same time as its iron and coal industries expanded. The region's production of grain, corn, oats, and dairy products grew during the 1840s and 1850s.[45] The new structural relationships between land, energy, and society are clearly indicated by the fact that the region could increase multiple areas of economic activity at the same time without needing to decide between alternatives.

By heating homes and factories, driving steam engines, and smelting iron, anthracite coal created the early stages of a shift from the organic to the mineral energy regime. Burned in homes, it supported dense concentrations of residents in cities and allowed mid-Atlantic residents to use the remaining forests for lumber. As a source of industrial fuel in factories, anthracite facilitated a geographic shift of manufacturing to urban centers and the extensive growth of heat-intensive operations. Steam vessels and railroads created new patterns of travel for goods and people. When applied to iron manufacture, anthracite led to rapid growth and an industrial geography of production clustered along the banks of the canals. While organic energy sources might have been able to support any one of these developments, they could not have enabled them all. Collectively, these uses of anthracite began the shift to a mineral energy regime.

Roots of Dependence

This was just the beginning. While in 1820 it was difficult to convince any consumers to adopt anthracite, by 1860 the mid-Atlantic had become dependent on ever-increasing flows of coal. This change was technological, social, and economic. Technologically, mid-Atlantic residents altered their built environment in ways that required the continued availability of anthracite. They constructed dense concentrations of homes and factories in cities that demanded more heat and power than organic sources could supply. Capitalists invested in iron furnaces that could only operate in a world of energy abundance. Merchants established patterns of trade that depended on the power of steam vessels to travel quickly and without reliance on wind or currents. As people gained familiarity with burning coal, they became accustomed to its use and benefits. The higher heating value of anthracite compared with firewood, along with its lower cost, kept homes warmer in winter, lowered factory production costs, and freed land for other purposes. For most people with access to anthracite, life was better with coal than without it.

The growing dependence of the mid-Atlantic on anthracite coal was generated partly by boosters and partly by thousands of individual decisions. Energy boosters, often affiliated with the transport companies, actively encouraged people to adopt anthracite and worked to create large and growing markets. However, they were not all-powerful. It took thousands of individual choices about where to live, how to heat their homes, and where to locate factories, to create a new built environment and set of cultural expectations in the mid-Atlantic. Of course, these individual decisions were not made in isolation. They were structured by an economic system that encouraged the pursuit of profit and material transformations of the landscape that made anthracite coal cheap and abundant. These collective efforts, choices, expectations, and forces pushed the mid-Atlantic steadily down a development path that depended on ever-increasing supplies of mineral energy.

By the dawn of the Civil War, using anthracite was no longer a question. While an individual family could decide not to purchase a coal-burning stove, eastern seaboard cities would have faced acute heating crises had everyone made that choice. A manufacturer could decide whether to use wood or coal for heat and whether to locate a factory in a city or in a rural area, but the dense concentration of industrial laborers and shops in Philadelphia and New York could not have been sustained without continuing supplies of anthracite. Shippers could still decide to rely on sails for power, but they increasingly struggled to maintain economic viability against steam vessels that could travel more quickly and reliably. In short, the regional economy would have suffered enormously if anthracite suddenly ceased to be available. The loss of coal supplies would have destroyed the iron industry, transformed trade networks, and forced an exodus of industries and people from urban centers. Residents of the mid-Atlantic had stepped into a brave new world of fossil fuel consumption from which they could only turn away with great difficulty. Anthracite had become a necessary part of life.

Expanding the Transport System

Synergistic feedback loops are one of the key characteristics of the mineral energy regime. In an organic energy regime, the dependence on land for the production of goods and energy means that there are finite limits to growth based on the law of diminishing marginal returns: increasing production eventually leads to higher costs per unit until a stationary state is reached. In a mineral energy regime, no such limits are encountered. Sustained growth is possible as long as additional stocks of mineral energy can be brought to market. This logic of the mineral energy regime, however, is not inevitable. It relies on material transformations of the natural world to ensure that ever-increasing supplies of energy can be delivered to consumers. In the mid-Atlantic, the construction of the canal network was only the first step in altering the built environment to suit human needs. This growth was sustained over time through regular expansions of transport infrastructure systems that enabled the delivery of ever-increasing flows of anthracite.

In other words, the anthracite canal network was not a static technology that was built and then left alone. Transport companies continually expanded their systems in order to ensure that concerns about coal supply would never impede consumer demand. Over the antebellum period, canals were widened and deepened to allow more and more coal to reach

Canal boats being filled with coal. (*Harper's Weekly* 17, no. 6 [1873], Harvard University, Widener Library, P 207.6 F)

markets. Eventually, canals were supplemented by railroads, and by the dawn of the Civil War, railroad companies had surpassed canals as the primary carriers of coal. Large transport infrastructures ensured that anthracite remained cheap and abundant for mid-Atlantic consumers and reinforced the patterns of the mineral energy regime.

The growth of the canal network was rooted in the economic desires of transport owners and operators to maximize their profits. They knew that it was essential to keep markets fully supplied with anthracite coal in order to provide a favorable return to shareholders. While coal retailers and miners occasionally favored curtailing supply because it increased the price of coal, transport companies earned revenues from the shipment of coal regardless of the price to consumers. The incentive structure of transport companies, who generally charged flat rates for shipments, was to encourage low coal prices since they would lead to increased shipments.[46] The belief that supply would drive demand was explicitly understood. During an 1834 investigation of the emerging anthracite industry, members of the trade were asked: "Is not the consumption of Coal increased by having a consistent supply in market?" All respondents replied in the affirmative. Miners, merchants, and transport officials agreed with the statement, issuing lines such as "There can be no doubt that the consumption of coal is increased by having a constant supply in market" and "Yes—a constant supply of any staple necessarily increases its consumption." The transport companies were among the most emphatic in their agreement. The Lehigh Coal & Navigation Company responded: "There can be no doubt but that the consumption of coal is greatly and permanently increased by having stocks on hand in the spring . . . and to that in a great measure may be attributed the extraordinary increase [in consumption]." The Delaware & Hudson Canal Company concurred: "The consumption of coal is unquestionably increased by having a constant supply in market, as that produces low and uniform prices."[47]

This was not mere rhetoric. The transport companies devoted large sums of capital to enhancing the capacity of their systems. The Lehigh Coal & Navigation Company changed their descending-only navigation system to a full canal in 1829. The Schuylkill Navigation Company expanded their canal several times: in 1825, the canal was three feet deep and could support boats carrying 25 tons of cargo. In 1840, the company widened and deepened the canal so that boats carrying 50 tons could travel the route. In response to pressure from the Reading Railroad, the company closed the canal for most of 1845 and expanded it to support 180-ton boats. Similar improvements were undertaken on the other canals: the Delaware Division was expanded in 1841, 1854, and 1857; the Delaware & Hudson in 1842, 1845–46, 1850, and 1853; and the Morris Canal in 1841, 1847, and 1856. These investments significantly lowered the cost of shipping coal, since a heavier boat could be pulled with only minor additions of power—usually an extra mule or two. The improvements on the Delaware & Hudson Canal, for example, decreased shipping costs from $1.34 per ton in the 1830s to $.91 per ton in 1846. Most of these savings were passed on to consumers as the price of anthracite fell steadily during this period.[48]

In addition to expanding canals, anthracite boosters also extended the energy landscape by building railroads. The developers of railroads were often bitter competitors of canal developers, engaging in extensive economic battles to win market share, highlighted by the thirty-year struggle between the Schuylkill Navigation Company and the Reading Railroad. The dynamics of the competition were fascinating, involving capital, technology, politics, and debates over corporate privileges, and have been discussed extensively elsewhere.[49] In the context of this account, however, the most notable feature of this competition was that it did not dramatically influence where coal went. Eastern seaboard cities, with their growing populations and industries, were the desired end points for railroads as well as canals. As a result, railroad tracks often followed the paths of canals. The switch may have influenced how coal traveled, but not where it went.

Railroad competition came to the Lehigh and Wyoming Valleys as well. In 1838, the Beaver Meadow Railroad was built in the Lehigh region, much to the consternation of the canal company. Canal employees reportedly made a habit of cutting timber on the hills above the teams building the railroad and sending the logs cascading through the construction zone; both sides were said to have armed their men with muskets. However, the Beaver Meadow Railroad never emerged as a major competitor. Because it did not have links all the way to the eastern seaboard, it depended on the canal to deliver its goods to final markets. In 1855, Asa Packer pioneered the development of the Lehigh Valley Railroad, which eventually managed to control most of the shipments previously handled by the Lehigh Canal. In the Wyoming Valley, the Delaware, Lackawanna & Western Railroad, built during the 1850s, became the dominant shipper of coal from that region after the Civil War.[50]

In many analyses of the anthracite canal and railroad companies, the central story has been the competitive dynamics between rival shippers.[51] But the synergies merit equal attention, particularly because their similarities shaped the development of the mineral energy regime. Each of the companies worked to build demand for coal, thereby creating a larger base of consumers. By providing multiple sources of supply, rivals generated a more reliable market, helping customers feel more confident that it was worth the investment in new stoves or equipment required to convert to anthracite. Even their competitive actions had the general effect of increasing the market. By lowering the cost of coal in rate wars or increasing production to gain market share, the companies gave consumers further incentives to use anthracite because it constantly became cheaper and more plentiful. Combined with the fact that canals and railroads often followed similar routes—it was not uncommon, for example, to see a towpath along one side of a river and tracks along the other—the similarities of the network were more crucial to the development of the mineral energy regime than their differences.

An Unequal Landscape

The energy landscape of anthracite transport systems was composed of a series of narrow tendrils that operated in a highly specific and limited spatial geography. Where people lived in relationship to canals—at a terminus in Philadelphia or New York, at the beginning in the anthracite regions, along the route, or not connected at all—structured their experience of the emerging mineral energy regime. Some people and places received large amounts of coal while others were mostly excluded. The broad brushstrokes of these coal shipments can be seen in Map 2.1, which indicates the scale and direction of flows. It reveals that eastern seaboard cities received the vast majority of anthracite shipments while large swaths of the mid-Atlantic were passed over. The most significant changes were felt in cities at the ends of canals, followed by the coal regions and towns along the canal paths. The lives of those in the countryside were minimally affected by these changes, as were those of many who lived outside the mid-Atlantic.

The shift from an organic to a mineral energy regime was most pronounced at the places canals terminated. Homes and factories in Philadelphia and New York City consumed the most coal, used it in the most diverse ways, and most quickly adopted the characteristics of a mineral energy regime.[52] These cities led the region in the use of coal for home heating, steam engines, and factories: all the categories of consumption except iron production. By 1860, most Philadelphians and New Yorkers burned anthracite in their homes, and businesses requiring heat for their operations largely relied on coal. Many of the steamboats burning anthracite served the trade needs of these cities. Although Philadelphia and New York did not dominate the production of iron, each city contained many enterprises that used anthracite to transform iron into finished products. Overall, Philadelphia and New York had clearly developed new relationships with

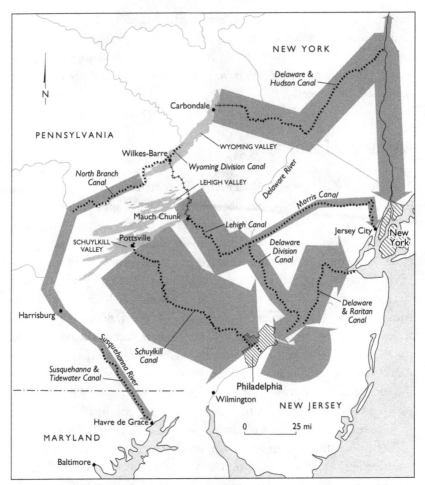

MAP 2.1. Coal flows, ca. 1855. Arrows are weighted to indicate the volume of coal flows.

land, energy, and limits that were no longer characteristic of an organic energy regime.

The anthracite regions exhibited a different set of transformations. Due to the rise of the coal industry, the rapid influx of population, and the booms and busts associated with mining districts, residents of towns near coal mining centers such as Pottsville, Mauch Chunk, and Honesdale experienced sweeping social changes.[53] However, these upheavals were not specific to the development of a mineral energy regime. In fact, in the 1820s and 1830s, much of the activity in the anthracite regions was characteristic of the organic energy regime. The main tools of coal mining were pickaxes, wheelbarrows, wagons, donkeys, and canals. Most people not involved in the coal industry farmed. Though the anthracite regions supplied the raw material that would make the mineral energy regime possible, the production of coal during that time occurred largely in the context of the organic energy regime.

With the rising use of steam engines for coal mining during the 1840s and 1850s and the increased production of iron, the anthracite regions began to take on characteristics of the mineral energy regime. Steam engines were deployed to drain water from underground coal mines, haul anthracite to the surface, and ventilate increasingly elaborate shafts and tunnels. In addition, a few towns in the anthracite regions—particularly Scranton and Wilkes-Barre—began to develop diversified industrial economies in the mid-nineteenth century. Entrepreneurs in these cities took advantage of their proximity to coal and cheap transport opportunities by canal and railroad to establish thriving manufacturing businesses.[54]

The regions along the canals followed a similar script. At first, very little coal was consumed in the regions along the paths of the canals. Between 1820 and 1840, the amount of coal consumed along the lengths of the Schuylkill and Lehigh Canals was only around 5 to 10 percent of total shipments.[55] Plenty of wood remained available to heat homes and manufacture goods, and as a result, the limits of the organic energy regime hardly appeared to local residents as a meaningful constraint. With the introduction of the anthracite iron industry beginning in 1840, several towns along the paths of the canals began to be more deeply integrated into the mineral energy regime, particularly Reading, Phoenixville, Bethlehem, and Allentown. Between 1840 and 1860, for example, there was a twenty-fold increase in coal consumption along the path of the Schuylkill Canal, comprising about 20 percent of total shipments.[56] The concentration of iron production along canal banks was encouraged by the ability of these networks to deliver coal, raw materials, and finished products cheaply and abundantly.

The growth of industrial enterprises in the anthracite regions and along the paths of transport networks points to a significant feature of canals: they enabled the benefits of the mineral energy regime to spread to multiple places. This possibility was rooted in their material characteristics: even though they were designed with the anthracite trade in mind, canals could also carry a wide variety of other goods to any point along their paths. The iron works along canals, for example, did not simply acquire coal from up-river. They also brought in lime and ore from below and then shipped their finished products cheaply to markets. However, such a result was by no means an inherent feature of energy transport systems. For example, oil pipelines and electricity transmission wires did not transport multiple products nor did they generate comparable levels of regional growth.

Throughout the rural areas of the mid-Atlantic, the patterns of the organic energy regime persisted during this period. Transporting coal over-land ten miles typically cost as much as the coal itself, so any location distant from a navigable waterway was unlikely to receive bulk shipments.[57] The predominantly rural population experienced little change in their daily lives from the development of coal canals and anthracite consumption. Their patterns were still governed by the organic energy regime, although such limits rarely mattered in a region where land and forests remained abundant. Charcoal iron producers could still take advantage of uncut forests to increase their output in rural Pennsylvania. Farming communities could find plenty of streams to support mills and congregated along their banks. On the whole, rural residents of the mid-Atlantic experienced little of the mineral energy regime during the antebellum era.

Anthracite was also delivered outside the mid-Atlantic. Some of the coal shipped to Philadelphia and New York City was then transported to other locations along the eastern seaboard. From centralized wharves, merchants loaded anthracite onto steam vessels that could travel along the coast and up navigable rivers. By the 1850s, Philadelphians were exporting more than a million and a half tons of anthracite annually, an amount that constituted more than 90 percent of the city's coastal trade as measured by tonnage.[58] Most of these shipments were directed toward other cities in the mid-Atlantic and New England. Boston, the third-largest market for anthracite, began importing coal as early as 1824, averaging annual imports of 75,000 tons of anthracite between 1835 and 1840, 250,000 tons between 1847 and 1849, and over 400,000 tons during the 1850s.[59] Several other cities also received shipments, including Providence, Lowell, Hartford, New Haven, Wilmington, and Albany. In addition to serving home heating markets, anthracite supported industrial development at these locations. As early as 1825, workers at the Springfield Armory in Massachusetts used anthracite to make gun barrels. In the 1830s, anthracite was burned to make bricks in New Orleans, for dyeing, print-making, and heating purposes in Rhode Island, and for heating and manufacturing purposes at the Lowell textile mills.[60]

Coal was not shipped everywhere, however. Very little anthracite was delivered south of Baltimore. Of the coal exported from Philadelphia in 1855, more than 90 percent went to the mid-Atlantic or New England. Only 6 percent was shipped to southern and western states, and less than 2 percent traveled overseas.[61] Some of this discrepancy is explained by climate: the warmer winters and larger forest reserves of the South meant that the home heating market was less promising. But the South also trailed the North in the industrial consumption of anthracite, a fact that helped to shape the different industrial development patterns of the North versus South in antebellum America.[62] In addition, foreign trade never became prominent: small quantities were shipped to the Caribbean islands but these exports were only a fraction of overall shipments. Despite the hope of some boosters, anthracite had a value-weight ratio that was not conducive to large-scale shipments across the ocean.[63]

Thus, the experience of new coal flows was significantly influenced by where people lived in relation to the paths of the anthracite canals. Moreover, these geographic differentiations were not neutral. Economically, environmentally, and physically, the distribution of costs and benefits accompanying the development of the mineral economy favored certain parties over others. On the whole, those living in cities received the large majority of the benefits while those living in the anthracite regions bore many of the costs.

Cities garnered the greatest economic benefits from the anthracite trade. In Diane Lindstrom's analysis of the relationships between Philadelphia and its hinterland, she notes that while all regions may have been advantaged by the development of an integrated economy, the urban core fared the best. Philadelphia had the fastest rates of population growth, the highest rates of return on investment, and the largest share of the transport savings, which were usually passed on to consumers instead of producers.[64] In addition, the varied uses of coal in cities gave rise to a diversified urban economy that was better able to withstand the booms and busts of the nineteenth-century economy. Though the towns in the anthracite regions and along the canal paths did benefit from the anthracite coal trade, their dependence on a single product (coal in the anthracite regions and iron in the canal towns) left them subject to significant recessions when the coal and iron markets experienced difficulty.[65] Moreover, urban capitalists owned much of the coal lands and iron factories and therefore siphoned dividends and royalties away from the sites of production.[66]

Residents of the anthracite regions bore most of the industry's negative environmental impacts. Over time, the anthracite regions were turned into a sacrifice zone: an environment whose health and vitality were tarnished to serve consumers living far away. The process of mining anthracite and breaking it into pieces suited for consumption generated enormous quantities of dust that settled on houses and fields, tainted drinking water supplies, and caused "black lung" inside the bodies of miners. Forests were stripped bare to expose the ground for mining and to provide the copious timber needed to support mine shafts and tunnels. As the scale of mining increased, streams and rivers were further polluted when acid and pollutants seeped from the mines. After coal was removed from underground deposits, the surface above could subside—quickly collapsing several feet, thereby destroying any property unlucky enough to have been built there. The anthracite regions became a scarred landscape to provide energy to other places.[67]

Consumers of anthracite experienced some harm from smoke pollution, but the high carbon content of anthracite ameliorated the potential harms. Anthracite smoke was far less offensive than bituminous smoke because there were fewer impurities. Therefore, while the air quality of Philadelphia and New York was never ideal, eastern seaboard cities fared better than urban locations dependent on bituminous coal like Pittsburgh, Chicago, and St. Louis.

Finally, the physical dangers of coal mining were borne by those working underground in the anthracite regions. Miners risked suffocation when ventilation systems failed, crushed limbs when mine shafts or tunnel supports fell, and death from explosions, fires, floods, and gas leaks. The range of physical threats was so pervasive that nineteenth-century anthracite miners had less than a fifty-fifty chance of surviving fourteen years of employment without a fatal or crippling accident.[68] To be sure, workers in cities also experienced physical risks as the use of steam engines and mechanized equipment became more common in factories, but few occupations were as dangerous as coal mining. Therefore, those living in the anthracite regions experienced a disproportionate share of the costs of the anthracite industry while recouping fewer of the benefits than those living in cities.

A Nation at War

By 1860, the mid-Atlantic was a very different place than it had been forty years before. The rising use of anthracite coal altered more than how people heated homes and manufactured goods; it changed the ways that people lived and worked. For example, anthracite coal enabled expansions in the size of cities and the density of industrial production that would have been impossible in an organic energy regime. Whereas the mill towns of rural New England had characterized American industrialization in the first third of the nineteenth century, the factories of Philadelphia and New York City became the center of the nation's industrial growth by mid-century. In 1860, Philadelphia and New York each had roughly a hundred thousand industrial employees, a fifth and eighth of their populations, respectively.[69] Only a handful of American cities had more than one hundred thousand residents at the time, meaning that the number of industrial workers in Philadelphia and New York was greater than the total population of nearly any other city in the United States.[70] In addition, there was a substantial growth of industrial centers along the paths of the canals and along the eastern seaboard. One historian of the mid-Atlantic economy noted that anthracite coal helped give rise to "one great manufacturing complex from Wilmington to New York. From 1843 to 1860 this megalopolis was probably the most rapidly growing large industrial area in the world."[71] Anthracite, canals, and industrial cities grew together synergistically.

The coal-fired growth of the mid-Atlantic set it apart from other parts of the nation. These regional divergences would soon take a momentous turn with the outbreak of the Civil War. Different energy endowments between North and South were one of the factors driving the conflict. Southern states relied on human labor, and their fear of losing that system contributed to their belief that secession was their only option.

This gap in energy practices was not as pronounced forty years earlier. In 1820, New England, the mid-Atlantic, and the South were all part of the organic energy regime. Though they harnessed power in different ways—small

farms and mill towns in New England; grain farms and artisan shops in the
mid-Atlantic; plantation agriculture in the South—there was a shared dependence on muscles, falling water, and plants.[72] In such a world, there
were relatively few options for increasing energy availability. Slavery was
one. Though slavery in the American South was particularly violent, brutal,
and reprehensible, it was not an uncommon approach to labor shortages.
Throughout world history, many societies in the organic energy regime
have relied on variations of human bondage including slavery, corvée labor,
and serfdom.[73]

Anthracite offered a different possibility for increasing energy availability.
By 1860, coal provided additional power to many in the mid-Atlantic, serving as what scholars have described as inanimate "energy slaves."[74] However,
anthracite was far less appealing to elites in the South. There were no applications of coal that could assist with the heavy labor demands of growing or
picking cotton and tobacco (anthracite offered relatively few benefits to
farmers in the North as well). The warmer climate and large forests of the
South meant that home heating was less of a constraint. In addition, coal
was more expensive and less available because the South lacked the transport
facilities of the mid-Atlantic. The nonadoption of anthracite was not simply
the result of a bias against technology: in 1838, there were many steam engines in the South at rural locations including saw mills and sugar refineries.[75] Rather, it was a reflection that for the rich and powerful in the South,
the organic energy regime, in the form of slave labor, seemed far more suited
to the region's economy and environment.

These differences in energy regimes were intimately connected to different political opinions about the proper policies to support the nation's development. To protect their growing manufacturing economies, northern
politicians sought a stronger federal government and protective tariffs. For
southern politicians whose electorate imported many of their goods, tariffs
would increase the cost of commodities. They also believed that greater
states' rights offered a more compelling framework for governance. Different energy regimes were linked to different visions of politics.

Once the Civil War began, the location of America's industrial heartland north of the Mason-Dixon line gave the Union a great strategic advantage in the conflict. The mid-Atlantic was able to use large quantities of

coal to manufacture armaments and deliver them to the Union Army using its extensive network of railroads, canals, and steamboats. As in most wars throughout history, the side able to deploy more energy emerged triumphant. The pioneering of the mineral energy regime in the mid-Atlantic not only reshaped the region, it transformed the future of the nation.

3

Pennsylvania's Petroleum Boom

O N AUGUST 27, 1859, a remarkable event occurred in a remote area of western Pennsylvania: Edwin Drake and his driller William Smith struck oil. Unlike the spewing geyser of crude oil typically depicted in movies, their discovery was far less dramatic. In fact, it took a full day before they realized their good fortune. Because it was late in the afternoon on a Saturday, the men stopped work to observe the Sabbath. They had reached a depth of sixty-nine feet and the drill bit had just slipped an extra six inches through a crevice in the rock. Drake returned to the nearby town of Titusville to join his family while Smith and his two children stayed by the well in a modest room attached to the building housing the equipment. On Sunday, Smith performed a routine check and noticed a film on top of the water. Fashioning a makeshift ladle out of a piece of tin rainspout, he gathered a sample of the greenish black liquid and excitedly sent one of his sons to fetch Drake. That Monday, they attached a hand crank to the well and began drawing up several gallons of oily water an hour. Word of their accomplishment spread rapidly, and within days, thousands began flocking to the town of Titusville to seek their fortune in black gold. The modern oil industry, so consequential to modern life, had been born.[1]

Over the next four decades, oil constituted a second great energy transition in the mid-Atlantic and beyond. Refined into kerosene, petroleum provided a cheap and abundant source of artificial illumination for a rapidly urbanizing and industrializing society. Processed into a variety of lubricants, petroleum greased the moving parts of factory machines and enabled railroads and steamboats to travel at ever-faster rates. Burned to provide power, petroleum fueled the growth of manufacturing and new forms of transportation. As with anthracite coal, the ever-increasing use of oil deepened the shift from an organic to a mineral energy regime.

But the use of oil was not simply a cause of the mineral energy regime; it was also a consequence of the mid-Atlantic's first steps away from the organic energy regime. The increasing use of anthracite from 1820 to 1860 had enabled the growth of urban and industrial cities like Philadelphia and New York; that boom in turn helped to create new demands. One was the desire for better and cheaper artificial lighting. In the rural and agricultural setting characteristic of the organic energy regime, the sun provided the great majority of people's lighting needs. Most work took place outdoors and during the daytime. People stayed up later during the long days of the summer and often went to bed earlier during the short days of winter. Interior lighting could be obtained fairly easily from open hearth fires or candles made from animal fats available from the farm. In industrial cities, this was no longer the case. Large factories were often constructed out of brick and frequently had only small windows. Moreover, the high amounts of capital invested in manufacturing equipment discouraged owners from closing the doors when the sun went down early in the winter, and as a result, the time clock began to replace the sun as the guide of human schedules. People increasingly began to engage in occupations requiring better light, such as bookkeeping or detailed work in textile production. Most large apartment buildings offered little natural light. City streets were dark at night, adding to the sense of danger when walking through unfamiliar communities.[2] A second demand was for better lubricants. As factory equipment grew larger and faster, the levels of friction increased, taxing the capabilities of lubricants derived from organic sources such as plant oils and animal fats. In other words, as coal enabled many in the mid-Atlantic to live and work in urban and industrial settings, these new patterns generated novel challenges that encouraged some people to investigate petroleum as a possible answer.

In addition to shaping why people looked for petroleum, coal also influenced how people acquired it. The availability of abundant mineral energy increased the oil industry's rate of growth. A proliferation of coal-fired steam engines pumped oil out of the ground, cheap iron allowed thousands of wells to be lined, and a well-developed railroad network rushed people and materials to and from western Pennsylvania. The world's first petroleum boom reflected a recurring pattern of the mineral energy regime: the use of mineral energy sources to solve problems created by the intensive use of mineral energy sources. One energy transition begot another.

Launching this transition required solving difficult problems of transportation. Like anthracite, petroleum was found in a rural and remote region far removed from urban centers of capital and consumption. Similar to coal boosters, oil pioneers were forced to contend with material characteristics of their product that presented both challenges and opportunities. Anthracite was known as stone coal because it was so hard: the lack of volatile gases made it difficult to ignite, but once lit, it burned cleanly and emitted much less pollution than other coals. The liquid nature of petroleum was also a blessing and curse for its boosters. Because it flowed, it could be pumped to the surface through narrow drill shafts with a relative minimum of human labor and be refined into a high-quality illuminating liquid. But controlling the flows of oil proved to be an immense challenge. Whereas anthracite coal could be easily stacked in a heap at the mouth of the mine, petroleum was incredibly difficult to store and transport. It poured out of wells and onto the ground. It seeped through wooden tanks. It leaked out of barrels. It evaporated. Turning the liquid nature of oil from liability to asset demanded huge investments in transport infrastructure.

Oilmen experimented with several approaches to oil transport in the decades following Drake's discovery. Their choices over whether to utilize wagons, barges, railroads, or pipelines not only shaped how oil traveled, but where it went and who benefited from the trade. The ability to control flows of oil was an essential component of the building of one of America's most influential monopoly powers of the late nineteenth century: John D. Rockefeller's Standard Oil Company. But the consequences of transport were felt beyond the oil industry as well. These systems favored certain cities over others and contributed to the unequal distribution of environmental harms. The spatial politics of oil infrastructure created winners and losers.

The Roots of an Energy Transition

The history of oil, like that of anthracite coal, begins hundreds of millions of years in the past. The surface of the earth was much warmer at the time, and shallow oceans and swamps covered much of the land. Tiny microorganisms known as plankton—consisting of both plant and animal species—lived on the surface of the water and sank to the ocean floor when they died. This organic matter combined with silt and other inorganic matter from rivers flowing into the sea. These sediments eventually hardened through a combination of pressure from overlying water, natural cements, and the crystallization of inorganic compounds. Over even longer periods of time, these hardened layers of sediment were buried further, thereby becoming subject to greater pressure and higher temperatures. Sediment became sedimentary rock, and the organic material trapped in these layers was slowly transformed into kerogen, a waxy substance, and then petroleum, which was diffused throughout the layers of rock. The creation of sedimentary rock and petroleum occurred in many places throughout the globe. But in certain places the petroleum seeped through porous rock formations until it became trapped by an overhead layer of impermeable rock like shale, sandstone, or limestone. There the petroleum gathered in pools now known as oil fields.[3]

In a few locales, including Baku, Mesopotamia, and western Pennsylvania, the oil fields formed near enough to the surface that small amounts of oil and gas naturally rose to the surface. For thousands of years, human groups living in these areas collected the petroleum and used it in rituals, to waterproof baskets and ships, to decorate bodies, to construct buildings, as a military weapon, and for medicinal purposes.[4] In North America, centuries before European settlers arrived, Native American groups collected petroleum from the oily waters of a small creek north of the Allegheny River for ceremonial and decorative purposes.[5] The Seneca tribe, for example, used petroleum extensively for skin coloring. They dug pits near the creek and waited several days for a thick layer of oil to rise to the surface. At that point, they skimmed the oil off the surface with ladles or laid blankets on the oily pools and squeezed the contents into receptacles.[6]

European settlers noted the presence of the oily waters in western Pennsylvania as early as 1755.[7] Because of its remote location and hilly geography, the region was only slowly settled by farmers and lumbermen in the eighteenth and early nineteenth centuries. Some of these farmers adopted the practices of the Seneca and gathered small amounts of oil by skimming it or collecting it with blankets. Most of this oil was used in patent medicines that could be rubbed on skin wounds like burns and consumed internally for conditions like rheumatism.[8] Because patent medicines were sold in quite small quantities, several dozen barrels a year were enough to supply the market. For the first half of the nineteenth century, the petroleum seeps near Titusville were little more than a curiosity and a peripheral side activity for a few farmers.

In the 1850s, several forces converged to encourage Americans to reconsider the potential value of oil. The most important was the huge increase in demand for artificial lighting occurring both in America and Europe. As the rise of the mineral energy regime enabled millions to move into burgeoning cities, urban residents began to desire larger quantities of indoor illumination to accommodate their new patterns of living and working. At the time, Americans and Europeans obtained light from a variety of means including open fires, candles, whale oil, camphene, coal oil, and manufactured gas. Before 1830, candles and tallow lamps were the most common form of artificial lighting. They were relatively cheap and easy to make, particularly for a rural population with farm animals, as they could be fashioned by dipping a wick into fat or tallow. Whale oil, particularly from the blubber of sperm whales, provided a much brighter glow, though it was costly. By the 1840s, camphene, a derivative of turpentine from pine trees, and burning fluids, a mixture of camphene and alcohol, became widely used synthetic illuminating liquids in America. Coal was also used to create artificial light. Several European companies invented a process for distilling a liquid from coal that could be refined into an illuminating oil. American firms adopted these techniques and over sixty factories were engaged in making coal oil by 1860.[9] In addition, wealthy residents of cities could obtain light from companies that manufactured gas from coal. By mid-century, urban gas works were providing light to factories, stores, and homes in more than fifty American cities.[10]

However, all of these lighting options had significant limitations. Candles offered a comparatively weak glow. The superior light of whale oil came at a price—between 34 and 79 cents a gallon at wholesale for regular whale oil between 1846 and 1856, while the more highly desired sperm oil cost between 88 cents and $1.62 per gallon in the same period.[11] Camphene offered comparable light quality to whale oil but it gave off a foul smell and was prone to dangerous explosions. Coal oil cost about seventy-five cents a gallon, and it was not broadly available because the industry was relatively young.[12] Manufactured gas was restricted to the homes of wealthy urban residents because of the high costs for installing pipes and the expensive monthly service charges. A large market was clearly in place for entrepreneurs who could offer a better solution.

Drake's discovery in western Pennsylvania was also the result of several advances in the use of coal over the preceding decades. For instance, the railroad system had helped circulate small bottles of petroleum-based patent medicines around America. Eventually, some began to notice the similarities between "rock oil," as it was known, and the kerosene produced by coal oil refineries. The use of coal-fired steam engines in the production of salt wells provided a further impetus. As drillers bored deeper and deeper into salt wells, some of these sites became unusable when small amounts of petroleum seeped in. For salt well drillers, petroleum was a nuisance because it ruined the brine. But their reports suggested possible linkages between drilling and petroleum production. The roots of the petroleum industry, therefore, were deeply grounded in possibilities created through the intensive use of coal.

George Bissell, a New York lawyer, and James Townsend, president of a bank in New Haven, were among those encouraged by the idea of a venture that would obtain large quantities of petroleum by drilling rather than collecting it on the surface. They teamed with a group of other wealthy men in 1854 to send a sample of western Pennsylvania oil to Benjamin Silliman, one of the nation's leading chemists, to analyze its commercial potential.[13] Silliman's investigation proved highly encouraging. He found that the refined oil offered a light that compared favorably with candles, whale oil, camphene, and manufactured gas. The flame was bright and steady, and it burned more slowly than other illuminating liquids. Silliman reported: "I have submitted the lamp burning Petroleum to the inspection of the most experienced lampists who were accessible to me, and their testimony was, that the lamp burning this fuel gave as much light as any which they had seen, that the oil was spent more economically, and the uniformity of the light was greater than in Camphene, burning for twelve hours without a sensible dimunition [sic], and without smoke."[14] Buoyed by this favorable report, Bissell, Townsend, and colleagues formed the Pennsylvania Rock Oil Company in 1855.

Edwin Drake joined the enterprise a couple years later. His involvement was highly circumstantial. Drake was not a likely candidate to pioneer an energy transition. He was not a particularly accomplished man, possessed few technical skills, and had spent most of his time working as a railroad conductor. He was not wealthy nor was he in great health. During the summer of 1857, he was on hiatus from the railroad recovering from an illness. Recently widowed, Drake was struggling to figure out how to support his family while living in a hotel in New Haven. But he happened to have the good fortune that Townsend was living there as well, and the two men engaged in long conversations about a petroleum venture. Because Drake was not working at the time and had a free railroad pass, Townsend and his backers agreed to send him to Oil Creek to explore the area and purchase land rights. Drake took the train to Erie, Pennsylvania, and then rode the mail coach the remaining forty miles to the small town of Titusville.[15]

After purchasing the designated lands, Drake returned to New Haven later that year and a new company was created, the Seneca Oil Company. In the spring of 1858, Drake traveled back to western Pennsylvania ready to begin operations. His backers realized Drake's background may not have impressed locals, so Townsend began sending letters addressed to "colonel" Edwin Drake in advance of his trip, creating a fictitious title intended to generate respect. Though the intrigue of a visiting colonel initially flattered many people, Drake did not long maintain his aura of authority. Most local residents found his idea of boring for oil to be a fool's errand, and salt well drillers seemed to agree. He quickly discovered finding a driller was far more difficult than he expected, particularly because he insisted on religious grounds that his employees abstain from alcohol consumption. He later reported that many considered him a lunatic. Because he was so persistent, a few drillers reportedly agreed to work with Drake simply to get the crazy man to leave, and he was forced to start his search over when they failed to show up at the appointed date.[16] But Drake was doggedly persistent and did not give up. Eventually, he discovered William Smith, a driller who also knew how to repair parts and machinery. Smith agreed to join Drake in the spring of 1859, and his expertise and mechanical abilities proved essential to the enterprise's eventual success.

Drilling proceeded slowly. Due to Titusville's isolated location, Drake had to travel as many as forty miles over primitive roads to find replacements when parts broke and could not be fixed. As the men drilled, the water from nearby Oil Creek often filled the well and caused cave-ins. Given that the men did not expect to find oil until a depth of five hundred feet, the slow pace discouraged the investors. Townsend, the project's most enthusiastic backer, kept the effort going with his own money when the rest of the company's principals were ready to quit. Eventually, Townsend lost hope as well and sent Drake a letter ordering him to cease operations in August of 1859. In a remarkable twist, however, the conditions that had made Drake's work so difficult ended up saving the project: Townsend's letter took so long to be delivered to the remote location that the men struck oil before it arrived.[17] Their plan was vindicated and the men were able to extract around eight to ten barrels of oil a day with a hand pump.[18]

What followed was a boom comparable to the Gold Rush a decade before. The Oil Regions, as the area would soon become known, were overrun with people hoping to strike it rich.[19] In a few short years, a relatively sparsely settled area was littered with derricks as oil production increased from dozens of barrels a year in 1858 to 450,000 barrels in 1860 and more than three million barrels by 1862.[20] Land speculation was one of the most common activities and properties that sold for dollars an acre before the discovery of oil sold for hundreds of thousands one day, only to be resold for millions a few months later.[21] The nation, as a popular song put it, had "oil on the brain," and western Pennsylvania was at the center of the action.

Edwin Drake's persistence may have proved that his ideas were not crazy, but it did not ensure that he was able to capitalize on his discovery. Over the next years, he bounced around several positions within the oil industry, but his investments never bore fruit. While others became millionaires, his finances and health continued to deteriorate. A little more than a decade after his strike, he was destitute. In 1873, the state of Pennsylvania made the charitable decision to grant him a modest pension in recognition of his accomplishment. Otherwise, he likely would have died penniless.[22]

The Great Difficulty

Drake's discovery proved that oil could be obtained in large quantities. But this did not ensure that an energy transition would take place. Oilmen quickly discovered that getting oil out of the ground was only a beginning step. The liquid nature of petroleum, combined with the lack of development in western Pennsylvania, made transport an acute challenge. As one contemporary observer noted: "the great difficulty which has hitherto attended the oil trade has been transport. It was easy enough to produce oil, but far more difficult to convey it to the consumer. The roads in the oil region are execrable; in fact, there are no roads. Everything has to be hauled through an immense slough."[23] Getting a heavy and bulky commodity to consumers using poor roads and leaky containers was a daunting proposition.[24]

Oilmen first turned to the organic energy regime to address their transport challenges. While coal-fired steam engines could help them drill wells, their transport options in the industry's first years were largely limited to organic possibilities. The nearest railroad stations were over twenty miles away, so they were forced to rely on the muscles of men and animals, along with the use of natural waterways. Oil transport typically occurred in two stages, each addressed by different people and technologies: local transport from the oil well to a centralized distribution point followed by long-distance transport to markets. For local transport, the only choice in 1860 was horse-drawn wagons carrying barrels over primitive dirt roads. This was brutally difficult work, and thousands of teamsters, mostly Irish immigrants, rushed to the Oil Regions following Drake's discovery in search of profitable work. Using horse-drawn carts that could carry five or six barrels weighing several hundred pounds each, the men loaded the oil and drove it over the rough roads to a point where it could be transferred onto barges or railroad cars. In good conditions, this was slow and arduous work. During rainy seasons, the roads became practically impassable, and wagons often sank up to their axles in mud.

Teamsters provided an essential function for the oil industry, and they quickly obtained a monopoly on oil transport. Despite their services, they were widely despised by oil producers and community members. Not only were their rates widely considered exorbitant—often as much as $3 or more per barrel, a price that often exceeded the value of the oil itself—they were seen as a social nuisance.[25] Teamsters were frequently depicted as a hard-drinking lot who spent most of their spare time boozing and fighting. They drove their horses so hard that it was rare for an animal to survive more than two years of service. Those getting in their way faced the prospect of feeling the "black snake" of a whip across their legs. Producers of oil felt unfairly robbed of profits by teamsters, while community members experienced them as a toxic presence. However, with no other way for getting oil to transport points, and faced with the ability of the teamsters to keep outsiders from entering the hauling business, there appeared to be no alternative except to tolerate an unwelcome presence. Raised in the Oil Regions, the muckraking journalist Ida Tarbell encapsulated local sentiment: "indispensable to the business [teamsters] became the tyrants of the region—working and brawling as suited them."[26] Similar to disparagement of Irish workers along canals, these sentiments reflected widespread anti-immigrant biases. A standard trope in newspaper articles of the time and early histories of the Oil Regions, the frustrations with the teamsters proved a pattern that would be repeated. Control over transport allowed a group to hold considerable power within the oil industry and make handsome profits despite widespread social critique.

Once teamsters took the oil away from the wellhead, it still needed to travel to distant markets. For this second stage, oilmen began by following the patterns of the organic energy regime. For several years, lumber had been floated down Oil Creek to its junction with the Allegheny River sixteen miles below Titusville. From this point, the lumber could be guided downriver to Pittsburgh. In its natural state, however, Oil Creek was often too shallow and its flows of water too irregular for reliable shipments to occur. This natural limitation had not detracted the region's lumbermen. Like Josiah White on the Lehigh River with anthracite coal, those in the lumber industry used pond freshets to turn the waterway into a more reliable medium for commerce.[27] This system involved setting up a series of temporary dams upstream of the point where oil barges were gathered. Over two or

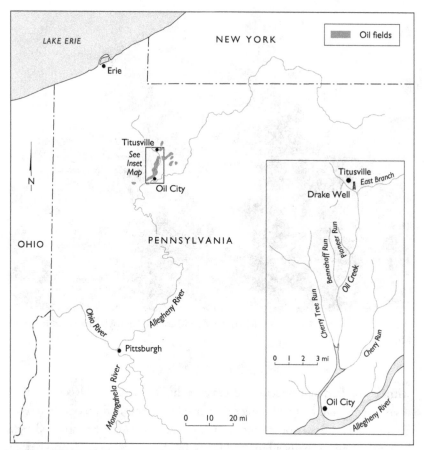

MAP 3.1. Oil Creek.

three days, the dams gathered large pools of water. When they were released in a coordinated fashion, the water rushed out in a long "wave" approximately two feet deep that could float several barges to the Allegheny
River.

Oilmen quickly turned Oil Creek into the world's first petroleum highway. Pond freshets were operated as often as three times a week during the
early 1860s. Oil was loaded onto shallow barges capable of carrying between 25 and 1,000 barrels and a single pond freshet often served a couple
hundred boats.[28] However, this coordination often created dangerous conditions. Whenever a pond freshet was scheduled, crowds would gather to

Pond freshet crash. (Courtesy of the Drake Well Museum, Pennsylvania Historical and Museum Commission)

witness the frequent wrecks and crashes that ensued.[29] A December 1862 disaster triggered by breaking ice destroyed 350 boats and 60,000 barrels of oil and caused $350,000 of property damage. In 1865, a fire sparked by a lantern spread to nearly a hundred boats and led to the loss of 8,000 barrels of oil.[30] Several people made a comfortable living by setting up small wing dams downstream to capture and resell the spilled oil resulting from such mishaps.[31]

Even when pond freshets operated smoothly, they were expensive and resulted in heavy losses. To get a barrel of oil to a seaboard market in 1860 cost an estimated $11.00 per barrel.[32] In addition, oil leakage and evaporation between the wellhead and the final destination meant that as little as 15–20 percent of oil production actually reached consumers in the early 1860s.[33] One observer of the oil trade noted that "the lighter oils of petroleum persistently penetrate the pores of every wood, so that in a voyage to Europe barrels often became entirely empty." The author went on to suggest that barrels could be treated with glue, glycerin, molasses, and tannin "which securely binds the most penetrating oils."[34] Given that desperate oilmen without other options were often willing to pay premium prices for poorly constructed receptacles, few barrel manufacturers bothered with such treatments when even an untreated container could be sold for a large profit.

Most importantly, the expansion of an organic transport network could not meet the exponential growth of a mineral industry. The finite water supply of Oil Creek could only support a few pond freshets a week, and summer droughts and winter ice limited transport further. As an industry observer noted in 1866: "a large portion of the year the river is not navigable. Sometimes in the winter it is ice-bound for months, while in summer it frequently becomes so low as to be fordable, when the smallest craft must be laid up from use."[35] Given that the average pond freshet shipped fewer than 20,000 barrels of oil, there was a severe constraint on total shipments.[36] Within a few years of Drake's discovery, the river was being used nearly to capacity. Moreover, the influence of mineral power in shaping people's expectations for fast and regular movement led even contemporary observers to lament the slowness of the process: "Transportation by the river is the cheapest of all modes of reaching the market; but in this fast age is a little slow."[37] A reliance on organic energy sources for transport presented a powerful constraint to the expansion of the oil industry.

From Organic to Mineral Transport

The widespread use of coal ensured that oilmen did not have to rely on nature's distribution of water or the limitations of organic energy sources. The extension of railroad tracks into the Oil Creek Valley in the early 1860s began the switch to mineral sources of energy for oil transport. At the time of Drake's discovery, thousands of miles of rails crossed the mid-Atlantic region, highlighted by the major trunk lines: the Erie and Central Railroads in New York and the Pennsylvania Railroad in Pennsylvania. Headed by the well-known capitalists Jay Gould, Cornelius Vanderbilt, and Thomas Scott, respectively, the trunk lines dominated the long-distance transport of manufactured goods from east to west and brought the rich agricultural yields of the midwest to the eastern seaboard. These tycoons quickly realized that crude oil could be a profitable commodity and were intrigued by the possibilities of the trade. However, because no rail line passed within twenty miles of Titusville, they would have to build expensive expansions of their transport networks. Since no one at the time knew whether the oil would continue to last, the large companies were wary of making such investments.[38]

The creation of a railroad to link the oil regions with the trunk lines was therefore initiated by local oilmen frustrated with the limitations of shipping oil by water to Pittsburgh. In 1860, they formed the Oil Creek Railroad and built a twenty-mile line from Titusville to Corry, where oil could be sent westward to Cleveland or east to New York City via railroad, the Great Lakes, and the Erie Canal. Completed in late 1862, the railroad shipped approximately 430,000 barrels over the next fifteen months.[39] The creation of the Oil Creek Railroad drew other parties to the region as well. By 1862, the Atlantic & Great Western Railroad, working with the Erie Railroad, had extended its tracks to Corry to enter the oil business. Not wanting to be left out, the Pennsylvania Railroad contracted with the Philadelphia & Erie Railroad to extend its tracks to Sunbury, so that it would have access to the Oil Regions.[40] By 1865, most oil was being transported long distances in railcars. This began an intense competition between the major trunk railroads that would play a significant role in the transport of oil over the next fifteen years.

Not everyone applauded. Energy transport systems create particular landscapes that favor certain places over others.[41] The shift to railroads altered both how and where oil was shipped. In a world of water transport, Pittsburgh was the "natural" outlet for oil, due both to its proximity to the Oil Regions and its river connections. Refiners in the Oil Regions prospered as well because high transport costs encouraged the processing of crude oil close to the site of production due to the fact that some volume was lost during refining. In a world of railways, a new order of oil flows emerged. Railroad rates were determined by competition far more than anything else. As a result, oil tended to flow toward those places where competing railroads were operating. In the new world of space constructed by the railroads, Cleveland and New York City were much better positioned than Pittsburgh because they were served by multiple railroads as well as water-based transport options such as the Great Lakes and the Erie Canal that provided a further downward pressure on rates. The oil refining business

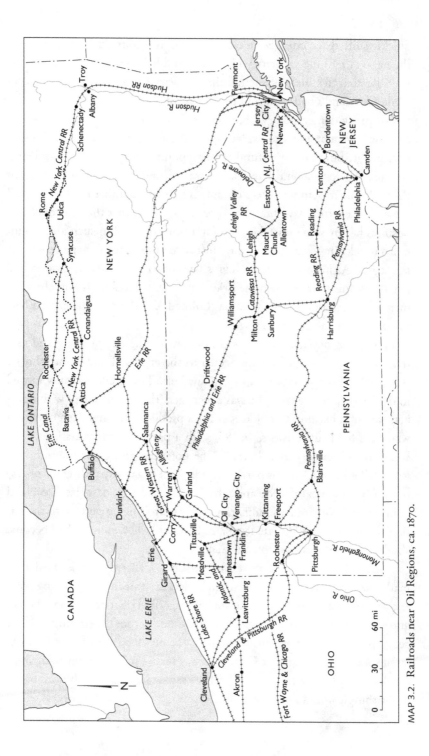

MAP 3.2. Railroads near Oil Regions, ca. 1870.

quickly shifted accordingly. In 1865, Pittsburgh accounted for 39 percent of the nation's refining capacity while Cleveland held 6 percent.[42] Eight years later, Pittsburgh's share of the refining capacity had dropped to 19 percent while Cleveland's had increased to 27 percent.[43]

For many contemporary observers, this was a puzzling state of affairs and some were at a loss to explain it. In the 1870s, one Pittsburgh booster noted: "Pittsburgh is the natural refining point of the oil of Western Pennsylvania. The city should have the entire refining of all the oil of Western Pennsylvania if facility to do so cheaply is to be the dominating motive, and she will at a future day obtain it. There is no doubt that the control of this business has by some mistake been for a time lost."[44] But such an account failed to take into account the ways infrastructure systems shape geographical logics. As historian Allan Nevins later observed: "Cleveland soon had two trunk-line railroads and the Erie Canal, while Pittsburgh was left at the mercy of the grasping Pennsylvania Railroad. On this fact above all others turned the fate of the oil empire."[45]

Human agency mattered as well, of course. The rise of Cleveland as a refining center was directly connected to the efforts of one man: John D. Rockefeller. Born in 1839 in upstate New York, Rockefeller's family moved to the Cleveland area when he was a teenager. Thrifty and adept with numbers, he soon became a bookkeeper for a produce firm and then opened a wholesale foodstuff business in 1859 with a partner. Four years later, they added an oil refinery. A believer in the potential growth of the industry, Rockefeller bought out his partner in 1865 and began expanding his operations. Over the next decade and a half, he turned a modest-size Cleveland refining company into an industrial giant controlling 90 percent of the nation's oil refining. By the late 1870s, his Standard Oil Company had become absolute master of the petroleum trade.[46]

Rockefeller had many exceptional personal qualities. He possessed a remarkable memory, fanatical attention to details, fearsome negotiating powers, and an ability to retain the top managerial talent from firms he acquired. Yet Rockefeller also benefited enormously from the contingencies of geography and transport infrastructure. The development of Standard Oil owed much to the fact that Cleveland was served by a wide range of shipping options. A person with Rockefeller's same talents and ambitions based in Pittsburgh would not have had the same opportunities for success.

To understand how Standard Oil was able to leverage control over the railroad transport system into a monopoly position, it is helpful to step back and review the structure of the oil industry in the nineteenth century. The industry was divided into several branches: production, transport, refining, and marketing. With the exception of refining and marketing, which were often combined within a single organization, each task was performed by different organizations. Producers would drill and collect the oil, one or multiple transport companies would gather the oil at a centralized depot and ship it to distant markets, and a refining organization would process the crude oil into a finished good and market it to consumers. Unlike today's oil industry, there was little vertical integration at the time.

For refiners, the transport of oil was their single greatest variable cost. To be sure, purchasing crude oil was often the most expensive aspect of their operations, but refiners had little ability to gain an advantage over their competitors because relatively standard market prices leveled the playing field. Transport costs, however, were far more fungible. They therefore served as one of the most significant opportunities for refiners to gain a competitive edge. It was standard practice by all the major railroads to post official rates specifying the costs of shipping goods to various destinations. It was equally common for agents to offer discounts—or "rebates" as they were known at the time—to shippers who provided large volumes of traffic or regular business. This practice was heavily protested by farmers and small manufacturers who were disadvantaged by the system, but even though many states passed laws making rebates illegal, they remained a regular practice in the nineteenth century.[47] The lack of enforcement of existing laws by government bodies thereby helped deepen the inequalities of the mineral energy regime.

Once the railroads began to ship oil, Rockefeller quickly began to build his company through the clever manipulation of railroad rebates. In her famous exposé of Rockefeller's company, Ida Tarbell declared: "It was the rebate which had made the Standard Oil Trust, the rebate, amplified, systematised, glorified into a power never equaled before or since by any business of the country."[48] The presence of multiple shippers in Cleveland greatly strengthened Rockefeller's hand because he could play competing transport systems against one another. He took advantage of this situation masterfully. First, he negotiated with all the shippers to obtain the lowest rates he could. These initial lower rates helped him undercut his competitors and expand his refining capacity. By 1870, Standard Oil was refining so much oil that Rockefeller could negotiate further discounts by offering railroads bulk shipments. These bulk shipments lowered the railroad's costs by utilizing their investments in tank cars more effectively, allowing them to ship Rockefeller's oil at lower rates.[49] This soon turned into a synergistic cycle whereby lower transport costs allowed Standard Oil to increase its business, resulting in even larger oil shipments. The company could then achieve further rate cuts, which put it in an even stronger competitive position. Whereas posted rates on oil shipments in the 1870s fluctuated between $1.25 and $1.40 per barrel, Standard Oil was consistently paying $.85 or less.[50] Using his financial advantages from lower transport costs, Rockefeller eliminated nearly all of his refining rivals during the 1870s by buying them out, or forcing them out of business by flooding their markets with cheap kerosene. Crucially, once Standard Oil obtained a large fraction of the oil trade, no other party could negotiate similar discounts because they could not offer the same volume of traffic. The cost advantage of railroad transport was the central pillar of Standard Oil's growth.

The power of Rockefeller's control over railroads was widely displayed in a very public confrontation with Joseph Potts of the Empire Transportation Company. Empire was one of several mid-size companies that gathered and stored oil in the mid-1870s. In addition, Potts worked directly with the Pennsylvania Railroad to coordinate most of the railroad's oil shipments. Given his involvement in many aspects of the oil industry, Potts realized that control over transport was contributing to Standard Oil's dominance. As he later told a federal committee investigating the role of monopoly power in American business, "we reached the conclusion that there were three great divisions in the petroleum business—the production, the carriage of it, and the preparation of it for market. If any one party controlled absolutely any one of those three divisions, they practically would have a very fair show of controlling the others. We were particularly solicitous about the transportation."[51] In 1876, Potts began an aggressive effort to challenge Rockefeller.

In collaboration with the Pennsylvania Railroad, Potts added refining to Empire's core business of transporting oil. Rockefeller and the other major railroads responded quickly and decisively. Rockefeller withdrew all oil shipments from the Pennsylvania Railroad and flooded the markets Empire tried to enter with cheap kerosene. The Erie and Central Railroads protested the Pennsylvania Railroad acquiring its own refineries through Empire and facilitated Standard Oil's efforts by offering discount shipments. For several months, the parties struggled against one another for access to crude oil, lower transport costs, and kerosene markets. The contest may have continued longer because Potts was widely regarded as a first-rate oilman, but in July 1877, railroad workers across the nation went on strike to protest wage decreases. When the Pennsylvania Railroad ordered militiamen to attack strikers in its Pittsburgh equipment yards, the conflict turned violent. Strikers set fires that destroyed numerous buildings and hundreds of railroad locomotives and passenger cars. By the time the violence was complete, dozens of strikers had been killed and the Pennsylvania Railroad had lost millions of dollars in equipment. Financially strapped, the railroad decided it could no longer support Potts's efforts and negotiated a deal with Rockefeller. Empire's lines and equipment were sold to Standard Oil shortly thereafter.[52] For contemporary observers, the very public defeat of the Empire Transportation Company reinforced the crucial links between control of transport infrastructure and industry dominance. Rockefeller's collaborations with the Erie and Central, along with his ability to negotiate with the Pennsylvania Railroad, allowed him to triumph over his would-be competitors.

The transport of oil by railroads, therefore, created clear winners and losers within the oil industry. Standard Oil clearly gained the most from this system. The railroad companies also did well. Once Standard Oil had achieved control over most of the oil flows, Rockefeller began to act as an "evener." He allocated a set share of traffic to each line, thereby ending the competition between them. As a result, the railroads were able to avoid rate wars against one another and could plan for steady business. Compared with shipments of many other goods, oil became a regular and profitable commodity.[53] The advantages that accrued to Standard Oil and the railroad companies came at the expense of others, most notably the small group of oil refiners not aligned with Rockefeller. In addition, the prices that consumers paid for refined oil—though significantly lower than for other artificial illuminants—were likely somewhat higher as a result of monopoly pricing than they would have been in a more competitive system.[54]

Railroads brought the expansive potential of the mineral energy regime to the long-distance transport of crude oil, albeit in a highly unequal manner. But they could not address the other dimension of oil transport: its movement from the well to a centralized depot. In 1865, Samuel van Syckel introduced a revolution in the short-distance transport of oil by building a gathering pipeline that connected a series of oil wells to a railroad depot.[55] His efforts were inspired by the prolific wells discovered along Pithole Creek earlier that year. Despite an estimated three thousand teamsters flooding to the area, transport was slow and cost as much as three dollars a barrel. Once again, organic energy sources were a constraint to growth. Van Syckel took out a $30,000 loan from the First National Bank of Titusville to build a pipeline with a two-inch diameter powered by three pumps.[56] The capacity of the pipeline, eighty-one barrels per hour, was estimated to do the work of three hundred teams working ten hours a day. Van Syckel charged one dollar per barrel and made a small fortune. It was described as "one of the most wonderful of the many wonders produced at Pithole."[57]

Most oil producers greeted van Syckel's breakthrough enthusiastically. It offered a cheaper way to transport oil and alleviated some of the bottleneck. The teamsters, on the other hand, recognized the pipeline as a profound threat to their livelihood. On multiple occasions they sabotaged van Syckel's pipeline, forcing him to post armed guards along the line day and night. An early employee later wrote that "all of the officials of the company, including the writer, were threatened by the teamsters with transportation to a warmer climate."[58] However, the protests of the teamsters did not succeed, due to their general unpopularity and the greater efficiency of the pipelines. As short-distance gathering pipelines spread throughout the Oil Regions, the numbers and social power of teamsters faded rapidly. Astute oilmen learned a valuable lesson: rather than negotiating or dealing with laborers and sharing the industry's profits, it was easier to replace them with technology powered by mineral energy. The ability of oilmen to avoid labor battles through technological innovation gave the industry a significant advantage compared with coal over the course of the twentieth century.[59]

By the late 1860s, the transport of oil was largely accomplished with mineral energy sources. Crude oil flowed through short pipelines to railroad depots where it was shipped by rail to refining centers. Oil had left the age of wood as iron storage tanks, iron pipes, and iron railcars replaced wooden barrels, wooden wagons, and wooden boats. As long as Pennsylvania's mines kept producing more coal, Pennsylvania's oil production and transport could continue unabated.

Thus was born a landscape of intensification. Railroads and gathering pipelines ensured that transport constraints would not impede the growth of the oil industry. From a total supply of dozens of barrels a year in the 1850s, output skyrocketed to nearly two and a half million barrels in 1865 and more than five million barrels by 1870.[60] But these systems influenced more than simply how oil traveled: they structured where oil went and who benefited. Cleveland's gain came at Pittsburgh's expense, and manual laborers lost a valuable trade when they were replaced by gathering pipelines. The rising tide of oil did not raise all boats.

Consuming Oil

The development of railroads and short-distance pipelines enabled oilmen to deliver their product in ever-increasing quantities to urban markets. Refined into kerosene and lubricating oils, petroleum lengthened the day and greased the wheels of industry. The steadily increasing consumption of petroleum deepened the shift to the mineral energy regime in the mid-Atlantic and beyond.

In the first decades of the oil industry, lighting was its first and most important market. For those living in industrialized nations today, it is easy to take bright, cheap, and reliable artificial lighting for granted. The widespread use of electric lighting controlled with the flick of a switch has made turning night into day a regular and unremarkable activity. But for the vast majority of those living in 1860, no such simple option existed. Urban residents of the mid-nineteenth century experienced light and its absence in very direct ways. Artificial illuminants were expensive and typically cast a weak glow. They required regular tending, emitted soot, reduced oxygen levels, heated rooms to uncomfortable temperatures, and came with a great risk of fire. Therefore, it was not mere exaggeration when contemporaries claimed that "as far as an illuminator is concerned, petroleum is the great blessing of the nineteenth century."[61]

Early petroleum boosters benefited greatly from this preexisting demand and prior investments in lighting infrastructure. Not only did many people want a high-quality illuminating oil, there were few technological or knowledge barriers to the adoption of kerosene. Whereas early anthracite boosters were forced to contend with the challenges of encouraging consumers to buy expensive stoves and then teach them complicated methods of igniting stone coal, petroleum boosters faced an easier path. In the 1850s, many firms produced lamps costing as little as a dollar that could be filled with whale oil, camphene, or coal oil. Because many consumers already owned and operated these lamps, they had learned the techniques of filling, lighting, trimming, and maintaining the flame. Substituting petroleum-based kerosene for another illuminating oil, therefore, was a relatively simple process. In fact, some early consumers may not have known that their first purchases of kerosene were derived from petroleum instead of coal oil.[62]

But even if an established market existed, this did not mean petroleum could be delivered directly to consumers. Crude oil pumped out of the ground is an agglomeration of water, multiple hydrocarbons, and an assortment of impurities. Most of the water was typically removed from the oil in separating tanks at the well. However, the remaining crude oil was a mix of hydrocarbons and impurities ill-suited for most purposes: it burned unsteadily, released large amounts of soot, and often smelled foul. To be useful, crude oil needed to be refined. Following techniques developed by coal oil refiners, oilmen learned to heat large quantities of crude oil and then separate the hydrocarbons as they vaporized at different temperatures. These fractions could then be treated with chemicals to remove impurities. The middle fractions were the most valuable because they could produce high-quality kerosene. The heaviest parts of crude oil were used to make lubricants and for asphalt and pitch. Light fractions, known as naphtha, gasoline, and benzene, were often burnt off in the 1860s because they were considered too volatile to use safely and there were few established applications.[63] There was no need to squeeze every drop out of a barrel of oil when it was so cheap and abundant.[64]

Refining, in a certain sense, was alchemy. Depending on where crude oil was obtained, it might hardly resemble the output of another well. One observer described the differences in 1865: "Petroleum coming from different localities often differs in consistency from the fluidity of naphtha to the viscidity of tar. In color, specimens range from extreme yellow to deep black, and some have a greenish or reddish hue."[65] Some oil was good for making lubricants while other fields produced oil that could be more easily transmuted into kerosene. This variation forced refiners to adapt their processes to the particular characteristics of the crude oil they received, continually changing the levels of heat, the length of treatments, and the mix of chemicals. In the same way that anthracite breakers and merchants transformed a naturally varying substance into an abstract commodity by creating classifications, oil refiners altered the complex mixture of hydrocarbons into a few standard products whose origin was unknown and irrelevant to consumers. Kerosene, the main product of most refineries, was marketed to customers primarily as "standard white" while "water white" was a premium product that offered a slightly superior flame.[66]

For consumers, the provenance of their kerosene mattered little. They cared much more about the brightness of the light, its safety, the smell, and the price. Kerosene drew particular praise for its bright light and even glow. One commentator claimed, "its use is characterized by a clear, strong and steady flame that is most agreeable to the eye."[67] Benjamin Silliman's report on kerosene noted that the light was "pure and white without odor."[68] Another observer argued that it "surpassed all others, except gas, in brilliancy."[69] Only manufactured gas, which was often described as "the most perfect substitute for the light of day" and "as bright as sunlight," was consistently rated higher than kerosene.[70]

Kerosene was further credited for its safety and lack of smell. Though today we rarely think of light as having a smell or being dangerous, this was not the case in the nineteenth century. Camphene and burning fluids offered bright light, but they emitted an unpleasant odor that could permeate a house or apartment. Moreover, they were highly volatile and came with the risk of fire and explosions. As noted in 1865: "the older burning fluids, manufactured from strong alcohol and oil of turpentine . . . invariably exploded when their volatile vapors, mingled with atmospheric air, came in contact with a light. They have cost hundreds of lives in our country."[71] When suitably refined, kerosene was a safe illuminating oil with a relatively benign odor.

Kerosene, however, did not always perform as expected. In 1876, it was estimated that there were 5,000 deaths annually from fires triggered by exploding lamps, many of which were burning kerosene that had been mixed with volatile naphtha by unscrupulous refiners.[72] These safety concerns encouraged government agencies to investigate kerosene, and the decentralized nature of American governance quickly led to a proliferation of safety measures. In the 1860s, local municipalities and cities like Philadelphia were often the first to act and passed laws specifying where refineries could be located, how oil could be stored, and what safety standards kerosene had to meet. Some states passed similar measures, though by 1880, more than a third of the states in which kerosene was sold had no regulations. More effective regulation came from overseas. Because many European nations imported large quantities of kerosene, they were able to implement trade standards that typically demanded higher levels of safety than the patchwork of American rules. As a result, European consumers often had access to safer kerosene than their American counterparts.[73]

While the quality of its light, its lack of odor, and its relative safety were compelling for consumers, kerosene's main advantage was that it got cheaper over time. As part of the mineral energy regime, it was subject to synergistic feedback loops between production, transport, and consumption. In 1863, kerosene cost just over fifty cents per gallon wholesale in New York City but this price plummeted to forty-one cents a gallon in 1867 and to less than twenty-five cents in 1871.[74] By contrast, coal oil and whale oil cost at least seventy-five cents a gallon around 1860 and the price was often well over a dollar.[75] Camphene sometimes sold for as little as forty cents a gallon but it was not as desirable due to its smell.[76] Gaslight may have seemed an "artificial sun," but its brightness was only available to the wealthy residents of urban cities who could afford the costs of installing pipes and the high service charges; it was simply not a realistic lighting option for most Americans.

The price advantage of kerosene was even more powerful when one factors in the quality of its light. Analyzing the cost of the light output of various illuminants in America in 1870, economist William Nordhaus found that kerosene had a seven-to-one advantage over camphene, a twelve-to-one advantage over manufactured gas, and a twenty-to-one advantage over sperm whale oil. Similar benefits were obtained overseas. In Britain, the price of achieving a million lumen-hours with kerosene in 1860 was £1,500, but this declined to £500 ten years later. By the end of the century, the same service cost only £200. Consequently, Britons increased the amount of light they received from kerosene from about 3.3 billion lumen-hours in 1870 to 1.5 trillion by 1900.[77]

Moreover, the output of kerosene could be steadily expanded while illuminants derived from organic energy sources faced finite limits to growth. Candles, whale oils, and camphene did not get steadily more abundant and cheaper. A shortage of fats and tallows in continental Europe during the nineteenth century resulted from the fact that the production of candles required the allocation of land and was therefore subject to the negative feedback loops of the organic energy regime. The same was true for camphene, whose main ingredient, turpentine, came from resin-bearing pine trees in the American South. And despite the common rhetoric of the inexhaustibility of the oceans, whaling vessels were already being forced to travel longer distances in search of prey by the 1850s. The output of the American whaling industry actually peaked in 1846, years before the introduction of petroleum illuminants.[78] It is doubtful that the oceans could have continued to provide American consumers with average yields of 117,950 barrels of sperm oil and 215,913 barrels of whale oil, as the industry had produced between 1835 and 1860.[79] While petroleum has rightly been linked with numerous environmental harms, kerosene may have helped to save some species of the world's whale populations from extinction.

Coal oils and manufactured gas were also part of the mineral energy regime but they were not able to expand at such a rapid rate. The high fixed costs of gas limited its installation to factories, city streets, and the homes of the wealthy. And coal oil refiners quickly discovered that it was much cheaper to refine petroleum than coal. Their operations required a separate stage of distillation where coal was broken into small pieces and heated in retorts to produce a liquid that could be refined. But with a naturally occurring source of liquid energy, coal refiners were at a disadvantage because petroleum demonstrated that "nature distils free of charge."[80] As noted by an industry observer, most coal oil refiners were forced out of business or quickly became petroleum refiners: "the discovery of petroleum prostrated the whole business, and threatened its projectors with overwhelming loss, from which they were happily rescued by converting their oil factories into refineries, which was done with very little trouble."[81]

Given its high quality and low price, kerosene quickly came to dominate illuminating markets in the mid-Atlantic and beyond. From the very beginning, international markets absorbed large amounts of kerosene. As much as two-thirds of American kerosene production was exported from 1867 to 1884. These sales ended up playing an important role in helping the United States government pay off the debts from the Civil War. European nations consumed roughly 90 percent of American oil exports, but kerosene was also sold anywhere that Americans traded with during the 1860s including Asia, Africa, and South America. Within America, kerosene consumption was concentrated initially in the eastern seaboard cities, where demand was highest and transport facilities were the best. However, small amounts of kerosene were soon sold throughout the nation since it could be transported to country stores along the same networks that distributed other commodity goods.[82]

Kerosene, therefore, was part of a democratization of light in the nineteenth century. Wealthy people could afford gaslight or whale oil, but for most of the population these sources were prohibitively expensive. One 1865 company pamphlet emphasized that kerosene would "give a good and cheap light in the houses of the poor."[83] Another author noted "the civilizing influence" of "an illuminator for the homes of the poor."[84] While the production, transport, and refining of petroleum were anything but egalitarian, kerosene's low price did bring it within the reach of a much wider segment of the population.

As kerosene use expanded, both in the mid-Atlantic and abroad, lighting increasingly became part of the mineral energy regime. With lighting a limited and expensive resource in the organic energy regime, certain patterns of social behavior were encouraged, such as scheduling evening gatherings during times of the month where the moon was full, thereby making night travel easier and safer.[85] In preindustrial times, those living on farms often slept much longer hours during winter as a result of having less work and less light.[86] Kerosene helped change these patterns. With cheap and abundant light, it was easy for people to have social gatherings in the evenings, do detailed work at home, or spend more time reading. In cities, it even stimulated the rise of evening versions of newspapers, as improved forms of lighting in streets and at homes made this a viable commercial business.[87] As a kerosene booster reported to *Chemical News* in 1864: "the effect that this illuminating agent has produced throughout the country is very striking. It has entirely displaced all other means of lighting except gas, and is used even in cities by many who desire an absolutely steady light . . . Kerosene has, in one sense, increased the length of life among the agricultural population. Those who, on account of the dearness or inefficiency of whale oil, were accustomed to go to bed soon after sunset and spend almost half their time in sleep, now occupy a portion of the night in reading and other amusements; and this is more particularly true of the winter season."[88]

A second way that petroleum deepened the hold of the mineral energy regime was through its use as a lubricant. Although lubricating oils were only a small percentage of the overall consumption of petroleum during the nineteenth century, they played a disproportionately important role in facilitating industrial growth. Lubricants derived from animals and plants had greased axles, waterwheels, and other moving parts in machinery for thousands of years. However, with the application of steam power to machinery and vehicles, the levels of friction and resistance grew exponentially during the nineteenth century, creating new challenges: "by the middle of the nineteenth century, the rapid growth of the factory system, the invention of new machines, and the expansion of steamship and railroad transportation had reached the point where the scarcity of efficient lubricants had become a serious bottleneck."[89] More powerful machinery could only function with high-quality lubricants.

Whereas much of kerosene's success came from rendering the natural variability of crude oil into a standardized product sold according to just a few grades, the wide range of industrial operations meant there was a market for hundreds of varieties of lubricants. Some machines required heavy lubricants that could withstand high heat, while others performed best with a lighter oil that would not gum up the gears. Refiners experimented with different processes and oils to create lubricants that were eventually classified in the broad categories of spindle oils, machine oils, and cylinder oils.[90] They also sought oil from particular fields. The "Venango first sand" of the Franklin field, about fifteen miles southwest of Titusville, produced the best oil for making lubricants and sold at a much higher price than oil from other areas.[91]

Lubricants sustained the synergistic relationships of the mineral energy regime. As abundant supplies of coal gave rise to more powerful machines, the increased levels of friction could have provided a limiting constraint to growth. Petroleum-based lubricants addressed this concern thereby facilitating the construction of larger, faster, and more powerful industrial operations. Once again, the mineral energy regime was called upon to address problems caused by the use of mineral energy sources.

The Sacrifice of the Oil Regions

The dramatically increasing consumption of oil came at great cost to the landscapes of western Pennsylvania. While consumers in the mid-Atlantic and beyond benefited from a cheap source of energy, the costs of its production were not evenly shared. The environment of the Oil Regions was sacrificed to meet the world's desires for kerosene and lubricants.

The destruction began with wood. Forests were clear-cut both to provide the material to construct derricks and also to generate space for drilling equipment to be installed. Once oil was discovered, the degradation often got much worse. Drillers focused so intensively on finding oil that they often failed to erect storage facilities until oil was discovered. Many oilmen simply dug large holes in the ground in a desperate effort to collect the petroleum once it began to flow. These pits only caught a fraction of the output, and as a result, the first days of production simply poured on to the ground and seeped into drinking supplies. In 1862, it was estimated that three-quarters of oil production was lost.[92] This practice was hardly discouraged. One writer seeking to provide "useful information" on the oil industry noted that "[storage tanks] cost about two hundred dollars, but this expense need not be incurred till the oil is reached."[93] Even if people wished to have barrels on hand ahead of time, it was often impossible to obtain them. A British observer of the early oil trade observed: "Great difficulties arose from the want of barrels, which could not be made fast enough. The owners of the wells tried to stop the flow of oil, but the wells would not cease to flow. 'Oil Creek' became literally what its name imported, for the oil was necessarily allowed to run to waste into the stream, the surface of which was covered with oil for miles."[94] In the rush to supply storage barrels and tanks, manufacturers often sped up the process by using unseasoned wood and skipping the step of treating the inside of the barrels with glues and sealants. As a result, even if barrels were available, they usually ended up leaking badly.

As the ground became saturated with oil and the landscape dotted with large containers of crude, fire became a regular and deadly occurrence. The lighting of a lantern, sparks from a steam engine, or smoking could unleash a deadly conflagration. When a flowing well caught fire in the early 1860s, the scene appeared biblical: "It seemed as though the earth was vomiting flame threatening to fill the whole valley with a sea of fire." The author went on to observe that the "scene was grand and awful, and had it not been for the suffering and loss of life that attended it, would have been interesting beyond description."[95] Hundreds of men died in fires and countless millions of dollars of property went up in smoke. Despite this danger, a sufficient number of prospectors deemed the potential rewards of a petroleum strike to outweigh the risks of a fiery demise.[96]

Mud may have been far less dramatic than flowing wells or raging fires, but it became a central feature of life in the oil-producing regions. As one 1865 observer noted: "If you wish to live in mud, to walk in mud, to ride in mud, to see nothing but mud, to have the color of your clothing obscured by mud, to inhale nothing but air burdened with gas and petroleum . . . by all means come to Oil City . . . Here King Petroleum reigns, seated upon his muddy throne."[97] While sweat and money were thrown in great quantities at the production of oil, few saw fit to invest in basic infrastructure such as quality roads or sanitation facilities. As a result, what passed as roads were frequently little more than wide dirt paths that became a mixture of mud and oil deeper than a man's knee. Clean water often cost more than oil in Titusville, and the stench of human waste was at times overwhelming. In short, "Petrolia was hell on Earth, teeming with mud, haphazard derricks, constant engine noise, shacks, and skiffs, all awash in flowing oil and blowing soot."[98]

Ecological desecration was not confined to the industry's early years, nor did it escape the purview of observers at the time. When the United States government sent Stephen Peckham to analyze the oil industry for a special report in the Census in 1880, he compared the landscapes to the vagaries of war: "The development of the oil territory proceeds, after its existence has been demonstrated, without regard to any other interest. Nothing that I ever beheld reminded me so forcibly of the dire destruction of war as the scenes I beheld in and around Bradford at the close of the census year; and

Pioneer Run: the sacrificial landscape of petroleum. (Library of Congress)

nothing else but the necessities of an army commands such a complete sacrifice of every other interest or leaves such a scene of ruin and desolation."[99] And while precise measurements were never available for the oil that flowed to waste, his report noted that conservative estimates showed that anywhere from five thousand to twelve thousand barrels of oil were flowing to waste every day in 1879 and 1880, with the actual losses likely to be even higher.[100] To put this into context, each month western Pennsylvania oilmen were spilling the equivalent amount of oil that was lost in the 1989 Exxon Valdez disaster.[101]

For the most part, urban consumers were spared from experiencing any of these harms. Because kerosene burned relatively cleanly, it produced little indoor pollution. The one major exception was the presence of urban refineries. Though cities competed to attract refineries because they were sources of tax revenue, jobs, and growth, these enterprises came at a cost. An 1881 newspaper report describing a visit to refineries in the New York harbor bemoaned the "nauseating stenches which poisoned the atmosphere for miles around" and informed readers that the smell of the discharged water was "quite offensive."[102] The wastes also ruined the local fishing industry.[103] Refineries in Cleveland polluted the Cuyahoga River so significantly that the city was forced to find new sources of drinking water.[104] The urban refining of petroleum, therefore, came with environmental costs for those living nearby.

Although the sacrifice of natural landscapes to extract natural resource wealth occurred in other booms such as the production of anthracite coal, several factors made events in the Oil Regions particularly devastating. The first was the motivation of the oil speculators. When pondering the internal improvements necessary to develop the anthracite coal regions, boosters mixed hopes of financial gain with a broader sense of regional and political development. To be successful, such improvements needed to be built to last for decades, and it was expected that benefits would accrue over long periods of time to a wide range of parties. By contrast, oil investment was largely a matter of short-term financial gain for individuals. People had no idea how long the oil would last, and they rushed to make their money before the boom ended.[105] During the first decade of oil extraction, they invested little into permanent infrastructure. To the extent that those developing the oil industry believed it would offer a social benefit, it was largely through the indirect means of economic growth. Those developing the oil regions were fortune-seekers, not nation-builders.

A second factor shaping the environmental consequences was the use of mineral energy sources in production. For the first several decades of the anthracite coal trade, organic energy sources—human and animal muscles—provided most of the industry's power. Mineral energy, primarily coal burned in steam engines, was not used intensively until the 1840s. Limited amounts of organic energy mitigated the rate and scale of landscape transformation. By contrast, oilmen used coal-fired steam engines from the earliest days to drill as many holes as quickly and deeply as possible. Within a few years, "nothing was heard throughout the valley but the working of engines."[106] By 1870, more than half of the steam engines in the nation were at work in the Oil Regions, and they used more horsepower than any industry except anthracite coal.[107] The energetic abundance of coal provided a mechanism for the rapid and wanton development of western Pennsylvania.

Government actions also exacerbated the environmentally destructive patterns of the oil industry. In the early 1860s, both Pennsylvania and New York passed laws simplifying the process of incorporation, and Pennsylvania relaxed restrictions denying "foreign" corporations, including those chartered in other states, the right to own property. These changes made it easier for speculators to tap capital flows from distant cities and channel this money into drilling operations.[108] In addition, property ownership rights were granted high accord in the American legal system, and there were few constraints on actions that took place on private property. Those who wished to develop their property for oil production had full right to do so with relatively little regard for potential impacts on the surrounding area. As a result, even if a landowner did not want to commence drilling, he or she would likely find their property tarnished by the actions of neighbors. Moreover, because the oil under one property might flow to parts of a neighboring property, a landowner who delayed development risked losing any chance to profit. These legal decisions eventually became formalized under the "rule of capture," which held that drillers were entitled to all the oil that they could pump from a well, even if this meant taking a disproportionate share from a pool that extended beyond the surface land rights they controlled. Property owners were put in a direct race against one another to extract the mineral wealth before it went to another party, thereby accelerating the rate of development. Careful and measured production was a losing proposition under such conditions: intensification was more logical.[109]

The liquid nature of oil exacerbated these factors. The California gold rush also operated according to a logic of economic growth above all else, but neither gold nor the massive quantities of rock removed to find it flowed in the same way that oil did. The fact that petroleum seeped out of wells, ran into streams, and leaked out of storage tanks made it much harder to control. The materiality of oil, combined with human disregard for spills, played a significant role in the sacrifice of the environment of the Oil Regions.[110]

Edwin Drake is widely credited with pioneering the oil industry. His persistence proved that drilling could be effective, but an energy transition only occurred once boosters overcame the substantial obstacles to controlling the fluid nature of petroleum. Oilmen turned first to organic energy systems to fulfill this need, though the limitations of wagons and waterways encouraged industry insiders to tap the potential of the mineral energy regime. The deployment of railroads and gathering pipelines created a landscape of intensification that facilitated the continual growth of oil flows.

While kerosene offered a large and growing market, there was very little use of oil to provide heat or power during the petroleum industry's first decades. If petroleum were to do more than light the world and provide lubrication for machinery, boosters would need to create new markets. And it would be a revolution in the transport of oil that would facilitate this development. Long-distance pipelines would replace railroads with revolutionary consequences for the consumption of oil.

4

Pipelines and Power

ON JUNE 4, 1879, a large crowd gathered in "intense excitement" to witness the world's first test of a long-distance oil pipeline. As early evening began to settle in the central Pennsylvania town of Williamsport, they heard a "strange" and "distinctly audible" noise as air was forced out of the pipe. A few minutes later, a steady flow of oil began to pour into the collecting tank below. The assembled group began to cheer loudly and filled small bottles with petroleum to take home as souvenirs. Byron Benson and other officers of the Tide-Water Pipe Company gave brief speeches and a "spirited celebration" ensued. Newspapers labeled it the dawn of a "new era."[1]

The creation of the Tide-Water pipeline marked a watershed in the early oil industry. Over the previous several months, scores of men had labored in the forests of the Allegheny Mountains to construct a pipeline that would ship oil from the prolific fields of western Pennsylvania toward the seaboard. Their efforts were a blend of the organic and mineral energy regimes. Thousands of tons of coal were consumed to create iron pipes and power pumps that pushed the oil on its journey. But the rigorous labor of human and animal muscles hauled the pipes from railroad depots into unsettled parts of western Pennsylvania and connected them into a single line stretching more than a hundred miles. The work was hard, the risks were many, but so too were the rewards: at stake was the future of the oil industry.

The tale of the Tide-Water pipeline reveals two central patterns of oil in nineteenth-century America. First, it illustrates the contingencies and power relationships that characterize the building of energy transport systems. More than simply the inevitable result of a relentless search for lower-cost ways to ship oil, the Tide-Water pipeline was a deliberate response to the social, political, and economic climate of the oil industry in the 1870s. In particular, it was an attempt to overcome the dominance of John D. Rockefeller's Standard Oil Company. Oilmen knew that Rockefeller was benefiting enormously from preferential rates given to him by the railroads. By creating a new system for transporting oil, Benson and the Tide-Water Pipe Company were seeking to overturn the conditions that had enabled Standard Oil to control nine-tenths of the nation's refining business. Pipelines were not simply a mechanism for moving oil; they were an explicit attempt to transform who controlled the flows of petroleum and who would profit from them.

Second, the Tide-Water pipeline initiated a series of developments that turned out to have profound implications for American energy history and the nation as a whole. As with other energy transport systems, the creation of pipelines served to intensify the consumption of oil. In the pre-pipeline era, petroleum was used predominantly for light and lubrication. The development of pipelines, in conjunction with the discovery of new oil fields, facilitated the creation of new oil markets for heat and power. Although oil had once been too valuable for these applications, the low cost of shipping it along pipelines encouraged Americans to reconsider how they would use it. Pipelines created a new landscape of intensification in the mid-Atlantic.

These new uses of oil, combined with the expansion of kerosene and lubricant markets, furthered the dependence of the mid-Atlantic on mineral energy sources. And as oil began to be discovered in new regions including California, Oklahoma, and Texas, the development of new oil consumption practices in the mid-Atlantic accelerated the rise of the mineral energy regime in other parts of the nation as well. These changes in energy flows had significant implications for American history more generally. Oil played an important role in pioneering the second industrial revolution and ushering in the politics of the Gilded Age.

Early Pipeline Attempts

The recognition that Standard Oil benefited enormously from its transport advantages encouraged some oilmen in the 1870s to begin experimenting with a new infrastructure for shipping petroleum. Crucially, pipeline developers were motivated by dissatisfactions with the industry structure, not from impersonal market forces autonomously generating technological advances. There was no shortage of railroad tank cars that made pipelines necessary to relieve the bottleneck. Nor were the cost of shipments too much for consumers to bear: before the first pipeline was built, kerosene was cheaper than other artificial illuminants and it was winning market share around the world.[2] There was nothing inevitable about the rise of oil pipelines.

When considering alternatives to railroads, pipelines came to the forefront of people's imaginations because they had been used in the local transport of oil since 1865. However, the development of a long-distance pipeline was a very different proposition from the gathering pipelines pioneered by Samuel van Syckel. Gathering pipelines had a small diameter (usually two inches) and ran only a short distance (typically under five miles). The oil flowed by gravity or was powered by small pumps when there was an elevation gain. Gathering pipeline companies operated as intermediaries between producers and shippers. Long-distance pipelines, by contrast, had large diameters (five inches and above) and usually ran more than a hundred miles. Powerful pumps were needed to propel the oil across the landscape and their operators acted as intermediaries between gathering pipeline companies and refineries. In other words, the two systems involved different capital requirements, technologies, and customers. As a result, long-distance pipelines were not a straightforward extension of existing practices.

Given these challenges, it is not surprising that the initial attempts to build pipelines were not entirely successful. In 1874, David Hostetter began construction of a 32-mile pipeline from the Butler oil field south of Titusville to a point near Pittsburgh. The history of the Columbia Conduit details the myriad challenges involved in such an endeavor. "Doctor" Hostetter was a colorful man who took his title from selling Hostetter's Bitters—a patent medicine made from whiskey and wormwood. He was also involved in oil production and manufactured gas works in Pittsburgh and was frustrated with what he considered to be unfair rates from the Pennsylvania Railroad. He therefore sought to build a four-inch pipeline from the Oil Regions to the outskirts of Pittsburgh with pumping stations every five miles. He and his workers ran into trouble, however, when they had to cross the tracks of a branch of the Pennsylvania Railroad. Because the railroad saw the pipeline as a threat to its oil shipments, it moved with force against the potential competitor. Like the teamsters attacking van Syckel's line during the previous decade, as soon as the pipes were laid under the tracks, railroad men ripped them out and sued Hostetter. Not content to rely on the law to uphold their claims, they built fortifications out of railroad ties and kept armed guards on site to prevent the completion of the pipeline. Frustrated and ready to give up, Hostetter leased the pipeline to Byron Benson, Robert Hopkins, and David McKelvy in April 1875.[3]

Benson, Hopkins, and McKelvy had been working together in the oil and lumber industries for several years. Compared with many of the dramatic and flamboyant oilmen of the era, they were pragmatists. While others focused exclusively on drilling for oil, Benson and Hopkins entered the business in 1865 and sold lumber for derricks and barrels to provide regular income that supplemented the more speculative field of petroleum production. In 1870, they met the young lawyer McKelvy and formed a partnership. One of their colleagues, J. G. Benton, first alerted the men to the pipeline opportunity. Benton had an idea but needed capital. He realized that if the line was split in the middle at a public crossing of the railroad, the men could make regular oil shipments by carting the oil over the tracks in horse-drawn tank cars. Benson, Hopkins, and McKelvy agreed and struck a deal with Hostetter. Benton identified a nearby public highway and built a storage tank at either side of the line. When the oil arrived at the north side of the tracks, it was pumped from the storage tank into a wagon with a large container, pulled across the railroad tracks by a team of horses,

Byron Benson. (Courtesy of the Drake Well Museum, Pennsylvania Historical and Museum Commission)

deposited into the storage tank on the south side, and sent by pipe to Pittsburgh. The railroad company tried to thwart this plan by leaving railroad cars parked on the tracks to block the wagon, but a court forced them to stop this practice because it was a public highway. With this work-around complete by summer 1875, the pipeline was able to ship five thousand barrels a day and earn a good rate of return. This success, however, drew the attention of Standard Oil. Rockefeller reportedly paid Hostetter a million dollars for the line in the fall of 1877, and Benson, Hopkins, and McKelvy received a quarter of that sum to terminate the lease.[4]

Henry Harley of the Pennsylvania Transportation Company put forward a more ambitious pipeline plan in 1876. Like Joseph Potts's Empire Transportation Company, Harley's company owned a network of gathering pipelines and storage tanks for oil. Seeking to move into long-distance transport, he proposed a 230-mile pipeline to Baltimore that would deliver crude oil to the eastern seaboard. To lend legitimacy to his project, he employed the noted Civil War general and civil engineer Herman Haupt, who had led early efforts to construct the Hoosac Tunnel, a railroad passageway in Massachusetts. Despite having completed the survey, drawn up the technical plans, and raised some capital, Harley was forced to abandon this effort when he was arrested for fraudulent dealings in oil: his company had oversold the oil holdings in its storage tanks and went into bankruptcy. Harley's eye for promotion was keener than his aptitude for maintaining account books. As with Empire, Standard Oil took advantage of the company's weakened state and purchased its gathering pipelines and storage tanks the next year.[5]

In 1878, Benson, Hopkins, and McKelvy purchased the rights to Harley's proposed pipeline to Baltimore using half of the money they received when Standard Oil bought the Columbia Conduit. They formed the Seaboard Pipe Company and obtained subscriptions for many of the shares. However, questions over the feasibility of the project led to its collapse. Potential investors worried about the lack of independent refiners in Baltimore, declining production in the Butler oil fields where the line was to originate, and the uncertainty of obtaining an unbroken line of property rights for 230 miles.[6] In all three cases of early pipeline development, capital requirements, difficulties in obtaining land rights, and competitive pressures proved insurmountable.

The Tide-Water Pipeline

Despite being bought out of control of the Columbia Conduit and failing to attract adequate funding for the Seaboard Pipe Company, Benson and his colleagues remained intrigued by the potential of pipelines. In November 1878, they turned their attention to an alternate route and established the Tide-Water Pipe Company. The men came to an agreement with Franklin Gowen, the outspoken president of the Reading Railroad, to construct a 110-mile pipeline from the newly discovered Bradford oil field east to Williamsport, where the railroad company would take the oil to refiners in Philadelphia and New York City. The Reading agreed to provide half the needed capital in return for the opportunity to enter the oil trade. Because the Reading's tracks did not extend west of Williamsport, it had previously been reliant on transfers from other railroads in order to obtain any oil shipments. Therefore, the Reading was one of the only major railroads operating in the mid-Atlantic that was not already under Standard Oil's sway. Gowen was eager to increase the railroad's business and hoped a pipeline would give him direct access to oil.

While the concept of pipelines had been proven through the construction of small-diameter gathering lines, the company's directors, engineers, and workers had to face a number of technical and competitive questions given the new scale of their effort. Could a pipe sustain the pressure required to pump the oil over the Allegheny Mountains? Would oil be tarnished by extended contact with iron? Most importantly, given the vigorousness with which Standard Oil had attacked the Empire Transportation Company and acquired the Columbia Conduit, how could the company expect to withstand Rockefeller's anticipated response? The combination of these challenges led many in the region to dub the effort "Benson's folly."[7] Newspaper accounts reported that observers watched the pipeline's efforts with "great curiosity" but that many "looked upon it doubtfully."[8]

Technologically, the construction of a long-distance pipeline was an ambitious project, much like the building of the Brooklyn Bridge a few years later. To begin with, practically all the parts had to be designed and made to order, including pipes, fittings, and valves. The company decided to use sixteen- to twenty-foot wrought-iron pipes with a six-inch diameter and submitted orders to the National Tube Company and the Reading Iron

Works. These were larger than any pipes previously used for oil: each pipe length weighed 340 pounds and collectively they were estimated to weigh over five thousand tons. And because the heavy pipe segments were so unwieldy, the company had to invent new tools that would allow workers to manipulate them. The company's engineers designed the first pipe tongs that enabled the workers to screw the pipes together. However, simply designing and ordering the parts was not enough. Because Standard Oil was such a large purchaser of products from local manufacturing enterprises, Tide-Water officials feared that Rockefeller could use his influence to have the products be manufactured poorly or delivered late. Company officials, as a result, ordered parts from suppliers outside the Oil Regions, though the move angered some locals who thought area businesses should be supported.[9]

Another challenge was the design of pumping stations that could force the oil over large elevation gains without exceeding the pressure capacity of the wrought-iron pipes. Most pumps at the time were direct-acting, which meant that each stroke of the piston produced a surge of energy, much like the hand-operated air pumps used to inflate bicycle tires today. This was fine for water transport systems where pipe pressures rarely exceeded fifty pounds per square inch, but unsuitable given the force required to move copious quantities of oil over mountains.[10] Working with the Holly Manufacturing Company, the Tide-Water's engineers developed a tri-plex pump that maintained a steady output of pressure through the use of three pistons timed to rise and fall at different times. Rather than the surges of power from a direct-acting pump, the new system could deliver seventy horsepower at a steady level of pressure that would propel the oil without tearing the pipes apart. In reviewing the new design, the president of the pump company reportedly announced that he fully understood pressure for the first time.[11]

These technological advances in materials and parts were not matched by corresponding innovations in labor practices: it was grueling, difficult, and dependent on the power of human and animal muscles. Much like carting wagons loaded with petroleum barrels to Oil Creek, the labor of pipeline construction was neither glamorous nor easy. And similar to the building of coal canals, while the Tide-Water pipeline would play an important role in entrenching the mineral energy regime, the labor that constructed it was drawn from organic sources. The work began in the winter of 1879. The first task was to deliver the lengths of pipes from railroad stations to the line's projected path. Because the pipeline was to be built through the forests of the Allegheny Mountains, there were few existing roads and long distances between railroad stops. Often groups of teamsters had to cart the lengths of pipe fifteen to twenty miles over hills and valleys using primitive paths. Once the pipes were delivered, teams of eleven men positioned the heavy pipes in their proper place and screwed the lengths together with pipe tongs. At the height of construction, over eighty men were at work connecting the pipes, while forty to sixty teamsters were employed to haul supplies.[12]

Finally, the natural landscape provided another set of difficulties. It was much easier to obtain the rights-of-way for the pipeline in the Allegheny Mountains because there were few people living in the area. The relative ease of obtaining property rights, however, was largely a result of the rough terrain. Not many people wanted to live in a place full of hills, cliffs, and ravines because it was poorly suited for agriculture or manufacturing. As a result, the construction teams were forced to carve out an undulating path for the pipeline full of rises and falls. They also had to work with a significant elevation gain: the pipeline ascended over fifteen hundred feet to a maximum elevation of twenty-six hundred feet. A severe winter exacerbated the challenge as crews were forced to work around the clock to complete critical sections while navigating through five-foot snow banks.[13]

The technical obstacles were formidable, but the company was confident that these challenges could be met with sufficient money, time, and sweat. For most observers, however, these were minor issues compared with the competitive threats facing the enterprise. As was expected, Standard Oil moved quickly to thwart the Tide-Water company's plans. Rockefeller knew that rights-of-way were one of the pipeline company's greatest vulnerabilities. At this time, pipeline companies did not have the right of eminent domain, in large part because Standard Oil and the railroads had worked to defeat legislative efforts by independent oilmen to achieve this goal in 1873 and 1878.[14] Therefore, the Tide-Water company had to purchase land outright or obtain rights-of-way from landowners for the entire length. Standard Oil agents immediately began efforts to buy a north-south blocking line that would prevent completion of the east-west line. They challenged the leases obtained by the pipeline company and sought to purchase strategic property rights. Not all their approaches were legal: two Standard Oil employees were found to be impersonating Tide-Water officials negotiating deals for land rights and were subsequently arrested

Sledding the pipes for the Tide-Water pipeline. (Courtesy of the Drake Well Museum, Pennsylvania Historical and Museum Commission)

for fraud.[15] As late as May 1879, Standard Oil was willing to spend considerable sums of money to buy two small farms that would break the path of the pipeline.[16] To protect its project, the pipeline company dispatched several survey teams to hide the true path of the line and masked the recording of deeds. At one point, the company feared Standard Oil had cut off all chance of a continuous right-of-way. Only by resurveying several properties did one of the company's employees—"a natural sleuth on titles and boundaries"—discover that a narrow sixteen-foot band of land was unclaimed. They purchased this land and work was able to continue.[17]

Standard Oil pursued the fight on several other fronts as well. When the pipeline was being built, there were seven independent refineries in New York that had signed agreements to get their oil from the new company. Rockefeller purchased control of six of them before the line was completed.[18] Through its influence in several newspapers, Standard Oil published negative articles about the pipeline and its founders.[19] The railroads were also threatened by the new pipeline and offered any resistance they could. As soon as the pipe was laid under the tracks of the Northern Central branch of the Pennsylvania Railroad, for example, the railroad sent twenty-five men in the early morning hours to rip the pipes up. This "army of occupation" secured the area by building fires and preventing the pipeline workers from approaching.[20] Court injunctions upheld the Tide-Water company's land claims and the pipes were replaced.[21] In addition, the railroads delayed and misplaced shipments of pipe and supplies along their lines, a problem that was only solved by hiring people to journey with the goods to ensure that they were actually delivered to the appointed location.[22]

Despite the obstacles, the Tide-Water pipeline was completed in late May 1879 at an estimated cost of $750,000.[23] Oil entered the pipeline on May 28, moving at about the pace of a man walking. A couple days later, the pressure in the pipes rose rapidly. After shutting down the pumps, the cause was soon discovered. A few pieces of wood and rope were found inside the line, though it could not be determined whether this was deliberate sabotage or simply a mistake of careless workers. With the obstacle removed, the pumps were restarted and the oil arrived in Williamsport in the early evening of June 4, setting off an enthusiastic celebration.[24] For the Tide-Water officials, the success of the pipeline was a vindication of their efforts and an impressive technological accomplishment. It would later serve as the model for the 1937 Kern and Hammerstein musical film "High, Wide, and Handsome" produced by Paramount Pictures and starring Irene Dunne, Randolph Scott, and Dorothy Lamour. Set in Titusville in the nineteenth century, the musical centers on the attempts of oil-drilling farmers to defeat an evil railroad magnate by building a pipeline.

The completion of the Tide-Water pipeline demonstrated the feasibility of pumping oil long distances in pipes. But this technological accomplishment did not determine the fate of the industry. Several questions were unanswered. Would Benson and his partners profit from their innovation? What would be the reaction from Standard Oil and the railroad companies? Would other pipelines be built, and by whom?

Rockefeller and the Railroads Respond

It did not take long for the railroad companies to take action. The day after the pipeline's first successful shipment, the heads of the Erie, Central, and

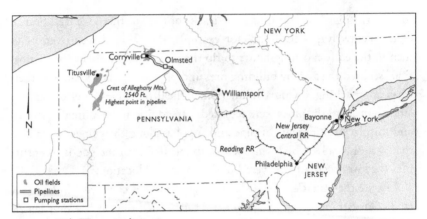

MAP 4.1. Tide-Water pipeline, 1879.

Pennsylvania railroads gathered in Saratoga, New York and agreed to wage
a rate war that they hoped would put the new competitor out of business.
They lowered the prices for delivering crude dramatically: from more than
a dollar to less than twenty cents a barrel from the Oil Regions to New
York.[25] Standard Oil agreed to support the railroads and withheld any shipments from the pipeline. For the next six months, all parties shipped oil at
extremely low rates. Tide-Water officials could find buyers for only about
fifteen hundred barrels a day, a quarter of the line's capacity, and lost an
estimated $100,000. But this was small change compared with the railroad
companies: their losses were estimated to be as high as ten million dollars.[26]
The pipeline's cost savings provided a competitive advantage the railroads
could not overcome. Defeated, the railroads ended the rate war in early
1880, and came to an agreement allocating a certain percentage of the oil
traffic to the Tide-Water pipeline.[27] Rates were restored to their previous
levels, but the business of oil transport would never be the same. As Cornelius Vanderbilt, head of the Central Railroad, presciently observed shortly
afterwards: "The oil business is sealed; that is settled; there is no question
about that; we [the railroads] won't any of us have the oil business long."[28]

While the railroads were never able to respond to the new technology,
Standard Oil quickly recognized the promise of pipelines and began to pay
its new competitor the highest form of flattery: imitation. In the months
leading up to the completion of the Tide-Water line, several of Standard

Oil's executives had been pushing Rockefeller to develop a series of long-distance pipelines. He rejected these suggestions largely because he wished to retain friendly relations with the railroad companies who were giving him such an advantage in transport costs.[29] Under the status quo, Standard Oil had little reason to undertake a risky endeavor. Monopoly power, despite its vast resources of capital, discouraged innovation.

Once the Tide-Water proved the success of long-distance pipelines, however, Rockefeller wasted little time following suit. And he did so with the thoroughness, expertise, and ruthlessness that characterized his refining operations. Standard Oil's first pipeline was directed toward its Cleveland refineries. Drawing on his connections to the Atlantic and Great Western Railroad, Rockefeller negotiated an agreement by guaranteeing the railroad one-third of his oil shipments to the west and southwest in exchange for being able to lay his pipeline along the right-of-way. This deal revealed that railroad companies would remain important to the development of oil pipelines, even if they would no longer be the primary carriers of crude. Because railroads held land rights that crisscrossed the region, pipeline entrepreneurs faced extreme challenges in obtaining rights-of-way on their own.[30] This also put Rockefeller in a unique position. Thanks to his close relationships with the railroad companies and ability to offer guarantees on shipments of refined oil, he could make deals that no other party could match. It also caused the spatial geography of the mid-Atlantic's pipeline network to mirror railroad tracks. Pipes ran next to rails as one energy landscape was laid on top of another.

Work on the Cleveland line began in the fall of 1879 and was completed in March 1880. By investing about a half million dollars into the line, Rockefeller lowered the cost of shipping oil to Cleveland from thirty-five to fifty cents per barrel by railroad to twelve to twenty cents by pipe. Standard Oil allowed competitors to purchase oil from the pipeline as long as it did not exceed a set quota. For example, one refiner was allowed to purchase 85,000 barrels of oil a year for a transport cost of twenty cents a barrel, but Standard Oil cut off shipments when this amount was exceeded.[31] From the very beginning, Rockefeller employed pipelines to discipline competitors.

Standard Oil's pipeline to Buffalo reveals another way in which Rockefeller used the new technology to deepen his advantage. In 1881, a group of independent oilmen led by the Kalbfleisch brothers built a pipeline from

Pipeline workers. (Hagley Museum and Library)

the Bradford oil field to Buffalo. The four-inch Buffalo & Rock City pipe-line began operations in August of 1881, charged ten cents per barrel, and had a daily capacity of 5,000 barrels. Having heard of the independents' plan, Standard Oil built its own three-inch pipeline to Buffalo at about the same time and bought out many of the independent refiners in the city. With few customers for its shipments, the Buffalo & Rock City company sold their line to Standard Oil at the beginning of 1882. Standard Oil then tore up its own pipeline and used the Buffalo & Rock City line for deliveries. Rates were immediately increased to twenty-five cents per barrel.[32] Notably, this was the only other major attempt to build a pipeline by an independent company for the next decade.

Standard Oil also constructed a series of trunk pipelines to its refineries on the eastern seaboard. The company first made a deal with the Erie Railroad, paying $50,000 for access to its rights-of-way and promising to maintain a certain level of oil shipments along the railroad. Workers began constructing the six-inch pipeline from Olean, New York to the New York City harbor in July of 1880, working from both ends. The line was completed as far as Saddle River, New Jersey by December of 1881, about sixty miles from Bayonne, New Jersey. Shortly afterwards, Standard Oil began to lay a sec-

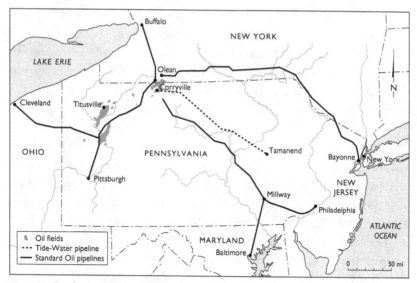

MAP 4.2. Pipeline network, 1884.

ond six-inch pipeline next to it, doubling the total capacity to approximately 24,000 barrels a day. In 1884, the line was extended to Bayonne with a branch supplying oil to refiners on Long Island. Standard Oil also built a 260-mile six-inch pipeline to Philadelphia in 1882. The line began in Colegrove, Pennsylvania and traveled to the Atlantic Refining Company's refinery at Gibson's Point in Philadelphia. The following year a 70-mile branch was added to Baltimore. In addition, Standard Oil still owned the Columbia Conduit pipeline to Pittsburgh.[33]

While its pipeline network was under construction, Standard Oil and the Tide-Water pipeline engaged in a series of negotiations and confrontations. At several points, Rockefeller attempted to purchase the Tide-Water line as he had the properties of Empire and the Columbia Conduit. Benson's son reported that Rockefeller offered to buy the Tide-Water Pipe Company in May 1879 before the line began operations. This offer was rejected—not necessarily for ideological reasons, but because Benson felt the reported offer of $300,000 was not compelling. To strengthen its position, the company continued to expand its operations. In early 1880, the company began building refineries at Bayonne and Chester, Pennsylvania. In the winter of 1881–1882, the pipeline was extended to Tamanend, Pennsylvania so that oil could be shipped directly to Bayonne on the New Jersey Central Railroad. In 1882, many of the officials at Tide-Water reportedly were willing to sell to Rockefeller for five million dollars, but it appears Standard Oil thought this price too high.[34]

Standard Oil also engaged in two efforts to take control of the company. In 1882, Standard Oil gave $20,000 to a dissatisfied stockholder of the Tide-Water company who used this money to sue the managers for negligence because the line was not operating at full capacity. The cause was soon discovered—someone had put a plug of wood into the pipeline—and the case was dismissed. The following year, a group of stockholders with known ties to Standard Oil held an impromptu board meeting and elected themselves as directors of the company, presumably with the intention of negotiating a sale. It was widely reported that many in the Oil Regions believed Standard Oil to be behind the effort. In a case decided primarily on technical questions of corporate elections, the original board of directors was reinstated.[35]

In the fall of 1883, the independent bid of the Tide-Water company came to an end. Due to a law passed earlier in the year by the Pennsylvania legislature prohibiting the merger of competing pipeline companies, Standard Oil could not legally acquire the Tide-Water company.[36] Instead, the two companies came to a pooling agreement that meant they began to operate as collaborators, not competitors. The Tide-Water company was allocated 11.5 percent of the traffic of the Oil Regions, giving Standard Oil control over the balance.[37] For Tide-Water officials, the agreement guaranteed them oil shipments equal to the capacity of their pipeline, adequate markets for their products, and the assurance that they would remain an independent corporate entity. It was a partial victory. The terms were better than most other competitors of Standard Oil had achieved, which indicated that the introduction of a new technology had enabled the company to mount a formidable challenge against a monopoly power. In 1913, the company president boasted that those who invested in 1882 had received dividends totaling 2000 percent of the initial investment and that the value of the shares had increased fifteen-fold.[38] However, the agreement also demonstrated that technological innovation alone could not transform the dynamics of the industry. By agreeing to limit its traffic, the Tide-Water company effectively ended its bid as an independent actor. It would not build a broader network of pipes to compete with the Standard Oil system nor would it offer relief to other independent oil producers. Benson and his colleagues would prosper, but never again be a revolutionary force in the transport of oil.[39] Critics of Standard Oil bemoaned this result, as a *New York Times* article observed: "The Tide-water Pipe Line . . . [has] fallen under the control of that despotic, unscrupulous, and lawless organization . . . Standard will probably be hereafter absolute master of the petroleum business of the United States."[40]

With the eventual domination of pipelines by Standard Oil, it is clear that the story of the Tide-Water pipeline is one of unintended consequences. New technologies can be thought of as opening spaces in which industry structures can be transformed.[41] Benson and his company used pipelines to become bigger players in the oil industry. But the ability of Standard Oil to appropriate the threat led to an even greater degree of monopoly power. Rockefeller wielded his significant financial resources to invest heavily in the new technology and control its development. The railroads did not adapt and lost their role in the trade, as Vanderbilt had predicted. And while these contests mostly took place between various capitalists, private actions were structured by state decisions. By privileging the property rights of individual landholders, government authorities stacked the deck against small companies. The fact that the Pennsylvania legislature did not pass a bill giving pipeline companies eminent domain privileges until 1883 greatly enhanced the ability of Standard Oil to control the new technology, because it meant pipeline enterprises were essentially forced to find railroad allies. Since Standard Oil had the closest relationships with most of the railroads, they were uniquely situated to prosper. As a result, the actions of the Pennsylvania legislature favored entrenched interests.

By 1884, the transition to pipelines was largely complete. The building of the Tide-Water pipeline "was the beginning of an industrial change which in a few years would turn three-quarters or more of all the crude oil produced away from the rail heads into silent channels underground."[42] Combined with Standard Oil's comprehensive network of pipelines serving its refineries in the New York harbor, Philadelphia, Baltimore, Cleveland, Buffalo, and Pittsburgh, the transport of oil switched from railroads to pipelines within a few short years.

The Spatial Politics of Pipelines

The history of the Tide-Water pipeline is a tale full of conflict, intrigue, and subterfuge. It reveals the importance of competitive dynamics, technological innovation, and the structuring role of the state in the building of infrastructure systems. While these intra-industry power struggles have captured the interest of many energy analysts, they provide only a partial account of the Tide-Water's historical significance.[43] Pipelines were not simply important for determining who made money within the industry; they also shaped the unequal allocation of costs and benefits of the production and consumption of oil more generally.

As with the shift from waterways to railroads, the development of pipelines altered the flows of oil in ways that benefited some locations more than others. In a world of railroad transport, Philadelphia was at a relative disadvantage because it was served by fewer competing railroads than Cleveland and New York. The construction of two pipelines toward Philadelphia helped put its refiners in a more favorable position, and, as a result, the city increased its oil refining capacity from just over two thousand barrels a day in 1873 to more than twenty thousand in 1888 and nearly fifty thousand by 1897.[44] But pipelines proved less beneficial to other locations, particularly Pittsburgh and the Oil Regions. Because not all of a barrel of crude oil could be refined into a profitable product, refiners in Pittsburgh and the Oil Regions had benefited from an era of higher transport costs due to their proximity to oil wells. With pipelines lowering shipment rates, this comparative advantage was greatly reduced. Combined with the fact that labor and materials were often much more expensive in the Oil Regions than in seaboard cities, pipelines contributed to the decline of refining near the site of production. And pipelines accelerated the losses to Pittsburgh's refining trade, as the city processed less than 3 percent of the nation's crude oil by 1895, compared with nearly 40 percent three decades before.[45]

Yet the change in oil flows was not as dramatic as it might have been. Because the railroads played such an important role in structuring where pipelines were built, oil often traveled along similar routes whether by rail or pipe. Since Standard Oil had already built large refineries in the New York harbor and Cleveland in the railroad era, Rockefeller chose to direct most of his pipelines toward these locations. As a result, by 1888, refiners in Cleveland, Philadelphia, and New York City possessed nearly three-quarters of the nation's total refining capacity.[46] The fact that Standard Oil controlled oil flows by railroad and pipeline shaped a convergence between the spatial geography of pipes and rails. Prior investments in transport infrastructure had a powerful influence on the shape of future developments.

Pipelines and railroad tracks may have shared a common geography, but they had material differences that shaped their consequences. Pipelines carried a single product in a single direction to a single point.[47] This meant that they transported a nonrenewable resource away from the Oil Regions without creating a reciprocal trade in goods. Some residents of western Pennsylvania recognized this at the time. Commenting on debates over whether Pennsylvania should authorize a bill granting eminent domain privileges to pipeline companies in 1875, one local newspaper argued that "what we want in this section . . . is to have a means of transportation for articles into the county as well as out of it. These railroads accomplish, but pipes do not."[48] The only possible reverse flow along pipelines was capital, but because overproduction rendered the price of oil quite low during this period and Standard Oil owned most of the pipeline capacity, the bulk of the profits were sent to Rockefeller's headquarters. Pipelines negatively affected the possibilities for the industrial development of the Oil Regions or the areas along their paths.

This arrangement can be usefully contrasted with the canals in the anthracite regions. As multi-product systems capable of shipping goods in two directions, canals generated a number of amplifier effects throughout the eastern mid-Atlantic, best embodied by the proliferation of iron-producing towns along their banks such as Reading, Bethlehem, and Allentown. Because canals could transport a range of goods up- or downstream, they supported the spread of industrial activity to several places. Cities like Scranton, Wilkes-Barre, and Pottsville all grew to be regional industrial centers in the anthracite regions with thriving businesses that went beyond simply the extraction of coal. No city in the Oil Regions, by contrast, ever developed in comparable fashion. Titusville, Oil City, and Corry remained relatively small towns with little activity outside the oil trade. Though pipelines were not the only reason for the lack of industrial development in western Pennsylvania, they contributed to this result since they funneled a valuable

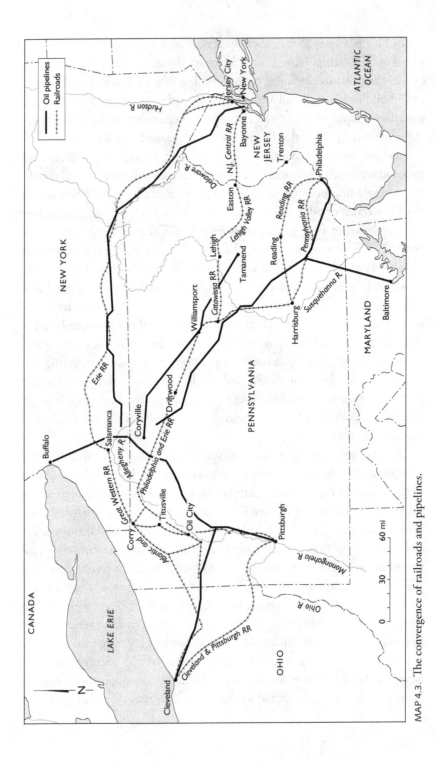

MAP 4.3. The convergence of railroads and pipelines.

resource away and returned very little of value to those living at the site of production or along the transport corridors.

Pipelines were further distinct from railroads because they operated continuously, invisibly, and with little human interaction. Unlike railroads where tank cars needed to be hitched and unhitched, connected to storage tanks, and filled and emptied, pipelines operated around the clock with steady flows of oil. Trains could be seen crossing the landscape while most pipes were buried underground. Pipelines did require a few humans to keep them operating—usually a foreman, two engineers, two assistant engineers, four firemen, a telegrapher, and line walkers for every pumping station, in addition to a management team coordinating the buying and selling of oil—but this was far less than the labor system needed to keep a railroad running.[49] Moreover, the labor of operating pipelines was focused on keeping the pumping stations in working order, not actually touching the oil. Oil could be drilled at the wellhead, shipped in a gathering pipeline to a storage tank, then pumped to the seaboard in a pipeline and delivered to refinery stills without a human hand ever touching it. The invisibility of pipeline transport, therefore, was part of a material and cultural practice in which oil became an abstract commodity.

The environmental consequences of the oil industry were also influenced by the shift in transport systems. In a direct sense, pipelines were prone to slow and steady leaks along with the occasional dramatic burst.[50] But their indirect effects may have been far more significant. Pipelines heightened a geographic separation between the regions in which oil was produced and those in which it was consumed that exacerbated the environmental consequences of extraction. The production of oil came at great environmental cost. But users who lived hundreds and even thousands of miles away did not need to worry about oil flowing into their streams or ruining their soil. They had little personal connection to the massive deforestation of large regions in pursuit of liquid gold. Even if they experienced some soot and odor from the burning of kerosene in their homes, it was likely cleaner and more pleasant than candles or camphene. For the most part, the users of oil gained the benefit of cheap energy without assuming responsibility for its environmental damage. One of the reasons that fossil fuel energy production has been so environmentally destructive is that those who benefit from energy sources rarely have to live with the environmental damages associated with its production. While this happens for a number of cultural and political reasons, it also has a crucial material dimension: the construction of transport infrastructure systems makes it much easier for consumers to ignore and avoid responsibility for the environmental harms of the energy they use. Pipelines, by operating continually and out of sight, are perhaps the quintessential example of such a dissociating technology. Ultimately, pipelines helped retrench the ecological sacrifice of the Oil Regions because capitalists and consumers had little direct reason to demand environmental protections for a region they did not inhabit.

In these ways, pipelines benefited some far more than others. Financially, they advantaged Standard Oil at the expense of the railroad companies and rivals of Rockefeller. Consumers gained by being able to obtain kerosene at lower prices. Pipelines served refineries in cities that provided a range of good jobs, though they also forced some urban residents to live with the toxic pollutants discharged by refineries. For those living along their paths, pipelines might offer the minor benefits of payments for land rights, but this came with the great risk of the land being ruined by leaking and bursting pipes. Residents of the Oil Regions received remarkably few benefits from the development of pipelines, as they sucked away a valuable resource while returning very little in their wake.

A Landscape of Oil Intensification

One unanticipated consequence of the Tide-Water pipeline was that a new technology ultimately reinforced Standard Oil's control over the industry rather than overturning it. A second was that it helped introduce new patterns of oil consumption. Once limited to providing light and lubrication, petroleum gained new markets as a source of heat and power as a result of the lower shipment costs enabled by pipelines. Although it was not an explicit goal of their pioneers, pipelines gave rise to a new landscape of intensification.

The extensive use of petroleum as fuel oil, and later as gasoline, was a development that few people in the oil industry anticipated in the mid-1870s. The problem was not technical. Crude oil could be burned with fairly minimal processing; refined into fuel oil, it was a particularly clean and efficient form of energy. Since the early 1860s, many industry observers had recognized that petroleum could offer numerous advantages in powering steam engines or supplying heat for industrial processes. Compared with coal or wood, fuel oil offered a higher output of energy per weight and it burned with fewer impurities. Moreover, its fluidity could be a benefit: oil flowed by gravity into boilers, thereby increasing loading precision and avoiding the labor costs of shoveling coal or wood. The liquid nature of oil that frustrated early boosters became a great boon once its materiality could be adequately controlled.

The problem was price: oil cost far more than coal. An 1864 report on fuel for steam vessels noted that oil on the eastern seaboard was ten times more expensive than coal, leading the author to conclude that *at the relative prices of coal and petroleum, this substance can never be made to compete successfully with coal, as an economic fuel* (italics in original).[51] An 1868 analysis of petroleum in marine ships noted substantial promise but reached the same conclusion regarding prices: "It is therefore evident . . . [that] the excess of the heating power of the petroleum over that of the [coal] is so very much less than its excess of cost, that there is not the slightest probability, as long as these ratios exist, of petroleum ever taking the place of coal as a steam fuel."[52] Even as late as the early 1880s, a careful analyst of the oil industry argued that since coal was "cheap, plentiful, and safe" there was little chance for petroleum to enter these markets: "I do not look for any considerable increase in the use of petroleum for steam purposes in the United States."[53] Because oil was so much more expensive than coal, it simply did not make sense to burn it for power purposes. It would be like warming one's home by burning mahogany wood: yes, it could provide heat, but mahogany is much more valuable when transformed into value-added products like furniture. Around 1880, petroleum was similar to mahogany in that refining it into kerosene and lubricants could warrant much higher profits than simply burning it for heat or power.

Moreover, the illuminating market was large, growing, and profitable. Much as the desire to find a source of cheap and abundant artificial lighting drew Edwin Drake to Titusville, kerosene continued to be the animating force behind Standard Oil's rise to power: during the 1870s, illuminating oil represented approximately 85 percent of the output of the nation's refineries. Overseas markets, particularly Europe, absorbed as much as two-thirds to three-quarters of American kerosene production.[54] To put the scale of this trade into perspective, kerosene was the nation's fourth most valuable export, trailing only cotton, wheat, and meat.[55] Kerosene was big business.

Kerosene remained extremely attractive to consumers because of the quality of its light, the ease of its use, and the competitiveness of its cost. Over the course of the 1870s, advances in refining and declines in the price of crude oil had resulted in continually cheaper kerosene. Whereas a gallon of kerosene cost seventy cents wholesale in New York City in 1865, the price had fallen to twenty-six cents in 1870 and below twenty cents by 1873.[56] As this was a substantially better value than other options such as whale oil, camphene, gaslight, or coal oil, consumers increasingly turned to kerosene when it was available. While some refiners specialized in the production of lubricants, paraffin wax, and other petroleum by-products, these played a much smaller role in the industry's development.

But a quick glance around our current world reveals that while lighting markets launched the oil boom, they have not been responsible for most of the industry's growth. It is as a source of heat and power for factories and vehicles that oil has reshaped the modern world most substantially. For this transformation to occur, Americans needed to treat petroleum less like mahogany and more like pine. This, in turn, meant that oil needed to compete with coal on a cost basis. Since a barrel of oil offered about a quarter of the heating power of a ton of coal, approximately four barrels of oil were needed to match a ton of coal. During the first quarter-century of the American petroleum trade, oil was significantly more expensive than coal because both its purchase price and its transport costs were higher than coal.[57] In the 1880s, these conditions began to change: lower shipment rates via pipelines, along with the discovery of new oil fields in Ohio, allowed oil to be a compelling alternative to coal.

Pipelines were essential to this transition. In a world of railroad transport, oil could not compete with coal. In the last two decades of the nineteenth century, a ton of anthracite coal was selling for between $1.41 and $2.00 at the mine, with railroad shipment costs ranging from one to two dollars to many locations in the mid-Atlantic. A ton of coal, therefore, could be delivered to a wholesale stockyard for approximately three dollars.[58] To match coal, crude oil would have to be available at seventy-five cents or less per barrel in major market centers. But the transport costs of shipping four barrels of oil under prevailing railroad rates in the 1870s precluded such a possibility. It is extremely difficult to determine the costs of nineteenth-century railroad shipments. Not only were official rates rarely followed, it is not even clear that the accounting systems of the railroad companies enabled them to accurately assess the shipment costs of individual products.[59] However, the available evidence suggests that transport alone made oil more expensive than coal. A conservative estimate of the costs of oil shipments via railroads before pipelines is at least seventy-five cents a barrel, and more likely closer to a dollar.[60] As a result, simply shipping four barrels of oil on railroads exceeded the cost of a ton of coal delivered without even taking into consideration the cost of the petroleum itself.

Pipelines transformed this economic logic. As with the railroad companies, the costs of pipeline operations were closely guarded industry secrets, so we only have approximate values. But several sources reveal that a long-distance pipeline could ship oil for a fraction of the cost of railroad transport: about twenty cents to send a barrel of oil to the seaboard in the 1880s, with the price declining to around ten to fifteen cents during the 1890s.[61] The actual costs may have been even lower: one analyst suggests that Standard Oil achieved costs of six to ten cents per barrel in the mid-1880s.[62] With pipelines, therefore, the cost of transporting four barrels of oil fell below the cost of shipping a ton of coal. For the first time, the transport costs of oil no longer precluded it from competing with coal. The potential to create new patterns of demand was introduced.

Making oil competitive with coal was not, however, an explicit goal of pipeline developers. When these systems were built, their pioneers were hoping to profit from kerosene, not to create new markets in fuel oil. The Tide-Water and the Standard Oil pipelines all extended from the western Pennsylvania oil fields, where the price of oil had hovered around a dollar per barrel from 1878 to 1884.[63] Even if four barrels could be shipped for less than a dollar, the cost to consumers would still exceed coal by a significant margin. The introduction of pipelines was designed to obtain share of an existing market, not to create a new one.

It took a second development to launch the fuel oil market. In western Ohio in the early 1880s, several parties began to explore for natural gas deposits in the "black swamps" near the town of Lima. Gas flares had been discovered in the region since the early days of European settlement, but few expected to find oil in large quantities given that the region's geography was very different from western Pennsylvania (it was flat and most of the rocks were limestone and shale as opposed to the hills and sandstone around Titusville). In 1885, much to the surprise of industry observers, natural gas prospectors discovered impressive pockets of oil. As happened in Titusville a quarter-century before, thousands flocked to the region and the production of Lima oil began to skyrocket. More than a million barrels of oil were produced in 1886 from the Lima fields, nearly five million the next year, almost ten million in 1888, and over fifteen million barrels in 1890.[64]

Not all crude oil is the same when it comes out of the ground. And the Lima petroleum had one very distinct characteristic: it had high levels of sulfur. In today's parlance, it was "sour" crude; at the time it was sometimes called "skunk juice." With the available refining techniques in the mid-1880s, it was not possible to remove the sulfuric odor, and as a result, it produced extremely poor quality kerosene. As an illuminating oil, Lima oil smelled noxious; it also crusted the wick of lamps and clouded the glass. Unfit to be sold as kerosene, the oil had no clear market. About 80 percent of the more than five million barrels produced in 1886 and 1887 was sitting in storage tanks at the end of the year. As a result of expanding production and few consumers, the price of Lima crude dropped to extremely low levels—between fifteen and thirty cents a barrel between 1886 and 1890.[65] A large supply of mineral energy had been discovered, but there was little demand.

For producers of Lima oil in 1887, things looked bleak. Oil was being brought out of the ground faster than storage tanks could be erected and consumers were distinctly uninterested in purchasing it. As was the case with many other energy transitions, boosters would need to create new markets if they were to profit. Although Standard Oil let it be known that it was investigating ways to remove the sulfur smell from the oil to make it suitable for kerosene production, company officials described their initial efforts as a "complete and utter failure."[66] These disappointing results were notable because Standard Oil was aggressively seeking to develop other markets for petroleum products at the time. The company "increasingly distributed heaters, stoves, lamps, lanterns, irons, and other utensils, usually at little or no profit, as a means of expanding the consumption of Standard Oil kerosene and gasoline."[67] But the chemical composition of Lima oil defied their efforts. Skunk juice was much less like mahogany and a lot more like pinewood.

Desperate to find a market, Ohio oilmen sought to expand the use of fuel oil, in part reasoning that industries would have fewer objections to the sulfur smell than homeowners. Their first consumers were local enterprises that had been established near the Lima fields to take advantage of the natural gas deposits. Many of the cities in the region had offered free natural gas to manufacturers in the hopes of stimulating the local economy.[68] As a result, large numbers of glass works and iron mills were established in surrounding towns such as Lima, Tiffin, and Findlay. They were joined by several other factories dependent on cheap energy including brick works, lime kilns, and pottery plants. But because the dynamics of gas fields were poorly understood at the time, they were not managed well and only a few years later many were faltering badly. The presence of numerous energy-intensive factories suddenly finding themselves without an adequate supply of fuel opened up a promising market for Lima oil producers. In 1885, a paper mill and boiler manufacturing company were among the first to use Ohio crude as fuel oil, and several other factories began to follow suit shortly after.[69]

If transport was limited to railroads, the use of Lima crude in factories may have been a predominantly local phenomenon. Even if it could be purchased for little money at the site of production, the shipment costs along railroads still would have rendered Lima crude more expensive than coal in most areas of the mid-Atlantic. But pipelines facilitated the development of a much broader market. In 1888, Standard Oil built a 205-mile pipeline connecting Lima with Chicago and began to deliver 8,000 barrels of fuel oil a day for 60 cents, a price that included both oil and its transport. At this price, oil was competitive with coal, and its consumption rose rapidly. In 1889, oilmen were able to deliver 5.8 million barrels of Lima crude, the large majority of which was used as fuel oil.[70] By the early 1890s, Standard Oil had extended its pipelines from western Pennsylvania to Ohio, allowing Lima crude to travel cheaply to the eastern seaboard as well, significantly extending the availability of fuel oil. A new era in oil consumption had been opened.

Even when Standard Oil discovered a method of refining kerosene from Lima crude, the fuel oil market did not disappear. In the late 1880s, one of their scientists, Herman Frasch, developed a process that used metal oxides to bind the sulfur into particulates that could be filtered out of the oil. With this knowledge, Standard Oil constructed an enormous refinery near Chicago to produce kerosene from sour crude that began operating in the early 1890s. But the Frasch process was only capable of producing a yield of approximately 50 percent illuminating oil from Lima crude. The remaining balance could be used for little other than fuel oil. This was notably different than refining Pennsylvania crude, where yields of more than three-quarters of a barrel of oil into kerosene could be obtained and much of the rest could be turned into lubricants or other by-products. As a result, to maximize its profits from the remnants of Lima crude after kerosene was extracted, Standard Oil continued to promote the use of fuel oil.[71]

Pipelines thereby helped create what we can think of as an accidental landscape of intensification. Unlike the builders of anthracite canals, Benson and his colleagues were not seeking to create new markets. But once pipelines were introduced, they reshaped the geographic and financial logic of the oil industry. When cheap oil that could not be sold as kerosene was discovered, oilmen created new markets and pipelines provided a means through which the abundance of rural sites of energy supply could be connected with urban centers. Supply drove demand, and transport infrastructure investments facilitated the development of new consumption patterns.

Oil and the Mineral Energy Regime

The intensifying use of oil for heat and power served to deepen the hold of the mineral energy regime by encouraging the urban and industrial development of the mid-Atlantic and spreading these patterns to areas rich in oil but poor in coal. In factories, petroleum helped generate the second industrial revolution. And with the continued consumption of oil in homes and vehicles, petroleum brought the mineral energy regime into new domains of human life.

The first uses of oil for heat and power reflected patterns established with coal. Some of the new consumers, like the factories making glass or bricks in western Ohio, simply needed lots of heat for their operations. Converting boilers to handle fuel oil was a relatively straightforward proposition in such cases. But other enterprises required a more careful calibration of equipment in order to burn fuel oil effectively. Iron manufacturers, for example, discovered that it was necessary to develop new techniques like spraying petroleum into furnaces for it to be adapted to the smelting process. Oilmen also worked with railroad and steamboat operators to enter transportation markets. They noted that oil-fired boilers reduced the problems associated with cinders flying out of railroad engines that could set fire to the surrounding areas or harass passengers. On steamboats, boosters argued that oil occupied less cargo space, provided more motive power per unit of volume, and reduced the number of firemen needed to operate the ship. Once adequate equipment was developed to overcome challenges such as safely storing large quantities of oil onboard, many vessels began to convert to petroleum. Collectively, these efforts yielded considerable success as fuel oil consumption grew from under half a million barrels in 1884 to more than eight million in 1899, a jump from a fortieth of refinery output to nearly a sixth.[72]

In one sense, the use of oil in applications previously fueled by coal was simply a replacement of one source of mineral energy for another. But for the development of the mineral energy regime, this was more than mere substitution. One consequence of these new practices was the geographic spread of mineral energy consumption. In the late nineteenth and early twentieth centuries, large quantities of oil were identified in places that lacked the abundant coal reserves of the mid-Atlantic, including California, Oklahoma, and Texas. For these regions, oil offered an opportunity to gain some of the benefits of industrialization without the high costs of importing coal from other areas. As oil production soared in California around the turn of the century, for example, railroads in the state rapidly took advantage of this abundance: by 1909, they were consuming an estimated twenty million barrels of fuel oil a year.[73] In Texas, the Sante Fe Railroad had only a single oil-fired locomotive before the discovery of oil at Spindletop in 1901. In response to the flood of cheap oil, it had converted 227 engines to burn fuel oil by 1905.[74] In both of these cases, the expansion of the mineral energy regime owed much to developments in the mid-Atlantic where the techniques for producing, refining, and consuming petroleum had been established. In particular, the petroleum at Spindletop was so heavy and sulfuric that it made Lima "skunk juice" seem attractive.[75] Because Texas oilmen could draw on more than a decade of innovations in the refining of sour crude, they were able to develop markets quickly for a substance that might not have had many consumers otherwise. Oil, therefore, helped accelerate the rise of the mineral energy regime outside of the mid-Atlantic.

The use of oil in factories also contributed to a qualitative shift in the patterns of American industrial development by helping initiate what has been known as the second industrial revolution. Early industrialization was based on coal, iron, and steam engines, but a number of historians have argued that the late nineteenth century saw the development of new practices including increasing mechanization, faster machinery, larger corporations, and the greater application of scientific knowledge to manufacturing. Oil was a central component of this second industrial revolution. The fluid nature of oil lent itself to mechanization because unlike the laborious shoveling of coal, the flow of oil could be raised or lowered at precise rates with the turning of valves. Lubricants enabled the use of faster and more powerful equipment by reducing friction, and Standard Oil was a paragon of corporate growth in the late nineteenth century. Moreover, science proved essential to addressing refining problems like removing sulfur from crude oil, a challenge that was only addressed with the intensive application of chemical knowledge to industrial practice. Oil and the second industrial revolution went hand in hand.[76]

Moreover, while the competition between oil and coal was intense, it was not a zero-sum game. The expansion of fuel oil markets did little to dampen the mid-Atlantic's appetite for coal. Between 1860 and 1900, the production of anthracite coal increased more than five-fold from just over ten million tons to nearly sixty million tons annually. Pennsylvania's bituminous coal production practically doubled each decade during this period, growing from under five million tons to nearly eighty million tons a year.[77] To put this energy production into perspective, in 1900 Pennsylvania coal mining produced the energy equivalent of the annual yield of a forest four times the size of the state.[78] This coal was used to make copious quantities of iron and steel, manufacture railroad tracks, cars, and locomotives, power steam engines, and even to refine petroleum. Coal and oil served complementary purposes: furthering urban and industrial growth and the hold of the mineral energy regime.

Yet oil could also be used in ways that coal could not. Coal-fired steam engines, for example, operated most efficiently when they were large and operated constantly. They could not be started and stopped easily because operators needed to bring a great deal of water to a boil. This led some to investigate the possibility of a power source that could operate at lower levels of output and be turned on or off quickly. One answer to this challenge was the internal combustion engine: a device in which fuel was burned internally to provide power rather than by heating an external container of water. Early experiments into engines that consumed fuel directly date back many centuries, but its practical development occurred in the last third of the nineteenth century when engineers found solutions for igniting the fuel with spark plugs, compressing the fuel in the cylinder, and implementing a four-cycle engine. As the technology improved, many small producers adopted these devices quickly. Befitting the patterns of the second industrial revolution, internal combustion engines not only provided a more flexible form of power, they also replaced labor with technology. As one observer noted in 1896: "For small manufacturers the convenience of having a motive power at hand, easy to start or stop in a few moments, is so great, that small gas motors are rapidly superseding, not only steam, but manual labour."[79] By 1898, over a hundred companies were selling internal combustion engines in America and tens of thousands were in operation, bringing the mineral energy regime to a range of enterprises for which steam engines were unsuitable.[80]

Internal combustion engines were initially deployed as a source of stationary power that could be run with any combustible fuel including natural gas, manufactured gas, or petroleum. This would change dramatically in the early twentieth century with the rise of the gasoline-powered automobile. Many parties were interested in developing a "horseless carriage" in the late nineteenth century, and several power sources seemed promising, including steam engines, electric motors, and the internal combustion engine. Europeans, rather than Americans, took the lead in making the gasoline-powered automobile a reality. German engineers including Nicolaus Otto, Gottlieb Daimler, and Carl Benz made crucial innovations in the 1870s and 1880s while several French firms were at the forefront of developing experimental models in the 1890s. American entrepreneurs may have been at least a decade behind in 1895, but they soon closed the gap and opened a wide lead. Highlighted by Henry Ford's focus on mass production, American automobile manufacture skyrocketed from a few thousand cars in 1899 to more than a hundred thousand in 1909 and over a million and a half in 1919. By the end of World War I, three out of every four automobiles were being manufactured in America.[81]

Abundant supplies of gasoline in America created a synergistic relationship with the automobile. In the early years of the oil industry, gasoline had often been considered a waste product that was simply burnt off because it was considered dangerous. But in the context of the internal combustion engine, this volatility was considered a benefit as it made combustion easier. Flush with cheap gasoline as a result of booming oil production at the dawn of the twentieth century, the gasoline-powered automobile quickly eclipsed vehicles designed for steam engines and electric motors, comprising more than 95 percent of American production by 1909. This, in turn, created an immense demand for gasoline; sales grew nearly fifteen-fold in the first two decades of the twentieth century. It also increased the per capita demand for petroleum products: whereas a gallon of kerosene could supply a lamp used every evening for more than a month, automobiles could burn through a gallon of gasoline in less than an hour.[82] Both the oil and automobile industries benefited enormously from this positive feedback cycle.

Over the course of the twentieth century, the automobile has become perhaps the most visible and immediate example of the mineral energy regime in daily life. Unlike walking or riding a horse, drivers did not need to expend personal energy for travel—they could substitute gasoline instead. In this capacity, automobiles furthered the transformed experience of space and time begun with coal-fired steam engines on railroads and steamships. But instead of passengers being dependent on time schedules and fixed routes, cars put the energetic abundance of mineral energy sources directly into the hands of drivers. For the first time, quantities of power previously reserved for factories were suddenly available to individuals. As long as they could access abundant stocks of gasoline, drivers were no longer constrained by the limits of their muscles or the schedules of corporations. They could travel where they wanted, when they wanted, and along whatever route they wanted.

While new applications of fuel oil and automobiles in the late nineteenth and early twentieth centuries paved the way for the industry's continued growth, this expansion occurred without dampening the prospects for kerosene and lubricants. In the mineral energy regime, the size of the pie is not fixed, and several sectors can expand at once. Over the last two decades of the nineteenth century, kerosene became steadily cheaper and showed no signs of limits to growth. By 1885, wholesale prices of kerosene were as little as eight cents a gallon, a major contrast to three decades prior when whale oil often cost more than a dollar a gallon. The use of kerosene increased accordingly, as American annual per capita consumption grew from 1.5 gallons in 1874 to 3.6 gallons in 1884 and 7.4 gallons in 1894. As a gallon of kerosene could provide about 140 hours of light, this represented an increase from 210 to 1,036 hours of light a year, or from about forty minutes a day of lighting to nearly three hours.[83] The market for lubricants grew during this period as well. By 1907, it was estimated that 90 percent of the world's lubricants were derived from petroleum.[84] Moreover, these lubricants had a synergistic influence by enabling other applications of mineral energy. Internal combustion engines typified the need of advanced machinery for quality oils, as noted at the time: "Oiling the piston is a matter of much importance, and must be carefully performed. The high speeds and temperatures at which gas motors work necessitate a continuous and skillful use of good mineral oil."[85] Whether for light, lubrication, heat, or power, petroleum pushed the nation further into the mineral energy regime.

Oil and the Gilded Age

It is no coincidence that America's oil boom coincided with the Gilded Age. The last decades of the nineteenth century were a period of rapid economic and population growth fueled by increases in energy consumption, mechanization, and the concentration of corporate power. While the United States trailed Britain, Germany, and France in industrial output in 1860, by 1900 Americans produced more goods than all three countries combined.[86] During the same time period, the nation's population grew 250 percent while the urban population increased nearly 500 percent.[87] As the center of the nation's coal and oil industries, the mid-Atlantic was at the forefront of these changes. New York and Pennsylvania solidified their standing as the nation's wealthiest states despite having their populations grow at a rate slower than the national average. New York's share of population decreased from 12 percent to 9.5 percent, while its share of the nation's taxable wealth increased from 11 percent to 14 percent in 1860 and 1900, respectively; in Pennsylvania during the same period, population decreased from 9 percent to 8 percent, while its taxable wealth increased from 8 percent to 11 percent. In the domain of manufacturing and railroads, the story was even more pronounced. In 1900, the two states accounted for 30 percent of the nation's investment in manufacturing facilities and 22 percent of its railroad property, eclipsing the total of the next four highest states. In the South, where the use of mineral energy sources was much less common, the result was very different. North Carolina, South Carolina, Georgia, and Florida produced 10 percent of the nation's taxable wealth in 1860 but less than 3 percent by 1900 while experiencing only a slight decline in total population.[88] The uneven distribution of the mineral energy regime exacerbated inequality across the nation.

But it was not simply uneven growth that defined the Gilded Age: it was the unpredictable and chaotic nature of a rapidly changing economy. Periods of expansion and good times were followed by panics that led to bankruptcy and layoffs. Manufacturers and capitalists made great fortunes only to see them disappear as quickly. Though average wages rose considerably in the last third of the nineteenth century, millions of workers experienced a volatile labor market with few safety protections and frequent furloughs. The state offered little assistance. Despite many calls from citizens to protect workers and alleviate corruption, government bodies at the federal and state level typically implemented only halting and incomplete measures.[89]

Oil both reflected and shaped these trends. The mysteries of its production mirrored the unpredictability of the economy's boom-and-bust patterns. Given their inability to see underground deposits, oilmen continually struggled with the seemingly random nature of oil production. One day they might strike a gusher that would spew out hundreds of barrels of petroleum for a month or two before drying up completely. An entire field might produce large quantities of oil for a year or two before declining rapidly. Sometimes oil was found in places it was not expected, like western Ohio, while at other times it failed to appear at sites where the geology seemed most promising. The American economy appeared just as enigmatic. A financial panic in 1873 abruptly ended a period of strong performance following the Civil War and plunged the nation into recession for six years.

Following a decade of recovery, overbuilding of railroads and interruptions to the gold supply led to another severe panic in 1893 that crippled the economy for another four years. Ten more years of prosperity led to the Panic of 1907. Both oil production and the economy defied rational planning.

For a few businessmen, the answer to these wild swings was to use corporate power to bring order to unruly markets. No one embodied this logic better than John D. Rockefeller. His domination of the transporting and refining of oil allowed his company to regulate the market and achieve steady profits. In addition to being a model to other businessmen of his day, Rockefeller also facilitated the consolidation of other fields by pioneering the use of the trust. This innovative corporate structure offered at least two great benefits to capitalists seeking to control entire industries. First, it allowed a large number of corporate enterprises to be linked without raising public awareness. Even when Standard Oil acquired control of other companies, the trust allowed these companies to maintain their existing names and appear to operate independently. This made it extremely difficult for industry insiders as well as consumers to determine which oil companies were operating in coordination with Standard Oil and which were not. Second, it allowed a small group of directors to control myriad enterprises without being directly implicated for monopolistic behaviors. During legal hearings, the officers of Standard Oil could plausibly deny directing the actions of subsidiary companies because, according to the letter of the law, such orders came from the trustees of the Standard Oil Trust. Capitalists soon used trusts to achieve monopoly control in several other industries, including the sugar, steel, whisky, and meat trades. By 1898, more than eighty trusts directed more than a billion dollars of assets; in the next six years, more than two hundred additional trusts were formed controlling over $6 billion in capitalization.[90] While businessmen may have preached the virtues of laissez-faire in public, their practices reveal that they eagerly replaced the invisible hand of the market with the "visible hand" of managerial capitalism.[91] The Standard Oil Trust played a pivotal role in spreading this pattern of Gilded Age capitalism.

The consolidation of large industries, in turn, created vast disparities in wealth. For every Rockefeller or Andrew Carnegie, there were thousands of smaller entrepreneurs who were disadvantaged by the strength of corporate power. For laborers, this was a particularly challenging period because they typically worked long hours under dangerous conditions for modest pay. Moreover, they had few benefits and little job security since factories were frequently forced to shut down in response to economic downturns. In response, millions of laborers joined unions like the Knights of Labor and the American Federation of Labor to demand better conditions. Since most captains of industry refused to recognize unions, and the state often sided with capitalists, the late nineteenth century witnessed some of the most intense and violent strikes in American history. There were thousands of work stoppages during the Gilded Age highlighted by national events involving the destruction of property and state-sanctioned violence, such as the Railroad Strike of 1877 and the Homestead Strike of 1894. Recognizing that they were not receiving a fair share of the benefits of industrialization, workers used whatever organizational techniques were at their disposal to get access to shorter working hours, health care, wage protection, and disability insurance.[92]

For workers, petroleum was a mixed blessing. When they were introduced into factories, high-quality lubricants improved the safety of work environments as they allowed machinery to operate with less friction. However, this had the rebound effect of enabling the installation of even faster and more powerful machines that could result in higher levels of bodily harm when accidents occurred. Fuel oil eliminated the labor of shoveling coal because it could flow directly into boilers with the manipulation of valves. This reduced the available number of jobs and also gave management greater power by transferring agency from laborers to technologies. On the other hand, kerosene was a significant benefit for most workers because its steadily decreasing cost meant that illumination for their homes was not a great drain on their paychecks.

If oil helped usher in the Gilded Age, it may have also helped usher it out. The excesses of the period, particularly the unchecked power of corporations, led to a reform movement around the turn of the twentieth century that became known as the Progressive Era. As muckraking journalists like Henry Demarest Lloyd and Ida Tarbell publicized the monopoly practices of Standard Oil, government agencies began to take new action to regulate corporations, starting with the passage of the Sherman Antitrust Act in 1890 and the court-ordered breakup of Rockefeller's empire in 1911. These landmark victories proved to be a major rallying cry for progressives and gave momentum to a broad range of reform efforts. If oil could be controlled, it gave many confidence that other excesses of the era could be regulated as well.[93]

Assessing the legacies of petroleum's first forty years is complex, for there is no single narrative. From the perspective of intra-industry dynamics, oil was the epitome of monopoly control. But from the viewpoint of consumers, the low price of kerosene led to a democratization of illumination. Like anthracite coal for home heating, kerosene benefited the working classes by decreasing the cost of an everyday staple. Without doubt, oil helped entrench the patterns of the mineral energy regime in the mid-Atlantic and beyond. The production and consumption of oil grew at rates unimaginable in the organic energy regime. In factories, petroleum helped usher in the second industrial revolution, leading to greater levels of output using powerful machinery. Consumed in railroads, ships, and automobiles, oil increasingly moved transport from muscles, animal power, and wind to mineral energy sources. And kerosene and lubricants remained an essential part of urban industrialization.

These sweeping changes associated with oil were directly shaped by innovations in transport infrastructure. Though Byron Benson and his colleagues did not anticipate the rise of automobiles or the industrial consumption of fuel oil, their pioneering of pipelines made such a world possible. Oil at the wellhead might be found cheaply in places like Ohio, Texas, California, and Oklahoma, but it would only make sense to burn it for fuel purposes if it could be shipped at low cost and in large quantities. Pipelines produced a landscape of intensification that furthered the dramatic growth in petroleum consumption and the deepening of the mineral energy regime.

5

Taming the Susquehanna River

O N OCTOBER 14, 1910, Mayor J. Barry Mahool of Baltimore stood before a crowd gathered at the newly completed Holtwood Dam on the Susquehanna River. With much fanfare, he turned a knob on the powerhouse and declared "the big Susquehanna River is now working for Baltimore."[1] A "pulsating" current of electricity was sent forty miles in an instant and it was reported that lights were burning in Baltimore before the spectators even had a chance to applaud. A newspaper journalist predicted that "the waters of Pennsylvania's great river will light the streets, drive the trolley cars, and run the wheels of many mills in 200 towns and cities within a radius of 45 miles of the river."[2]

The journalist was both right and wrong. The raging waters of the Susquehanna River had been transformed into an energy source capable of providing heat, light, and power. But this energy would not be widely distributed. In reality, the power of the Susquehanna would be shipped over transmission wires to a small handful of cities with few benefits for the surrounding towns and villages. As with canals and pipelines, a local ecosystem was disrupted to serve the needs of distant consumers.

Electrification has been one of history's most consequential energy transitions. No other system has so radically altered people's everyday relationships to energy. Like coal and oil, electricity could provide heat, light, and power. But it was distinguished by its ease of use, convenience, and flexibility. Unlike the laborious shoveling of coal or tending of a kerosene lamp, the simple flick of a switch could turn on a light, activate a motor, or start an appliance. Consumers also discovered that electricity was clean and quiet: incandescent bulbs did not emit soot or consume oxygen, machines operated without the banging of steam engines, and there were no ashes to discard. Perhaps most important was that electricity could be used in a stunning variety of applications: indoor and outdoor illumination, urban transport, manufacturing, mining, domestic appliances, and even leisure. Because it could be delivered in both massive quantities and tiny increments, electricity could power large factories as well as small appliances appropriate for the home. For those becoming accustomed to replacing the exertions of their muscles with the consumption of power produced elsewhere, electricity was the culmination of a process several decades in the making.[3]

Yet electricity is not inherently a convenient form of power. Its benefits are obtained only with hefty investments in transport infrastructure. As with coal and oil, the materiality of electricity tested its boosters. Electricity is ephemeral: without an elaborate system of wires, the useful energy in an electrical current dissipates rapidly. But this challenge was also an opportunity. Electricity's propensity to flow meant that with the construction of transmission wires, it could be shipped long distances cheaply and reliably. As in previous energy transitions, choices over how, when, and where to build transmission wires structured who benefited from electrification and who did not. Wires were not passive conduits between producers and consumers; they advantaged certain parties but not others.

Unlike coal and oil, electricity is not a direct source of energy. It is a carrier, meaning that another source of power must be employed to generate electricity. Most electricity is generated by rotating a wire coil between the poles of a magnet—a process discovered by Michael Faraday in the early nineteenth century. If turbines are attached to the coil, the rotation can be powered by steam pressure or falling water. Once the electricity is generated, it can be transported to consumers through conductive materials like copper. Electricity, then, is a method of transforming mechanical energy into a form that can be delivered cheaply and used in an astonishingly wide variety of applications.

In the late nineteenth and early twentieth centuries, most electricity was generated by burning coal to produce steam or channeling falling water through turbines. Both relied on the transport of energy: in the former case, coal was shipped along railroads to urban generating stations while in the latter case hydroelectric power was transmitted along wires to distant consumption centers. The logic and roots of the long-distance transport of coal have already been covered earlier in this book. These chapters focus on waterpower because the pioneering developments in long-distance transmission wires were associated with hydroelectric dams.[4]

Hydroelectric dams and their transmission wires are hybrids of the organic and mineral energy regimes. Characteristic of the organic energy regime, rivers derive their power from renewable flows of solar energy. They are also subject to limits of growth: once the water has been dammed, there is little opportunity to increase the flow of energy. But hydroelectricity also shares certain features of the mineral energy regime. The creation of immense dams was only possible with the aid of mineral energy sources. Rather than being used at the site of production, as was common with waterpower in the organic energy regime, hydroelectricity was typically transported long distances to urban centers where it was integrated into a network with coal-fired generators. Moreover, consumers used electricity in ways that further reinforced the patterns of the mineral energy regime.

Completed in 1910, Holtwood Dam and its transmission wires produced a new landscape of intensification in the mid-Atlantic. Though Americans had already begun to consume electricity before the taming of the Susquehanna River, these developments marked a new era of long-distance power transmission in the region. The creation of an abundant supply of energy with the technological means to transport it encouraged boosters to find new applications of electricity. Once in markets, electricity furthered the shift to the mineral energy regime. Electric lights illuminated the night, electric streetcars transported urban residents through burgeoning cities, electric motors supported new manufacturing techniques such as assembly line production, and electrical appliances in the home altered the nature and experience of housework. Electricity even became an important part of recreation, as theme parks, radios, and movie theaters linked leisure with the consumption of mineral energy sources. In the early decades of the twentieth century, electricity became the quintessentially modern source of light and power.

Early Uses of Electricity

Americans had long been captivated by electricity. Scientists and showmen had used it since the late eighteenth century in theatrical displays designed to elicit feelings of awe and wonder from their audiences. In the mid-nineteenth century, electrical currents were routinely utilized in telegraph networks. But it was only in the last quarter of the nineteenth century that electricity was transformed into a source of energy through the pioneering work of innovators like Thomas Edison, Nikola Tesla, and George Westinghouse. With the development of dynamos, motors, wires, and incandescent lightbulbs, what was previously a novelty became a practical source of energy.

The roots of electrification, like the roots of American oil development, were shaped by previous energy transitions. Over the course of the nineteenth century, coal and oil had supported new levels of urban and industrial growth; these large cities and factories, in turn, created new demands such as the desire for better lighting and intra-urban transport. To solve these challenges of the emerging mineral energy regime, Americans embraced electricity, thereby further extending the mineral energy regime. Because the mid-Atlantic was the nation's most heavily urbanized and industrialized region in the late nineteenth century, it is not surprising that many important inventors worked there, including Edison and Tesla. But unlike the energy landscapes of coal and oil, the mid-Atlantic would not remain unique for long. Americans across the nation were quick to adopt electricity, and practices pioneered in the mid-Atlantic soon spread elsewhere. By the early twentieth century, electrification was a national process.

Lighting was the first major application of electricity outside of the telegraph network. In the last third of the nineteenth century, entrepreneurs such as Charles Brush created arc lighting systems in which an electrical current flowing between two electrodes produced a bright glow. In 1876, Thomas Edison invented the incandescent lightbulb, and in 1882 he demonstrated an integrated lighting system at Pearl Street in New York City. Just as gaslight and kerosene had been celebrated as leaps forward when they were introduced earlier in the nineteenth century, the electric light was widely hailed as the brightest and clearest form of artificial illumination.[5] But the brilliance of electric light was expensive. Users had to install costly wires and pay hefty monthly fees for service. As a result, whereas the relative cheapness of kerosene encouraged its adoption among a wide segment of the population, the first adopters of electric light were typically institutions with larger budgets: municipalities, stores, and factories. Residential electric use was extremely rare at the turn of the twentieth century: even as late as 1907, only one home in twelve was electrified.[6] For most people, kerosene remained a more economical option.

City governments were important early adopters of electric light. Many municipalities had invested heavily in manufactured gas lighting during the nineteenth century to address public safety concerns as their cities grew larger and more crowded. They hoped that illuminating streets at night would improve public safety and order, and many cities viewed electrification as an upgrade over gas.[7] But functional reasons alone do not explain the patterns of American street lighting. As the historian David Nye has demonstrated, the lighting of public spaces was intended to signify that a city was progressive.[8] Cities constructed elaborate lighting displays to convey an image of grandeur and advancement. The National Electric Light Association, a trade organization for the electric industry, encouraged these investments by emphasizing the symbolic importance of lighting in its promotional materials. One booklet declared "every dollar invested in an ornamental lighting system for business sections, residential districts, and parks is not only returned manifold in higher real estate values and in greater prosperity, but returned in prestige, in heightened civic pride, and in better citizenship."[9] A city with electric lights was a modern city.

Storeowners similarly rushed to adopt electric light for both functional and symbolic purposes. Not only did electric light make it easier to keep a store open after sunset and enhance window displays, it could be a central part of advertising. Spurred on by the "Great White Way" of Broadway in New York, stores vied with each other to create the most elaborate electric advertisements possible.[10] Department store owners like John Wanamaker in Philadelphia experimented extensively with electricity to draw customers into their buildings. This put pressure on competing stores to electrify, as the owners feared losing business if their enterprises did not appear to be on the cutting edge. When stores in one shopping district installed street-lights, other business districts often felt compelled to do the same. Based on the rapid pace of electrification among stores, many owners evidently believed the claims of boosters that "street lighting is necessary to attract business" and "crowds flock to [a] blaze of light like moths."[11]

Factory owners were also quick to replace gaslights with electric illumination. While gaslight offered a bright glow that enabled production to continue after sunset, it had several downsides: it gave off heat that could make factories uncomfortably warm, and leaking gas could cause headaches and start fires. Electric light was safer, healthier, and emitted less heat. Because of the reduced fire risk, insurers often reduced rates when electric lights replaced gas. Moreover, electric lights were flexible and could be moved around a room, unlike gaslights that were fixed in position. For jobs requiring precision work, such as many aspects of textile or craft manufacturing, being able to shift and redirect the light increased productivity and enhanced work quality.[12] Good illumination was such an important component of manufacturing that approximately half of the electricity consumed in factories at the turn of the century went to lighting.[13]

Lighting was electricity's first market, but it was eclipsed in the late nineteenth century by the streetcar industry. Earlier in the century, most major American cities had their commercial, residential, and industrial districts located within walking distance of one another. In 1850, for example, nearly all of Boston was packed within a two-mile radius of City Hall, meaning that a person could walk to and from nearly any point in the city in less than an hour.[14] Freed from the constraints of the organic energy regime and flush with industrial jobs stemming from the use of coal and oil, many cities expanded dramatically from 1850 to 1900. The populations of Philadelphia and Baltimore more than tripled during this period, Boston's quadrupled, and New York City's grew more than six-fold (some of this growth came from annexing surrounding areas).[15] More homes, stores, and factories led to a widening of the urban core, thus creating new intra-urban transport challenges as people had to travel further to get between residential, commercial, and industrial districts.

The first efforts to address this problem were drawn from the organic energy regime. Horse-drawn omnibuses and railways ran along city streets much as buses and trolleys do today. Omnibuses had large wheels and could travel flexibly over any city street like buses, while horse-drawn railways traveled along tracks following preset routes. These systems improved intra-urban transport but also had notable limitations. Horse-drawn cars were expensive and produced enormous quantities of pollution in the form of manure. Moreover, they traveled little faster than a person walking. If we take an hour's commute as a maximum distance people could live from their work locations, horse-drawn omnibuses and walking required urbanites to reside within three or four miles of stores and employment opportunities.[16] Some pioneers tried to attach steam engines to railway cars, but they were not a great improvement: people resisted their introduction onto city streets because they were noisy, polluting, and dangerous. Moreover, these transit systems were decentralized and unplanned, leading to wide variations in the quality of service.[17]

Streetcars powered by electricity offered the potential to overcome these limitations. Electric motors were quiet and did not pollute the urban core if the current was produced at a distant generating system. The amount of energy delivered to an electric motor could be increased or decreased much faster than in a steam engine, making starting and stopping quickly a realistic possibility. As a result, electric streetcars could travel more quickly along city streets and carry a greater number of passengers than horse-drawn omnibuses or any system based on steam engines.[18] In 1887, Frank Sprague developed one of the first functional electric streetcar systems in Richmond, Virginia, and others soon followed suit. Given the acute demand for improved urban transport, electric streetcars spread rapidly. In many cases, existing railways simply replaced their horse-drawn wagons with electric cars. By 1890, companies in more than two hundred cities had built or ordered electric streetcar systems and they were present in nearly all medium-size cities by 1902.[19] At this date, all but 6 percent of the nation's street railways had been electrified and nearly half of the nation's electricity was being used to power streetcars—more than was consumed in any other application including lighting.[20]

Controlling the Susquehanna River

These early uses of electricity during the last quarter of the nineteenth century encouraged numerous people to rethink the fate of the Susquehanna, a river with a curious human history. It is one of the longest and widest rivers in the eastern United States, but its particular geology and variable water flows impeded the efforts of European settlers to turn it into a conduit for transport or power as they did with most other rivers on the eastern seaboard. It would take the dreams and capabilities of the mineral energy regime to transform this waterway into a generator of electricity.[21]

The Susquehanna River drains an area greater than 27,500 square miles—over half of Pennsylvania as well as several counties in New York. It is formed by two branches that meet in the center of Pennsylvania and empty into the Chesapeake Bay. The North Branch begins in Lake Otsego in New York, near Cooperstown. It flows in a large S-curve, crossing through the Wyoming Valley and its anthracite reserves. The West Branch begins near Carrolltown, in western Pennsylvania. It generally runs eastward, though it meanders north and then south before joining the North Branch at Sunbury. The combined waters then travel south by southeast past Harrisburg and into the Chesapeake Bay northeast of Baltimore.

Parts of the Susquehanna River may be as old as the area's coal and oil reserves. Approximately 300 million years ago, the tectonic shifting of plates lifted up large sections of the eastern seaboard and drained some of the shallow lakes that covered interior areas. Streams coming out of the new mountains formed channels that were the antecedents of the current river. However, its path and direction has likely shifted many times. Roughly 150 million years ago, the central stem of the river may have flowed north rather than south. About 10,000 years ago, retreating glaciers produced its present shape as they left large banks of rocks that blocked streams and created lakes filled with melted ice. When the water burst through these temporary dams, the massive forces of the floods carved new channels including Pennsylvania's Grand Canyon, a thousand-foot gorge in Tioga County.[22]

The Susquehanna's last forty miles contain one of the river's most distinctive geological features: just south of Columbia, Pennsylvania, the river enters the Piedmont Province and drops nearly six feet per mile into the Chesapeake Bay. Large falls at the end of a river are extremely rare: most rivers begin with drops near their origins and then level out as they reach the sea. How this peculiar formation was created remains unclear. Some contend that it must have been a giant upthrust at the edge of the continent caused by earthquakes, while others see it as simply an odd layering of rocks

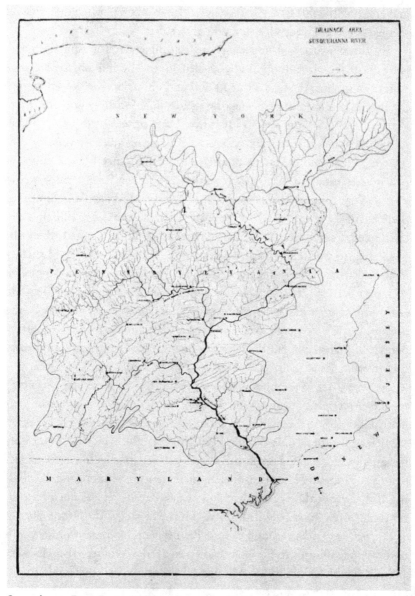

Susquehanna River Basin. (Hagley Museum and Library)

and erosion. The mystery of this stretch is further complicated by a series of strange potholes and scoops along the river's bed.[23]

The consequences of this geology are less enigmatic. The rapid descent at the end of the river dramatically shaped its use by humans. For Native American groups, the falls created pools and obstacles that slowed migrating fish such as shad, thereby making them valuable fishing grounds. More than a thousand years ago, Native Americans carved pictographs of fish into large boulders to signify important harvesting areas. European colonists experienced these rapids as a significant hindrance because they impeded transportation. Many early settlers hoped the Susquehanna would provide easy access to the interior of Pennsylvania. Captain John Smith led the first survey of the river by European settlers in 1608 and William Penn envisioned a sister city for Philadelphia that would be located where the Susquehanna and Conestoga Rivers met.[24] Yet the difficulty of getting boats up or down the choppy waters of the river's lower stretches inhibited their efforts. Smith was not able to travel any farther than the boulders and falls near the mouth of the river and no major city emerged to make Penn's dream a reality. Some goods could be transported down the river during periods of high water, but the flow was one-way, dangerous, and limited to certain stretches of the river and certain times of the year.

Because rivers were important transport corridors in the organic energy regime, Americans made several attempts to improve the Susquehanna's navigability during the eighteenth and nineteenth centuries, seeking to reach the rich agricultural lands of central Pennsylvania. But their efforts were only marginally successful. Nineteenth-century developments like the Susquehanna & Tidewater Canal enabled an increasing amount of goods, including anthracite coal, to reach the Chesapeake Bay, but it was not a reciprocal trade as few goods traveled upriver on the canal. With the completion of railroad networks through central Pennsylvania in the mid-nineteenth century, much of this traffic was diverted to overland routes. The reliability and geographic flexibility of the mineral energy proved preferable to nature's distribution of waterways.

Power production was the other major use of rivers in the organic energy regime. But for this purpose, the Susquehanna's variable water levels presented a great challenge. During the spring melt, the river often rose significantly and flooded. During the dry season in late summer and early fall, the great river was frequently reduced to a trickle, leading some to dub it the "mile-wide, foot-deep river."[25] These changing water levels discouraged power developments. It was difficult to site a mill along the river's banks because the full strength of a spring flood would provide too much power to control effectively, while lower water levels might not even reach a water-wheel. Moreover, spring floods were often accompanied by great blocks of ice cascading down the river that would destroy any bridges or buildings at river's edge. Most people in the region found it easier to establish mills along the tributaries of the Susquehanna where the water flows were more manageable. Not until the 1870s did a paper mill at York Haven use the main channel of the lower Susquehanna to generate power.[26]

As a result, the Susquehanna was an anomaly in the organic energy regime: a major river flowing through a large drainage basin that was only lightly used for power or transport. Compared with the Delaware and Hudson Rivers, its banks were far less settled, there were far fewer industrial enterprises, and levels of trade were much lower. It would take the emergence of the mineral energy regime and the increasing interest in electric power to tap the potential organic energy of the Susquehanna River.

The Most Marvelous Mechanical Feat

Within a month of Edison's Pearl Street station opening in New York City in 1882, America's first hydroelectric station began operating in Appleton, Wisconsin. Given the nation's long experience with waterpower, adapting such sites to produce electricity was often a relatively simple process. Numerous mills already had sophisticated water turbines in place, so attaching the existing equipment to a generator could repurpose them for making electricity. By the 1890s, this practice was common at several mills across the nation, including a few along the tributaries of the Susquehanna River. At such sites, the small generators typically produced enough energy to power the mill along with a few lights.[27] This reflected the general pattern in Pennsylvania: in 1902, there were fewer than fifty hydroelectric facilities, and the average capacity was under 100 horsepower (hp).[28] Because these installations generated relatively small amounts of power that was consumed locally, they, like the mills, were characteristic of the organic energy regime.

Yet other sites had much greater potential for hydroelectricity. At the end of the nineteenth century, New York was home to the world's largest hydroelectric undertaking at Niagara Falls. Boosters had long been intrigued by the incredibly powerful and constant flow of water as the Niagara River fell over one hundred and fifty feet on its thirty-mile journey from Lake Erie to Lake Ontario. Following the model of New England mills, in 1870 a diversion canal was built to provide waterpower for local enterprises. Twenty years later, a company owning Niagara water rights convened a distinguished international commission of scientists and engineers, headed by William Thomson (soon to become Lord Kelvin) to analyze the best way to exploit the power potential. In 1893, the company made the bold decision, for that time, to focus exclusively on generating electric power. Two years later, the first powerhouse was in operation, and by 1900, the facility was producing 50,000 hp. The capacity was more than doubled four years later, and in 1904, Niagara generated 20 percent of American electricity.[29] But while the Niagara developments were highly innovative in the production of electricity and would ultimately have a capacity of more than half a million horsepower, they did not revolutionize transmission. The vast majority of the power was used locally by factories that established themselves near the falls to take advantage of cheap power and easy transport along the Great Lakes.[30]

After pioneering hydroelectric developments through Niagara, mid-Atlantic entrepreneurs began to be eclipsed by boosters elsewhere—particularly California. This was, in large part, a product of the region's existing energy endowment. Blessed with abundant coal and sophisticated transport networks, those in the mid-Atlantic could easily use energy landscapes of the past to supply coal-fired generators in urban locations. Other regions with less access to mineral energy sources did not have the same flexibility. Lacking in native coal deposits, the Pacific Coast states developed a series of hydroelectric installations in the Sierra Nevada and Cascade Mountains and built some of the world's longest transmission wires in the first decade of the twentieth century.[31]

Even though the region possessed copious quantities of coal, mid-Atlantic boosters remained intrigued by the power potential of the Susquehanna River. At the dawn of the twentieth century, several parties contemplated erecting a huge dam that would turn the river's renewable flows into an enormous stock of power to serve distant markets. Their ambitious plans meant that such a facility would have many characteristics of the mineral energy regime. It could only be profitably constructed with the aid of mineral energy sources. Given the rural nature of the surrounding areas, there were no local markets for such a large supply of electricity. Instead of people moving to a site of energy abundance, these entrepreneurs planned to ship the energy of the river to urban centers. Moreover, to accommodate the fluctuating water levels, hydroelectricity needed to be integrated into a network of coal-fired power plants. A dam on the Susquehanna would have more in common with a coal mine or oil well than a mill along a river.

Starting in 1901, a number of boosters began surveying the lower Susquehanna and purchasing property rights. Cary T. Hutchinson, a consulting electrical engineer who became familiar with Baltimore's power situation while earning his doctorate at Johns Hopkins in 1889, led one group of promoters. James Harlow directed another, drawing on his engineering expertise derived from working on the generators at the paper mill near York Haven and developing water supply plants in Maryland. Much of this work was done in secret because rival groups hoped to acquire properties before their competitors. Moreover, they knew that if they tipped off locals to their plans, the prices for land would increase dramatically.[32]

By 1905, Hutchinson and his collaborators had acquired sufficient property rights to form the McCall Ferry Power Company and announce their plan to build a dam near an inn and ferry service that provided the site with its name. They chose the McCall's Ferry location because there was an island in the middle of the river allowing them to build the dam one half at a time, a natural tailrace for the powerhouse's water discharge between the island and east side of the river, and a bend in the river above the site that would prevent damage to the powerhouse by directing large blocks of ice to the west side of the dam. In addition, the river had high cliffs—only small amounts of land would be submerged in the reservoir created by the dam and no villages would need to be relocated. However, there were some disadvantages to the site: the surrounding area was very rural and remote, so the company would have to import laborers, erect housing, build construction plants, and supply any other facilities it needed.

The scale of the project was immense. The company proposed erecting a dam extending more than half a mile, making it the longest in the United

States at that time and comparable to the recently built Aswan Dam in Egypt.[33] A newspaper reported that the project was "considered by many experts to constitute the most marvelous mechanical feat in North America."[34] With the exception of Niagara Falls, its hydroelectric output would be the largest of any dam east of the Mississippi River. To tackle such an ambitious undertaking, the company combined the financial support of major New York City capitalists who raised ten million dollars for the project, and an elite group of engineers who had worked on the Panama Canal, including Hugh L. Cooper.[35] At least 400,000 cubic yards of concrete were estimated to be necessary to create a dam that was sixty-five feet wide at the base, over ten feet wide at the top, and as high as eighty feet. A local newspaper enthusiastically reported that this amount of concrete "would make a three-foot sidewalk from London, England, to Honolulu, via San Francisco, [with] enough left to pave every road in York county."[36] To supply the necessary materials, the company operated a rock quarry ten miles downriver and erected eight jumbo cement mixers next to the construction site; this was the largest concrete plant in the world at the time.[37]

Work began in the fall of 1905, and by the following spring more than a thousand laborers were on site. As with the building of canals and pipelines, construction was physically demanding and dangerous. The men had to haul materials, operate heavy machinery, pour concrete, and strain themselves in countless other ways. A sense of the difficulty can be inferred from the way the company scheduled its workers. They were divided into two teams: one that worked from 4 a.m. to 8 a.m. and noon to 4 p.m., and another that worked from 8 a.m. to noon and 4 p.m. to 8 p.m. Clearly the company did not expect workers' muscles to be able to sustain their output for eight straight hours at the desired pace. Workers also faced danger regularly. The current below the site of the dam flowed swiftly with dangerous rapids, and many laborers did not know how to swim. Several workers drowned during construction and others were barely saved by rescue boats.[38]

In another similarity to canal construction, the constitution of the labor force reflected prevailing social perceptions of ethnic difference. Christie Hutchinson, a lawyer for the company, told a newspaper "most of the force now is Italian, our superintendents finding that, on the whole, Italians are better workers than Slavs," though he did not explain how or why they had come to this conclusion. These workers were housed in simple shacks nearly a mile below the dam in a site that became known as "Little Italy." By contrast, the skilled "American" workers received higher wages and were offered room and board in company housing near the dam.[39] As in many large infrastructure projects in the early twentieth century, managers offered different levels of pay, living conditions, and opportunities based on ethnicity.[40]

In addition to the muscles of workers, dam construction required power beyond the scope of the organic energy regime to drill through rocks, run the concrete plant, and operate machinery. Engineers built a compressed air system powered by coal to supply the requisite energy. Compressed air was often used in major construction projects and mining in the late nineteenth century since it could supply power efficiently to many machines at once. In contrast to many small and inefficient steam engines, two large engines could compress air at high pressures in a centralized location. From this point, distribution pipes carried the air over a mile to wherever power was needed. Workers could then attach hoses to nozzles on the pipe to channel the compressed air into drills, augers, cranes, and the concrete plant.[41]

Due to the secrecy with which the project was begun, few people who lived in the vicinity of the dam had much idea of the changes under way. When one local citizen visited the construction site in 1906, he wrote to a newspaper that he would have considered the work a "false rumor" had he not witnessed it himself, but still found the scale of the effort hard to comprehend: "the only trouble to one familiar with these hills is to keep from doubting the evidence of his own senses and thinking that it must after all be only a dream."[42] Another reporter described the construction zone as a "most wonderful sight . . . the bed of the great river laid bare for a distance of three-quarters of a mile . . . It is something that should be seen, and it will never be forgotten. Nobody who has not witnessed such a sight can form the remotest idea of what it is from a description, and to walk about on the dry, rocky bed of what once was a roaring water-course, with water twenty feet deep, inspires very peculiar sensations indeed."[43]

Greater attention to the project soon initiated a wave of protest. Local fishermen opposed the project because they feared the dam would end their livelihoods by cutting shad off from its breeding grounds.[44] As one newspaper column noted, "[the dam builders] are looking out for [themselves], but we may well fear that they are not looking out for our shad."[45] Others complained because the reservoir behind the dam would submerge favorite local islands, such as the Indian Steps. These rock islands in the river were attractive spots for recreation, and local lore held that William Penn had bequeathed them to area residents.[46] These objections were often framed in anti-outsider and anticorporate rhetoric. One article described the project as a "scheme to grab the water rights of the lower Susquehanna" that was "financed by New York capitalists . . . with no native interest."[47] An editorial noted that "corporations have no souls" and emphasized that "the McCall Ferry Power company has its headquarters in Wall Street."[48] When a company executive was interviewed in a newspaper and declared that the "better class of citizens" in the area thought private ownership was desirable, a local official responded that only "a stranger to the mental habits of the people dwelling thereabout, would venture to assure them on moral grounds that it is for their betterment that a corporation should confiscate . . . their valued public lands."[49]

These critiques captured an early recognition among many locals that the benefits and costs of the dam would not be evenly distributed. Those who lived near the river and used it for fishing and recreation were threatened with losing access to these resources without any promises that they would receive cheap electricity. Given the links of the McCall Ferry Power Company to New York City and Baltimore, it was clear from the beginning that distant cities would be favored more than local communities. Therefore, even though some locals recognized that in the aggregate, the total value of hydroelectricity would be much higher than shad fishing, they knew they would bear the costs so others could benefit.[50]

These objections were powerful enough to draw the attention of Pennsylvania's Fish Warden, W. E. Meehan, who brought the issues to Pennsylvania's Attorney General Hampton L. Carson. Notably, there was remarkably little legislation governing the rights of private parties to erect a dam across the state's largest river. The company claimed the river was not navigable, which meant that state law, not federal, governed the project. As a result, they argued that Pennsylvania's Mill Act of 1806 gave them permission to erect a dam because they held the appropriate land rights on either side of the river.[51] Legal frameworks established in the organic energy regime, when legislators were pondering the small dams characteristic of rural mills, were mobilized to facilitate the mineral energy regime.[52]

By questioning whether the Mill Act was applicable, Carson obtained a temporary injunction in August of 1906, thereby halting the work.[53] On January 14, 1907, a compromise agreement was reached, allowing the company to proceed with work provided that it construct a fishway for the shad and facilitate navigation via locks if any party built a canal above the dam.[54] Shad fishermen would express dissatisfaction with the inadequacies of the fishway for several years to come, but their protests never seriously disrupted the project again.[55] Even as late as 1920, the company was still seeking to improve its standing among local communities by issuing a booklet aimed to "overcome . . . a great detail of misunderstanding" among "our neighbors" with the hope that familiarity with the plant will "let us have a place in their pride and enthusiasm."[56]

The company's neighborly relations were further strained as it acquired additional land rights. Rival interests drove hard bargains, and when one landowner refused to sell a key set of properties, the company was forced to lower the height of the dam from eighty to sixty-five feet.[57] When possible, the company proved willing to brandish the power of corporate capital. Because the dam would flood the tracks of a branch of the Pennsylvania Railroad running along the river, the company made arrangements to re-lay the tracks at a higher elevation (an expense of more than a million dollars). When a few landholders refused to sell their properties at prices considered fair by the McCall Ferry executives, the directors turned to the strength of the Pennsylvania Railroad, still one of the state's most powerful corporations, to resolve the issue. The Pennsylvania Railroad had eminent domain privileges, and the two companies worked out an arrangement whereby the railroad company used these rights to purchase the land at a cheaper price. While several landowners sued the two companies on grounds that the railroad could not use its eminent domain privileges for the benefit of the dam company, the courts ruled in favor of the more powerful capitalists.[58]

Even though the McCall Ferry Power Company successfully navigated the acquisition of land rights, thwarted legal obstacles, and made significant progress on construction, it met its demise with the collapse of the financial markets in the Panic of 1907. Even though the company had completed 80 percent of the work on the dam, it was unable to raise additional funds to finish the project. By March 1908, work had ceased entirely and

Holtwood Dam. (Hagley Museum and Library)

the river ran through fifteen forty-foot-wide sections of the dam that had been left incomplete.[59] The combination of prominent financiers and engineers was not sufficient to transform the falling water of the Susquehanna River into a profitable commodity.

The continued electrification of the mid-Atlantic and the large sunk costs in the dam, however, ensured that it would not sit idle long. A syndicate headed by John E. Aldred, who operated the Shawinigan Water & Power Company on the St. Lawrence River near Montreal, acquired control of the project early in 1909 and formed the Pennsylvania Water & Power Company (PWP). Two of Aldred's partners, Canadian bankers Herbert S. Holt and Edward R. Wood, invested enough money to warrant changing the name of the dam from McCall Ferry to Holtwood, a combination of their names. At the same time, Aldred and his colleagues acquired control of Baltimore's main electrical utility, Consolidated Gas Electric Light and Power Company (Consolidated).[60]

Over the winter and summer of 1910, the workers completed the dam by filling in the remaining open sections. PWP then built the powerhouse and installed turbines developed by the I. P. Morris Company of Philadelphia. General Electric supplied the generators and the transformers were purchased from Westinghouse.[61] By the fall of 1910, the dam and powerhouse were complete. The diffuse flows of the Susquehanna River that had defied the hopes of European settlers in the organic energy regime had been turned into a stock of concentrated energy capable of extending the mineral energy regime.

Transmitting Electricity

With the completion of America's largest dam and a powerhouse capable of generating more than 100,000 horsepower, Aldred and his colleagues suddenly had an abundant source of energy at their disposal. Yet with little local demand for their product, they had two choices. As in the case of the Lowell textile mills or the Niagara power plant, they could bring people and industries to the dam. Alternatively, as was typical of the mineral energy regime, they could ship the energy wealth of a rural site to distant urban centers. Given Aldred's acquisition of Baltimore's main electrical utility the year before, it was little surprise that they chose the latter option. This strategy, in turn, required a material connection between the trapped waters of the Susquehanna River and Baltimore's homes and factories. The ability of transmission wires to deliver electricity cheaply, abundantly, and reliably rendered the distance between sites of production and consumption negligible.

When PWP turned its attention to transmitting power to Baltimore at the beginning of 1910, it planned to erect the longest high-voltage line in the mid-Atlantic.[62] Fortunately, it could draw on earlier precedents and engineering knowledge. In particular, several of the engineers Aldred brought to Holtwood, including J. A. Walls, had prior experience operating transmission wires over the nearly ninety-mile distance from the Shawinigan Falls to Montreal.

Company engineers first directed their attention to acquiring rights-of-way for the transmission line. Their goal was to obtain a one-hundred-foot-wide strip of land for the entire forty-mile route to Baltimore: the broad path would allow them to build multiple transmission wires and keep trees away, thereby mitigating the risk that falling limbs would interrupt service. In Maryland, this process was relatively simple. The state passed a law in

1904 granting electric companies eminent domain privileges, and the company was able to force owners to sell them private lands at court-ordered "fair-market" prices. This quickly drew the ire of landowners who either opposed the presence of high-voltage transmission wires across their property or felt entitled to higher levels of compensation, but courts sided with the company.[63] In Pennsylvania, the company lacked eminent domain, despite the lobbying efforts of both the directors of the McCall Ferry Power Company and Aldred to achieve this privilege.[64] As a result, they were forced to pay higher prices for land rights north of the Mason-Dixon line. Even so, by the summer of 1910, all the necessary property rights had been acquired.[65]

At the same time the company was working to acquire land, it made decisions about materials. As was common in building long-distance transmission wires, the company opted for the greater reliability and strength of steel towers instead of cheaper wooden poles. The added capacity of steel towers was especially important as alternating current was shipped in three phases, each of which was carried over its own wire. A circuit consisted of the three wires put together, and a transmission line usually held one or two circuits. Steel towers capable of supporting two circuits—a total of six wires—were ordered from the Milliken Company of New York. For the wires, engineers chose aluminum wrapped around a steel core. Copper was the most common material for transmission wires at the time due to its high levels of conductivity, but aluminum was lighter than copper, had a higher melting point which was beneficial at high voltages, and cost only slightly more per pound.[66] Each wire could hold nineteen strands, thereby giving the circuits a normal capacity of 16,000 kilowatts (a kilowatt is about 1.33 horsepower) and a maximum capacity of 40,000 kilowatts (kw).

The use of aluminum wires demonstrates the synergistic feedback loops of the mineral energy regime. Before the introduction of electricity, aluminum was as expensive as silver because it was difficult to obtain pure samples. When the Washington Monument was completed in 1884, for example, its one-hundred-ounce aluminum cap cost more than two hundred times the daily wage of a laborer.[67] But in 1886, Charles Martin Hall discovered that running an electrical current through aluminum ore immersed in a solution provided an effective way of obtaining concentrated metal. Cheap electricity could be transformed into cheap aluminum that could, in turn, help transmit electricity long distances. Growth in one area fueled growth in another.

Company engineers also had to determine the line's operating voltage. Higher voltages reduced energy losses during transmission: the energy loss over forty miles on a 66,000-volt line was estimated to be one-fortieth the loss on an 11,000-volt line. But increasing and decreasing the voltage required expensive transformers and involved a loss of energy when the electricity was "stepped up" and "stepped down." Higher-voltage electricity was also more difficult to manage and necessitated more insulators along the transmission route. Therefore, engineers had to find the right balance between the transmission losses at lower voltage levels versus the capital investments and energy losses associated with higher voltages. The company ultimately decided to operate the line at 70,000 volts, resulting in about a 10 percent loss of energy between the dam's generators and the Baltimore substations.[68] Given that mechanical waterpower could only be transported a few hundred yards from a riverbank before the introduction of electricity, this was a remarkable advancement in the efficiency of power transmission.[69]

With these decisions complete, several hundred workers commenced construction in the summer of 1910. They began by building the steel towers, each of which was fifty to a hundred feet high and placed about five hundred feet apart. Construction teams were generally composed of a foreman, linemen, and grunts. Linemen were skilled workers who climbed the towers as they were being built and connected the steel beams. Grunts were responsible for hauling the materials and hoisting the beams to the linemen. The men lived in tents along the path of the wire and moved camp as they made progress.[70]

The labor of building a transmission line relied heavily on the power of muscles. The steel bars for the towers were hoisted into place using ropes and pulleys. To provide foundations for the towers, the men drilled holes in rocks and poured concrete foundations. Under good conditions, a team could erect a tower in a day or two. However, if the land was uneven or the ground was marshy, it could take up to a week. Supplies had to be hauled in by animals since most of the path ran through rural fields. There was also danger: a worker could fall off a tower, be struck by a tool dropped by a lineman, or be injured while using dynamite to create a base for the tower.

Transmission wire to Baltimore, showing two circuits. (Hagley Museum and Library)

One of the workmen, Evans Vickers, died when a stick of dynamite exploded unexpectedly.[71]

As the company was overseeing construction of the steel towers, it also built transformer stations at the beginning and end of the line. Next to the dam, the wires originated at a substation on the island in the middle of the river. Here the electricity was stepped up from 11,000 volts to 70,000 volts. The company bought a piece of property from Consolidated on the outskirts of Baltimore and built a second transformer station that reduced the voltage of the line to 11,000 volts.[72] From this substation, Consolidated shipped the electricity to its other substations and further reduced the voltage as it was distributed to customers.

By the end of July, the steel towers had been erected in York County and the northern section of Harford County.[73] The remaining towers were built over the next two months, allowing workers to string the wires. The men first attached a grounding wire along the top of the steel towers for lightning protection, then traveled the length of the line to install two circuits. They uncoiled the six aluminum wires and connected them to the steel towers; each wire was separated from the steel towers by three feet of porcelain insulators. In October, the line was complete and the company was ready to begin service.

Just as coal canals and oil pipelines were narrow tendrils that only connected certain places, the transmission wires extending from Holtwood Dam excluded many more than they served. Holtwood Dam was not linked with Philadelphia, Wilmington, Harrisburg, or Reading. In addition, because transformer stations necessary to reduce the voltage were expensive, the company did not build any more between Baltimore and the dam, thereby preventing local villages along the path of the wire from receiving service. Only a small percentage of the region's inhabitants obtained access to the Susquehanna's bounty.

Although the construction of Holtwood drew more comment from contemporary observers, transmission lines were as critical to the ultimate success of the venture. The fact that they allowed the energy to travel instantaneously to Baltimore's homes and factories with only small losses meant that the energy of the Susquehanna River was no longer restricted to the riverbed. As had happened with coal canals and oil pipelines, the building of transport infrastructure enabled a geographic separation between the sites of energy production and consumption.

Blending Organic and Mineral

Rivers that are developed for hydropower, navigation, or irrigation, as historian Richard White has suggested, can be thought of as "organic machines."[74] Their power derives from variable flows of renewable solar energy that are subject to finite limits to growth. Yet the pioneers of Holtwood Dam were not willing to accept these confines. The forces of the mineral energy regime were used to construct the dam and the transmission wires allowed them to ship the Susquehanna's power long distances into the heart of urban industrial economies. The river was further "mineralized" through its integration into a network with steam-powered electricity generators. By supplementing the Susquehanna's waters with the greater reliability of coal, Aldred and his colleagues were able to smooth over nature's caprices. Organic and mineral energy regimes were blended into a hybrid network.

The use of electricity reflected the patterns of the mineral energy regime both because consumers continually wanted more and also because they expected it to be available at all times, even if their own usage patterns shifted significantly. Within the electricity industry, this was known as base versus peak power. Base power was the minimal draw on the system that had to be provided at all times; peak power represented the maximum level of consumption in a day. Around five in the afternoon was the peak time for many utilities since factory machinery was still operating, lights were being turned on, and commuters were riding electrified streetcars. Demand could also vary by season: in the early twentieth century, users consumed more electricity during winter due to the greater need for artificial light (in our own era, summer has become the season of peak demand in many places due to the intensive use of air conditioning). But the shifting water levels of the Susquehanna River had a different set of variations. The flow was heaviest during the spring snowmelt and lightest during the late summer; winter ice reduced the levels as well. It varied much less over the course of a single day, but this meant that during certain seasons, large amounts of water were allowed to flow over the dam in the middle of the night when nearly all consumers were sleeping. Sometimes the Susquehanna provided far too much power capacity, sometimes far too little. By itself, Holtwood Dam was poorly suited for the patterns of American electrification.

Combined with the steam-powered plants already operating in Baltimore, however, Holtwood Dam could be used much more effectively. When the river flow was high and many consumers wanted electricity, the dam could supply the necessary power and coal could be conserved. When river waters were low, steam plants could be run at full capacity to meet demand. Supplementing water with coal meant that users would not have to adjust their consumption patterns to reflect the variations of the organic energy regime. Unlike the use of waterpower through most of human history, they would not have to make do with less when renewable energy flows dissipated.

This blending of organic and mineral energy regimes was made possible by Aldred's control of both PWP and Consolidated. In the short term, acquiring large blocks of hydroelectric power, even at low prices, was not a clear advantage for the Baltimore utility. Consolidated had already invested heavily in coal-fired generators capable of meeting the demands of Baltimore consumers, and it was not in their interest to let this capital stock sit idle. Moreover, Consolidated's chief engineer, H. A. Wagner, opposed a comprehensive integration because he thought the variable flows of the Susquehanna were less reliable than steam plants.[75] Without an interlocking directorate and shared management, it is difficult to imagine the companies agreeing to a deal that required Consolidated to put most of its steam power in reserve. But with Aldred serving as President and Chairman of the Board for both companies, he facilitated the negotiations. Looking back twenty-five years later, Aldred emphasized the importance of his controlling stake in Consolidated for the success of Holtwood: "One of the important elements necessary to make a success of this undertaking was the disposal of the power . . . In order to make possible the first and most important of these contracts, it was necessary for me to purchase control of the Consolidated Gas Electric Light and Power Company of Baltimore, which involved raising several million dollars."[76] As he stated to PWP's Board of Directors in 1910, his control over both organizations assured "close and harmonious relations."[77]

On August 29, 1910, the two companies signed their first ten-year power contract.[78] Under the terms of the contract, Consolidated agreed to absorb the bulk of Holtwood's output. The wholesale price of electricity from the dam was extremely cheap—less than half a cent per kilowatt-hour (kwh) at a time when Consolidated charged consumers more than ten times as much.[79] Even seven years later, when technological advances had lowered costs across the industry, large steam plants still had wholesale costs nearly 50 percent higher than Holtwood.[80] PWP was still able to prosper at this price and began issuing dividends in 1914, aided both by the abundant flows of the Susquehanna and the fact that the bankruptcy of the McCall Ferry Power Company eliminated the equity holdings of many initial investors.

Equally important for PWP, Consolidated agreed to supply steam-generated electricity at times of low river flow. This steam capacity, in turn, freed PWP to make contracts with other utilities for guaranteed electricity deliveries regardless of river conditions. The next deal was struck with Baltimore's electric streetcar company, United Railways and Electric, on February 11, 1911. PWP agreed to an initial supply of 16,000 hp; the contract also included a power-sharing clause whereby the steam-generating stations of United Railways would be available to PWP when needed. In 1912, Lancaster became the company's third customer. The local utility, the Edison Electric Company, had generating plants that were not in good operating condition, and found it preferable to purchase electricity rather than invest in new equipment. A ten-year contract was signed on October 9, 1912 to supply practically all of Lancaster's power needs using hydroelectricity supplemented by steam power from Consolidated and United Railways.[81]

All three deals reveal that the profitable operation of Holtwood Dam depended on its integration into a network with coal-fired electricity plants. The production of hydroelectricity may have come from the organic energy regime, but consumers expected a greater degree of reliability. By supplementing the river's flows with coal, Holtwood became part of an electrical network with several characteristics of the mineral energy regime.

Expanding Electrical Consumption

The completion of Holtwood and its transmission wires gave rise to a landscape of intensification. The dam was capable of generating far more power than existing demand could accommodate, thereby incentivizing the officers of Consolidated and PWP to create new markets. In 1910, for example, Consolidated's steam plants had produced over forty-five million kwh of electricity. But with the additional power from the Susquehanna River, less than half of this energy was needed the following year.[82] In order to obtain a return on its investments in steam plants, Consolidated knew that it must aggressively encourage new patterns of consumption. Similarly, PWP actively sought outlets beyond Baltimore for the Susquehanna's flows. Supply drove demand.

Residential consumers were one target market. Starting in 1910, Consolidated began an aggressive advertising campaign in local newspapers emphasizing that rates were lower in Baltimore than in other parts of the nation.

The next year, the company opened The House Electric, a store displaying lighting fixtures and electrical appliances. It was a major success, and three more branch locations were opened in outlying districts in 1913. These efforts enabled Consolidated to double its base of electricity consumers between 1910 and 1913.[83]

Consolidated gave industrial users comparable attention. After Aldred acquired control in 1909, the company formed an Industrial Power Department to work with local industries. Even though many Baltimore industries had already begun to electrify their operations, most produced their power in-house. This mirrored national trends: in 1910, private industrial plants generated more than half the nation's electricity, a greater share than utility companies.[84] Employees in the Industrial Power Department sought to convince factories that the large investments in Holtwood and Baltimore's steam plants allowed Consolidated to provide cheaper and more reliable electricity. In 1913, they undertook a private survey to determine the electrical capacity inside their service area. They discovered 537 local enterprises collectively could generate over 100,000 hp of electricity, mostly with steam engines. The company's improved ability to target potential customers was quickly put to use: later that year, the company was able to obtain contracts for an additional 19,000 hp of service.[85]

Aldred believed strongly that there were reciprocal benefits between Baltimore's industrial growth and the company's prospects. Like Josiah White, Aldred did not see a tension between public service and personal profit, trusting that the city's industrial growth and the company's success were mutually beneficial. In 1912, he led Consolidated and PWP to create what Silicon Valley executives a century later would describe as an incubator: the companies opened the Industrial Building in downtown Baltimore to provide small manufacturers with space and easy access to electricity to start new businesses.[86] Then in 1914, Aldred began to work with Baltimore officials to conduct an industrial survey of the city. Its overwhelming finding was that the city was not reaching its potential: "The one clear and emphatic impression left upon our minds by the data hereinafter presented is that the industrial growth of Baltimore has been less pronounced than it should have been, having in mind the general economic progress of the country and the forward strides of other cities no more favorably circumstanced." The report recommended that Baltimore residents make a more concerted effort to invest in manufacturing enterprises, noting "that which has been lacking is a collective consciousness and a communal effort."[87] Baltimore, the report suggested, needed more boosters.

Consolidated's efforts to build demand were highly successful. Over the decade following the completion of Holtwood Dam, Baltimore's electrical demand rose dramatically. The total number of electrical consumers (mostly residential) more than quadrupled, growing from 16,605 in 1910 to 79,469 in 1920. Electrical consumption grew twice as fast, jumping nearly 900 percent in those same years.[88] Consolidated's industrial base grew at a similar rate. In 1910, Consolidated served 1,333 industrial enterprises with a total capacity of 53,300 hp. They doubled the number of industrial consumers to 2,619 in 1920 while increasing installed capacity nearly six-fold to 290,153 hp.[89]

The managers of Holtwood Dam were also active energy boosters. Though their contracts with Consolidated absorbed a large amount of the Susquehanna's energy and provided steam power as a backup, PWP still faced the difficulty that the river sometimes was capable of producing more power than they could sell, particularly during times of high river flow and in the middle of the night. In 1913, for example, there was enough water to generate 100,000 hp for ten hours a day during six months of the year if customers could be found.[90] To take advantage of this cheap energy that would otherwise be wasted, the company built a factory in 1915 to manufacture ferrosilicon, a raw material useful in making steel, a booming industry as the nation prepared for war.[91] Like aluminum, the manufacture of ferrosilicon required huge quantities of energy. The factory was opened with a furnace that could draw 10,000 hp of energy at once. In 1917, its capacity was increased to 30,000 hp, and that year the factory consumed approximately 100,000,000 kwh of electricity. To put this energy demand into perspective, this single factory absorbed nearly twice the electricity of Lancaster—a medium-size city with several industrial enterprises and a relatively wealthy population.[92]

The landscape of intensification surrounding Holtwood Dam contributed to a higher rate of growth in Baltimore than other areas of the mid-Atlantic during this period. Edison Electric, the utility serving Lancaster, did not have the same incentives to encourage growth, and the city's consumption advanced at a pace less than half of Baltimore's.[93] Nor was the Philadelphia

Electric Company as active in generating demand. In 1920, the company only had 158,000 consumers despite serving an area with more than two million people, and the average resident used only 375 kwh of electricity a year. By contrast, Consolidated served a greater percentage of the population within its service area and the average consumption levels were about 15 percent higher.[94] The material transformation of the Susquehanna River and the sunk costs of PWP and Consolidated created unique pressures for these companies to be electricity boosters.

Increasing Supply

Landscapes of intensification are characterized by synergistic feedback loops. In this case, the creation of Holtwood Dam produced large quantities of surplus energy; that surplus encouraged members of Consolidated and PWP to build demand among potential consumers; the eventual success of these efforts created incentives for these companies to increase production. Demand began to drive supply, and PWP soon needed Holtwood to generate more power.

Because Holtwood Dam depended on the variable flows of the Susquehanna River, there were only limited options for increasing its output. But since waterpower was so central to the organic energy regime, PWP could draw on many well-established techniques for making it more abundant and reliable. The Lowell textile mills, for example, stored excess water at times of high flow in upstream storage reservoirs, then released this water at times of low river flow.[95] Nine months before the dam was complete, Aldred was already directing his engineers to investigate water storage possibilities higher up on the Susquehanna and along its tributaries.[96] The company also tried to enlist help from the state. In 1912, it helped form the Water Utilization Association of Pennsylvania, an organization intended to coordinate the efforts of various parties using waterways and seek legislative support for the creation of storage dams.[97] However, these efforts were only marginally successful: there were relatively few lakes and other suitable sites along the Susquehanna for storing large quantities of water.[98]

The company had more success by focusing on the dam and powerhouse. Though they did not own the riparian rights to create a permanent reservoir that was higher than the dam, they could store more water at times of low water flow by erecting flashboards—four-foot-high planks of wood attached to the top of the dam. Company officials estimated that this technique increased the efficiency of the plant at low water periods by 25 percent.[99] They also worked to improve the powerhouse's ten turbines. The first turbines had a capacity of 10,000 hp each. But by 1913, design innovations enabled the company to increase the output of each turbine to approximately 16,000 hp.[100] This allowed the ultimate capacity of the dam to exceed the initial estimates of 100,000 hp by a considerable margin.

Improving the capacity and reliability of transmission wires offered another strategy for maximizing the capacity of the dam. As Baltimore's demand increased and more power was shipped, it strained the capacity of the two circuits that had been erected in 1910. In 1914, the company built a parallel set of steel towers and installed an additional circuit, thereby immediately lowering transmission losses by 2.5 percent.[101] A fourth circuit was added in 1917. The company also worked to make the lines more reliable. During the first year of operations, lightning disrupted the flow of electricity to Baltimore twenty-three times, and an average of nearly six times a year over the next several years.[102] It was only when the company installed a fuse apparatus that these problems were addressed. The device automatically removed the voltage from the transmission line when lightning was detected and restored service immediately afterwards.

Reservoirs, flashboards, new turbine designs, and extra transmission wires were material interventions that helped PWP mitigate the variations of the organic energy regime. The company also adopted financial techniques to accommodate nature's uneven distributions of precipitation. PWP's income rose with high water and fell with low water, but such peaks and troughs complicated financial planning and did not present a stable picture to investors. So the company created a contingency fund in which it deposited extra funds during years of high river flow and made withdrawals during years of low river flow. Though this did not, of course, alter the patterns of the river, it served to mask nature's variability from capital markets. Reliance on the organic energy regime encouraged financial flexibility as well as technological adaptation.[103]

Ultimately, it was the employment of mineral energy sources that proved to be the most effective strategy for dealing with the limitations of organic

Dredging river coal from the lake behind Holtwood Dam. (Hagley Museum and Library)

energy flows. The company found a surprising source of mineral energy in vast quantities of anthracite coal dust that had settled in the lake behind the dam. The North Branch of the Susquehanna River, during its descent through the Wyoming Valley, gathered coal dust as it poured over banks of anthracite culm. Once Holtwood Dam was completed, much of it settled behind the concrete barrier. Within a couple of decades, company surveys estimated that the lake contained more than ten million tons of recoverable anthracite coal dust—enough to power a 30,000-kw steam plant for several decades. All they needed to do was dredge the bottom of the lake with barges and separate out the coal dust, thereby obtaining an essentially free source of abundant mineral energy. In 1925, PWP completed construction on a steam-fired power plant next to the dam; organic and mineral energy regimes were thoroughly intertwined.[104]

Consumption Patterns and the Mineral Energy Regime

The production of electricity delivered to Baltimore was a hybrid of organic and mineral energy regimes. The city's consumption patterns suggest that the use of electricity for lighting, streetcars, and industry served to reinforce the conditions of the mineral energy regime rather than the organic.

Like the use of kerosene, electric lighting created a further shift away from the patterns of the organic energy regime. With the flick of a switch or the turn of a knob, thousands of people found themselves able to illuminate the night. Moreover, they were able to do so in a manner that required virtually no labor. With kerosene, people still had the regular tasks of filling a lamp, trimming the wick, tending the flame, and cleaning the glass. Electricity provided unparalleled light with minimal personal exertion. Befitting the mineral energy regime, it also got cheaper over time. The cost of electric light in 1920 was only a quarter of what it had been twenty years before, a result of technological innovations and greater economies of scale. On the basis of lighting output, this was five times more efficient than kerosene lamps. However, because light was cheaper and more convenient, users consumed greater quantities, leading to bills that were comparable or even higher with electricity.[105] Low prices boosted demand.

Lighting also helped to stimulate urban and industrial growth. In prosperous areas, brightly lit streets helped overcome concerns about the safety of cities, though less wealthy areas did not receive comparable benefit. In public spaces and stores, conspicuous displays of light drew people into central shopping areas. In factories, electricity provided the illumination needed to keep industries running regardless of the time of day or season of the year. In fact, at Henry Ford's famous River Rouge factory, managers considered quality lighting essential. They believed there was "a direct relationship between the maintenance of adequate illumination and the production efficiency of the various departments" and that electric lights were "another production tool which is just as important as are modern types of machine tool equipment."[106]

The use of the Susquehanna River to power streetcars also deepened the hold of the mineral energy regime. In an organic energy regime, people traveled through cities using the power of their legs or the muscles of animals. This constrained how far they could live from where they worked and shopped. Streetcars created new possibilities for urban development. They could average speeds of eight or nine miles per hour, allowing people to live as far away as six miles from work locations and be able to commute within an hour's time. Express routes with fewer stops expanded the range of service even further. As a result, streetcars made it practical for urban areas to increase from a diameter of roughly five miles to twenty to twenty-five miles.[107] Streetcars also helped to transform everyday notions of time and space. Though technologies like steamboats, railroads, and telegraphs had been celebrated for conquering time and space since the 1840s, most Americans did not utilize these systems on a regular basis. By contrast, streetcars imparted an immediate and embodied experience of greater speed and access to wider areas of the city for millions of urban residents. The power of electricity, not the power of their muscles, was increasingly used for everyday transport. Electric streetcars were another example of the use of mineral energy sources to tackle a challenge that was, in large part, triggered by the rise of the mineral energy regime.

When streetcars were first being introduced, many Americans hoped that they offered an opportunity to reverse certain patterns of the mineral energy regime. The growth of cities had produced spaces that were seen as dirty and depraved, particularly by white, middle-class reformers of the Progressive Era. As one streetcar pioneer argued: "an increase of the tenement house system [leads to] an increase in vice, immorality, misery, crime, and the death rate." Echoing the vestiges of republican ideals, he and other streetcar boosters believed these systems could create a better nation through undoing urban growth: "The great advantage of increasing the available residence area, of encouraging the cottage system and discouraging the tenement system, will be readily conceded by all. The health and morality of a great city are universally proportional to the number of people beneath each roof. The electric railway is one of the great moral agents of the nineteenth century."[108] If coal and oil had led to dense concentrations of people within a city, boosters hoped electricity could be used to buck these trends. As with most utopian dreams associated with a new technology, the actual results were less decisive. Rather than rural renewal, streetcars helped create a new type of living pattern—suburbia. Those living in suburbs did have access to a greater amount of space than those living in the urban core, but this lifestyle was not necessarily accompanied by any of the morally uplifting qualities of independence and civic virtue that characterized Jefferson's vision for the nation.

Powering Baltimore's industries provided another way in which the hybrid nature of hydroelectricity served the mineral energy regime more than the organic. Consolidated devoted the greater part of its effort to increase consumption to the industrial sector and found a good deal of success.

Baltimore's railroads, shipyards, metal-working companies, chemical manufacturers, textile companies, and other enterprises invested heavily in electrifying their operations.[109] PWP's ferrosilicon plant was the clearest example of the ways in which the Susquehanna River was integrated into the mineral energy regime. Because its energy inputs were so high, producing large amounts of ferrosilicon would have been absurd in an organic energy regime. Not only would it have required massive exertions of effort and resources, it would have required trade-offs: less energy, less land, and less labor to provide other goods. Only in a world in which energy was incredibly cheap and abundant would it be sensible to open a single factory that could consume more electricity than a mid-size city.

The building of Holtwood Dam marked a radical transformation in the human history of the Susquehanna River. A mighty waterway that had mostly confounded the hopes and ambitions of European settlers until 1910 had been put to use generating electricity for distant markets. For residents of Baltimore, the dam provided an additional source of energy that could light homes, run streetcars, and power factories. But for those small communities near the Susquehanna's banks, the dam did more harm than good. It ruined the local fishing industry because shad were no longer able to swim to their breeding grounds, and it submerged favorite recreation spots without offering the compensation of cheap electricity. As in the development of the anthracite coal regions and the oil fields of western Pennsylvania, a local ecosystem was sacrificed to meet the ever-increasing energy demands of the mid-Atlantic's urban and industrial economy.

6

The Electrification of America

O N JUNE 28, 1914, Archduke Franz Ferdinand, heir to the throne of Austria-Hungary, was shot by a Serbian nationalist while visiting Sarajevo. A reserved man with little charisma, Ferdinand was not particularly loved in his native land. Nevertheless, his assassination led Austria-Hungary to issue an audacious ten-point ultimatum to the Kingdom of Serbia. When two of the terms were not met, Austria-Hungary invaded on July 28. Buoyed by a complicated series of alliances, the conflict spread quickly across Europe. Germany invaded Belgium, Luxembourg, and France; Britain declared war against Germany; and Russia attacked Austria-Hungary and Germany. Soon the Ottoman Empire, Bulgaria, Italy, and Romania joined the hostilities. By the following year, what was expected to be a short regional offensive had mired much of the European continent in an all-encompassing war.

For many Americans, the European conflict initially seemed a faraway concern and President Woodrow Wilson's stance of nonintervention was broadly popular. Why should Americans, millions asked, risk their lives to satisfy the ambitions of power-hungry European monarchs? Opposition to

war, though, did not prevent Americans from seeking to benefit financially. World War I was an industrial war, and the United States was already the world's foremost industrial power. American factories began to
accelerate production, both to expand the capabilities of the nation's armed
forces and to supply Europeans. Then in April 1917, in response to continued attacks on American merchant ships by German submarines, Wilson
successfully petitioned Congress to declare war on Germany.

The extra strain on the nation's industries as Americans prepared for war
soon generated an unfamiliar situation for those living in the mid-Atlantic:
periodic energy shortages. In late 1915, the cost of coal spiked and railroad
systems struggled to transport the higher levels of freight. Electricity out-
ages soon followed, interfering with the production of war materials. Philadelphia, the "Arsenal of America," was hit particularly hard. As hundreds of
thousands of workers flocked to the city to manufacture arms, munitions,
and ships, demand for electricity skyrocketed. The Philadelphia Electric
Company found itself providing more energy to war industries than any
other utility in the nation, but it often could not keep pace. The company
was forced to ration power distribution and on several occasions even cut
off service to consumers not involved in the war effort. Even these measures
could not avert a systemwide blackout in 1918 that left many consumers
without power for several days.[1]

Electricity shortages during World War I revealed Americans' dependence on a new energy system. Over the previous two decades, electricity
had been widely adopted, particularly in the nation's factories. Because it
was a safer, more flexible, and more efficient form of power than previous
systems, electricity enabled the rise of several innovative manufacturing
techniques, including the assembly line. Flush with electric power, industries in the mid-Atlantic and rest of the nation expanded their output substantially in the first decades of the twentieth century.

As American electrification increased, so did the need to expand the
transmission infrastructure. But who would build such wires and how
would they be operated? The convergence of electricity shortages and the
reform impulses of the Progressive Era stimulated a series of debates during
and after the war over the future of transmission wire networks. Government officials and industry insiders noted that some blackouts occurred at
times when neighboring utilities had spare capacity. By building intercon-

necting transmission wires between the systems, they recognized that power could be shared and the systems' overall efficiency increased. Yet if there was widespread agreement that interconnection would raise efficiency, there was far more debate about how such wires should be built and how the benefits should be allocated. Should the state take a greater role in coordinating the electrical industry? Would transmission wires better serve existing customers or could they be used to spread the benefits of electricity to previously excluded groups? While elaborate new systems were discussed by politicians, engineers, and citizens, the lower Susquehanna River once again proved consequential to the mid-Atlantic's transmission wire networks, as two more hydroelectric dams were constructed in 1926 and 1931. Reflecting the logic of capital more than technocratic efficiency or social equality, the wires reinforced the energy advantages of urban centers over rural areas.

Not all Americans had access to electricity by 1930. But where it was available, it furthered the hold of the mineral energy regime. In factories, electricity increased production and gave rise to new industries. In homes, electric appliances such as vacuum cleaners and washing machines brought mineral-based power sources into housework for the first time. Electricity even reshaped leisure practices: amusement parks, radios, and movie theaters all used this energy source to provide entertainment. Wherever its wires extended, electricity left few aspects of life untouched.

Electrifying Industry

Lighting and streetcars were electricity's first main applications. However, in the first decades of the twentieth century, factories rapidly began to electrify their operations and soon consumed the lion's share of the nation's electricity. In 1899, fewer than 5 percent of industrial motors ran on electricity; steam engines and waterwheels were much more common. By the outbreak of war in 1914, electricity supplied nearly two-fifths of the nation's industrial power. During the five years of wartime buildup, America's factories added so much capacity that electricity was the nation's primary source of industrial power by the time the Treaty of Versailles was signed.[2]

Electricity appealed to factory owners not simply because it was an additional source of power, but because it had unique qualities. As with waterwheels and steam engines, the energy of electricity was generated from falling water and burning coal. As a result, there was no great increase in the total power that could be produced through electrification. But compared with steam engines or waterwheels, electricity could generate power that was safer, quieter, more reliable, and more efficient: quality mattered as much as quantity.

One of electricity's most consequential characteristics was that a single block of power could be subdivided and easily transmitted to multiple workstations. Before electrification, determining how to take the power generated at a central waterwheel or steam engine and distribute it to many employees was a great challenge for industrialists. A tool shop, for example, might use one steam engine to power dozens of machines such as drills, presses, saws, and lathes spread throughout the building. In the nineteenth century, the most common approach to intrafactory energy transmission involved an elaborate array of metal shafts, leather belts, pulleys, clutches, and levers, known either as millwork or line-drive. In this system, the energy of the steam engine or waterwheel rotated a series of steel shafts positioned along the floor or ceiling. Workstations were placed directly above or below the shafts, and machines drew power from spinning leather belts connecting the machines to the shafts. When workers desired power, they switched a lever to engage the leather belts. By adjusting pulleys, workers could increase or decrease the amount of power delivered by the belts to suit the task at hand. When they were not using the machine, they used the lever to disengage the leather belts.[3]

Millwork was an impressive innovation that allowed a centralized power source to provide useful energy for many employees. However, this system had a number of inefficiencies. The friction from the spinning shafts and belts led to significant power losses: typically about a quarter of the energy of the steam engine or waterwheel dissipated as it was transferred from one end of the factory to the other.[4] The shafts and belts had to be kept spinning at all times while the factory was open, even though workers did not need power at every moment. Slight wobbles in the belts impaired precision work, and the delivery of power was inconsistent because the speed of the belts changed as workers connected or disconnected their machines. The systems were also loud, dirty, and expensive to maintain. The constantly rotating belts made a racket, and in order to combat friction losses, manufacturers

Edison's machine shop, late 1880s. Note the steel shafts, leather belts, and linear array of machines. (Library of Congress)

applied large amounts of lubricating oil to the leather belts: as a result, grease was constantly splattered throughout the workplace. Moreover, mill owners had to employ teams of workers to keep the systems running and replace worn parts.

Electricity helped industrialists overcome many of these limitations. At first, electric motors were employed to supplement millwork systems by acting as intermediaries between the main power sources and the spinning shafts and belts. With a steam engine or waterwheel, it was difficult to increase or decrease the power available to employees at a moment's notice, which exacerbated the volatility of power delivery to each station as workers engaged and disengaged their machines. Electric motors, by contrast, could supply a steadier level of power to the shafts and belts because they could respond quickly to fluctuating levels of consumption. They were also easier to start and stop. Therefore, many factory operators simply attached their waterwheels or steam engines to electric equipment to obtain a greater level of control over the line-drive system.[5]

But as industrialists experimented further with electricity, some realized that electricity could eliminate the line-drive system altogether. Instead of the heavy and cumbersome shafts and belts, thin wires could deliver the requisite power to each machine. This unlocked a host of new possibilities. First, electricity was more efficient. Much less power was wasted because, unlike the constant power losses from friction, it could be transported short distances over wires with negligible losses. Second, electricity was more reliable. Providing power directly to each machine eliminated the slight wobbles and fluctuations inherent in belt-driven systems and ensured that energy levels would not fluctuate based on the actions of neighboring workers. Such control could help achieve the long-held dream of manufacturing interchangeable parts. Third, electricity was more flexible. The line-drive system required all of a company's work operations to be laid out in linear paths connected to the overhead belts. To minimize power losses, factories were often dense, multilevel structures where the most energy-intensive operations were located closest to the power source. Electricity could be delivered anywhere in whatever amounts were desired, freeing operators to organize production according to the flow of parts, not the transmission of power.[6]

Henry Ford and his team of managers were among the first to capitalize on the revolutionary potential of electrical power. From early in their operations, they used the greater precision of electric motors to produce interchangeable parts, which was particularly important since one of their automobiles contained ten thousand or more components. In 1910, Ford opened a new factory in Detroit that was designed with electric light and power in mind; compared with traditional plants, it was more open, better lit, and more flexible. Over the next three years, his team experimented with several production methods that ultimately culminated in a new process whereby automobiles were manufactured by having each part attached as the car was transported through the plant on a conveyer belt. By 1913, the assembly line had been born. The gains in productivity were staggering: the time to assemble a Model T dropped from twelve hours in 1909 to about an hour and a half five years later, and the cost plummeted from nearly a thousand dollars in 1910 to less than $250 in 1920. The flexibility and precision of electric power was essential to the development of the assembly line.[7]

Other industries quickly embraced electric drive and assembly line production techniques, particularly young enterprises with relatively few investments in older power systems and the freedom to design a factory from the ground up. Manufacturers of electrical appliances such as radios, refrigerators, and irons built electrified factories, as did many of Ford's competitors in the automotive field. Companies needing a high degree of control of their power also transitioned quickly: bakers benefited from electric thermostats that kept ovens at a precise temperature, ready-made clothing manufacturers from small motors for individual sewing machines, and machine-tooling enterprises from controlled power at each workstation. The greater flexibility, efficiency, and precision of electric power were boons for a wide variety of industries.[8]

Many mines electrified their operations as well. Steam engines were poorly suited to providing power underground, because their sparks could trigger explosions of accumulated gas. As a result, they were limited to surface operations such as pumping water and driving ventilation systems. Most underground mining labor relied on organic energy sources: humans swung picks and hammers and loaded ore into carts that were hauled to the surface by mules. In some cases, compressed air systems, like the one used in the construction of Holtwood Dam, provided power for drills. However, the large pipes needed to deliver the compressed air were difficult to move from site to site within the mine, and power decreased the further it was distributed. Electricity was far more effective: it reduced the risk of explosions, wires for drills could be moved around the mine more easily than compressed air pipes, and power losses in distribution were lower. Given the mid-Atlantic's prominent mining industries, electricity was particularly important for the region's continued economic growth.[9]

The ability to manufacture new materials was another distinctive feature of electricity. Electrochemical processes, like the one pioneered by Charles Martin Hall to manufacture aluminum, used electrolysis to induce chemical reactions. Electrothermal processes took advantage of the high heats attainable with electricity: furnaces powered by electricity could exceed three thousand degrees Celsius—nearly twice as hot as fuel-based furnaces.[10] For plants like the ferrosilicon factory established by the Pennsylvania Water and Power Company, electric furnaces made it possible to produce materials that could not be obtained in significant quantities without such intense temperatures. By 1920, about 15 percent of all industrial electricity was being used to create new materials.[11]

Industrial electrification was often accompanied by another significant change for manufacturing enterprises: purchasing power produced elsewhere. Before the electrical age, factories generated their power onsite, most often with waterwheels or steam engines. When they first adopted electricity, most industrial consumers continued this pattern by attaching generators to their existing power equipment. But over time, utilities like Consolidated convinced industries that it would be cheaper and easier to purchase power. They noted that large facilities like Holtwood allowed them to produce electricity at lower costs and freed industries from needing to hire employees to maintain their power equipment. Moreover, factories only had to pay for the power they actually used. When they generated their own power, factories needed to produce enough energy to supply all machines, even if only a subset were being run at any given moment. With utility service, factories would only be billed for their actual consumption, further reducing costs. Whereas industries were producing nearly three-fifths of their electricity in 1910, they were generating less than one-half a decade later as utility companies came to supply the majority of industry's needs.[12]

Collectively, these industrial applications show that electricity was not simply an additional source of energy. Rather, its unique properties and ability to be delivered to individual machines by wires made new forms of manufacturing possible. These advantages were sufficiently compelling that industries not only added electrical power rapidly in the 1910s but also got rid of older equipment: from 1914 to 1919, the rate of growth in electrical motors exceeded the nation's total gain in industrial capacity.[13]

The Politics of Wires

The rapid growth of industrial electrification in the two decades leading into World War I was largely the result of decentralized decision-making. Utilities typically made their own determinations about whether to add generating capacity and which customers to target; operators of factories and mines decided whether, when, and how to electrify their processes. Their choices, to be sure, were not made in a vacuum. Government bodies influenced the provision of electrical service by giving utility companies monopoly privileges and rights to lay poles and wires along streets; patent protections encouraged inventors to improve electrical equipment; and many municipalities operated their own generating stations. In addition, boosters worked to convince industrialists to electrify their operations. Trade organizations like the National Electric Light Association published pamphlets touting the advantages of electrification, employees of utility companies visited factories to demonstrate the latest innovations, and manufacturers of electrical equipment promoted their products to managers. But still, most utility investment decisions were made on an ad hoc basis.

As World War I dragged on and the United States entered the hostilities, some began to question the wisdom of decentralized choices. Such fragmentation, they noted, exacerbated energy shortages that were becoming particularly acute. In the winter of 1917–1918, service interruptions plagued many utilities; industry observers expected the situation to be worse the following year if the war continued. Given the increasing importance of electricity to the war effort, many believed that greater centralized oversight was needed to address this critical industry.[14]

Electricity was not unique in this regard. The rise of the Progressive Era during the first decades of the twentieth century marked a significant shift in the patterns of American governance. Laissez-faire policies held wide sway during the nineteenth century, but by the 1880s many reformers had begun to speak out against its limitations. They decried the power of corporations like Standard Oil, the corruption of the patronage system, the failures of city governments to provide basic services, and the lack of women's suffrage. Whether it was addressing education, prohibition, immigration, or the economy, many Progressives argued that greater government involvement could be beneficial. In several cases, they shared a faith that scientific expertise could overcome waste and inefficiency.[15]

The reforms of the Progressive Era created new relationships between centralized planning, the state, and America's energy practices. Though government policies shaped the patterns of energy transitions in the nineteenth century, they generally did so in a "backstage" manner through corporate privileges, scientific surveys, property rights, and tax policies.[16] In the early twentieth century, many of these reforms started to intervene directly into the operations of energy companies, highlighted by measures such as the

creation of state-level public utility commissions with the power to determine utility rates in the years following 1907 and the court-ordered breakup
of the Standard Oil Trust in 1911.[17] Beginning in 1917, some reformers
turned their attention to the nation's electricity grid. The histories of the
War Industries Board, Superpower, and Giant Power reveal that many believed greater coordination in the construction of transmission wires offered a means to improve the nation's electrification, though there was less
consensus about what, exactly, counted as improvement.

World War I was a catalyst for new experiments in using government
expertise to shape the actions of the private sector. President Wilson took
unprecedented steps to manage the economy during the war, creating several boards with the authority to coordinate production, allocate resources,
set standards, and resolve labor unrest. In 1917, the War Industries Board,
headed by the financier Bernard Baruch, established a Power Section to
study the challenges of ensuring the nation's electric supply. It launched a
survey of the country's electrical generating stations to identify areas where
there were likely to be shortages, and recommended that war materials be
ordered from other regions whenever possible. Because of the dense concentration of factories in the mid-Atlantic, it is not surprising that the survey
identified Philadelphia, New Jersey, and Pittsburgh as locations likely to
overtax local utilities under conditions of heightened production. Concerned that shortages would grow worse, Baruch and others lobbied Congress to pass an Emergency Power Bill in the summer of 1918 to provide
funding for the construction of additional electrical capacity.[18]

While wartime planners' attention to coordination within the electrical
industry was not exceptional, the particular characteristics of this energy
source shaped their range of responses. The survey found that shortages
often occurred in one service area while a neighboring utility had excess
capacity. In the coal and oil industries, a logical response would be to stock-
pile extra production at times of low demand and then ship the surplus
energy to the neighboring region. But electricity could not be stored in
large quantities: it dissipated if it was not used right away. Interconnection
offered a quicker and cheaper option. If neighboring systems could share
their extra power through transmission wires, it would alleviate bottlenecks
without the need for new generators. Expanding the transport system offered an effective approach for the ephemeral nature of electricity.

The concept of interconnection was not new. Within the utility industry, it was generally recognized that sharing power would increase efficiency, and some, like Chicago electric financier Samuel Insull, strongly advocated the practice. Yet the practice was uncommon in the 1910s. Though many utility companies had worked to maximize the use of their installed equipment by encouraging a diversity of consumers in their service areas (this was known as improving the "load factor"), collaboration with neighboring utilities was much less common for three reasons. First, interconnection could lower revenues. As regulated monopolies, the rates of most utilities were directly correlated with the amount of capital invested in their systems. One of the main ways utilities could increase revenues was by building extra generating capacity and passing the costs on to consumers. Control was a second concern for utility executives. Sharing power required constant interaction with other organizations and dependence on their power plants. A failure in a neighbor's generators could render a utility unable to serve its customers through no fault of its own. Third, utilities often saw their neighbors as competitors. Though they usually operated with monopoly privileges in their service areas, many utilities hoped to expand into surrounding terrain. For these new markets, neighboring utilities were often bitter competitors, further discouraging collaboration. Interconnection was logical from an engineering perspective, but not necessarily from a managerial one.

Wartime exigencies allowed the War Industries Board to stimulate a few interconnections by identifying utilities with complementary demand loads and encouraging them to share power. But with the end of World War I in November 1918, the acute industrial demand for electricity was eased.[19] The War Industries Board was disbanded in 1919, along with many of the other measures coordinating the activities of government, industry, and labor. The first steps toward coordinating the nation's electric utilities came to a close.

The cessation of hostilities did not end discussions of interconnection. Many observers believed the war had shown that government intervention in the marketplace could produce positive results. Combined with the rising faith in scientific management and buoyed by the reform impulses of the Progressive Era, they were convinced that centralized planning could increase efficiency. This led to two major proposals to develop transmission wires in the postwar years: Superpower and Giant Power. Though neither proposal was implemented, they reveal the political dimensions of transmission wire development. Despite widespread agreement on the technical advantages of interconnection, Americans disagreed about how these systems should be implemented and who should benefit: transport systems were recognized to be about far more than simply the movement of energy.[20]

William S. Murray was a consulting engineer who had experience working with railroads and electric utilities during the first decades of the twentieth century. A strong believer in technical efficiency, Murray approved of the work being done by the War Industries Board and convinced Secretary of the Interior Franklin Lane to continue some of the Power Section's investigations. In 1919, he presented a plan for studying the electrical capacity of the industrial region on the Atlantic seaboard from Boston to Washington D.C., an area he dubbed the Superpower zone. Congress appropriated $125,000 for the analysis, which was performed in 1920 and printed the following year. Murray coordinated the survey and solicited contributions from dozens of technical experts, including electrical engineers, financial analysts, and utility executives.[21]

Murray and his colleagues focused on two problems. The first and most significant issue was that the lack of interconnection between electric utilities greatly increased the capital costs of what was already the nation's second-most capital-intensive industry.[22] When each utility was an island unto itself, it had to have sufficient generating capacity to meet peak demand. This forced each company to invest in small power plants with low efficiencies to support incremental growth. Interconnection between utilities would allow them to meet peak demand through the construction of a few large and efficient generators, not dozens of small ones, thereby reducing costs. The second problem was the high traffic levels of eastern railroads, many of which had experienced backlogs during the war. Coal was by far the largest article of trade, accounting for as much as a third of all traffic. If electricity was generated near coal mines and transported to urban centers by transmission wires, coal shipments could be reduced and the railroads would be able to provide better service for passengers and freight.

High-voltage transmission wires, according to Murray, were key to addressing both problems. His Superpower report proposed building several transmission wires along the eastern seaboard to enable power-sharing between utility companies, connect cities with large generating stations in remote areas (either steam plants at coal mines or hydroelectric facilities), and reduce the burden on railroad traffic. Murray and his colleagues emphasized that interconnection would avoid the duplication and unnecessary spending that were all too common when utilities failed to work together. They argued that the electric utility industry was characterized by "unnecessary waste of money, labor, and material incident to the present form of power production by unassociated units." Such excessive costs threatened the nation's development by leading to higher energy prices. Implementing the Superpower system, Murray estimated, could save hundreds of millions of dollars a year compared with a business-as-usual approach, thereby furnishing "adequate, reliable, and cheap power . . . to permit the normal expansion in our industries."[23]

The Superpower report was a curious mix of radical and conservative ideas. By proposing greater collaboration between utilities, Murray and his colleagues were suggesting a significant change in the management of the electrical industry. Decentralized development was argued to be inefficient, and therefore the report advocated that technocratic expertise supplement free-market forces. However, utility companies were not willing to cede control over their operations, and Murray was unable to develop a consensus about what policies should be enacted, who should finance the transmission wires, who would own them, or how they would be regulated. When printed in June 1921, the report hoped for "a broad policy in legislation, regulation, financing, and management" that would "remove the existing inhibitions" and "give positive encouragement" to collaboration, but did not specify the roles of private companies or government agencies. Superpower's technical proposals received positive coverage at the time, but they did not lead to the building of new transmission wires.[24]

If the Superpower report was bold in seeking an expanded role for technocratic expertise, it was quite conservative about the proposed uses of electricity. The report focused on serving the nation's industrial growth and paid little attention to issues such as the lack of access to electricity in the countryside or the higher rates typically charged to residential versus industrial customers. Greater efficiency was to improve existing applications of electricity, not to create new ones.

Other reformers saw the cost savings enabled by interconnection as a mechanism for much wider social reform. Two years after the publication of the Superpower report, a second major effort to transform the electrical system, called Giant Power, was begun in Pennsylvania under the leadership of Governor Gifford Pinchot and the engineer Morris Cooke. Pinchot had gained fame for his work to conserve the nation's forests and Cooke had established a reputation as an engineer and social reformer. Pinchot and Cooke, like Murray, believed that rational management of resources was an important goal. But technical efficiency was a means for them, rather than an end in itself. Their hope was to harness the potential of electricity to improve the lives of millions, not simply to increase profits or industrial output. Giant Power reflected a growing belief that electricity had transformative potential. As Pinchot put it: "[Giant Power] is a plan by which most of the drudgery of human life can be taken from the shoulders of men and women who toil, and replaced by the power of electricity."[25]

In 1923, Pinchot won approval from the Pennsylvania legislature to form a Giant Power survey and he appointed Cooke as the director. Two years later, Cooke and his fellow board members produced a report with recommendations for legislation. Pinchot wrote the introduction, arguing that electrification represented an energy revolution with widespread consequences for human life. He noted that steam power had freed humans from dependence on muscles, water, and wind, a revolution that had "altered the whole face of the earth for its inhabitants" and had produced "the safety and comfort which is now characteristic of human life in America." But he also contended that steam power had led to urban growth, industrial concentration, and the comparative disadvantage of those in rural areas. Reflecting long-standing republican ideals about the dangers of urban manufacturing and the virtues of farming, Pinchot declared that "steam brought about the centralization of industry, a decline in country life, the decay of many small communities, and the weakening of family ties."[26]

Pinchot was, in essence, reflecting on the shift from the organic to the mineral energy regime and hoping that electricity could address some of these challenges. Unlike steam engines, electric motors could be small and decentralized, allowing them to create new configurations of work and life. Electricity, he proclaimed, could usher in an "epochal change," but it must be managed with public interests in mind if it was to serve "the growing needs of humanity." Giant Power, he argued, "may bring about the decentralization of industry, the restoration of country life, and the upbuilding of the small communities and of the family. In this hope of the future lies the possibility of new freedom and great spiritual enrichment of individual life."[27]

But electricity could produce rural revival only if farmers had the option to purchase it. The vast majority did not, largely because urban utilities rarely provided service to rural residents: like coal canals and oil pipelines, electricity transmission wires privileged urban residents at the expense of those in the countryside. The Giant Power survey found that nearly 90 percent of Pennsylvania's farms lacked electrical service, and that almost half of those that did have service were supplying it themselves with independent generators or small cooperatives. As a result, utilities only served 6 percent of Pennsylvania's farmers.[28] This made sense for utility companies. Distribution wires were expensive, and in rural areas, each line could serve only a handful of customers. Better profits could be expected from urban residents and industries where shorter wires served a greater number of users. The Giant Power report also emphasized the disparity in rates charged by utilities, noting that residential consumers paid five to ten times as much as industries for electricity. Overcoming inequality and spreading the benefits of electricity were Pinchot's top priorities. Explicitly comparing Giant Power to Superpower, Pinchot noted that the "main object of the superpower idea is greater power to the companies. The main object of the Giant Power idea is greater advantage to the people."[29]

Despite the differences in political perspective between Superpower and Giant Power, many of the technical ideas were similar. Like Superpower, Giant Power hoped to achieve greater efficiencies and lower costs through large generating stations at the mouths of coal mines, high-voltage transmission wires (including lines operating at 220,000 volts and covering hundreds of miles), and the electrification of railroads. Interconnection was central to Giant Power, as Cooke favored "trunk transmission lines designed to transmit great quantities of power at high voltage, over great distances so as to give the whole territory thus integrated the advantage of the cheapest possible electric generation at the lowest possible transmission cost."[30] In addition to long, high-voltage transmission wires, Giant Power also included calls for the creation of distribution wires to rural consumers.

Pinchot and Cooke were willing to go further than Murray in articulating a new role for the state in the electric industry. Their report called for the Giant Power Board to coordinate the construction of generating plants, the siting of transmission lines, and the setting of rates. It would also be authorized to take the steps necessary to expand the access of Pennsylvania's farmers to electricity at affordable prices. Private utility companies would still be part of the system, but their overall influence and control would be significantly diminished.

The Giant Power report generated considerable controversy when it was published, particularly among industry insiders. Articles with titles such as "Pinchot Takes a Radical Stand" appeared in trade journals while Murray called the ideas "communistic" and "rotten at the core."[31] Critics also noted that it was unclear how the goals would be achieved since the details of the Giant Power Board were vague and unspecific. After several weeks of deliberations, a joint committee between the House and Senate of the Pennsylvania legislature voted against the proposal on February 8, 1926.[32]

Though the War Industries Board was disbanded at the end of the war and neither Superpower nor Giant Power were implemented according to the hopes of their authors, they illustrate a new level of government attention to energy transport systems in the Progressive Era. Interconnection was capable of increasing efficiency, but citizens, engineers, and politicians realized that it was not simply a question of whether transmission wires were built. Choices over the ownership, management, and geography of these systems would lead to different parties gaining the benefits of reduced costs. Such themes continued to reverberate in American politics even after the specific proposals were abandoned. Franklin Roosevelt shared many of Pinchot's concerns and made broader access to electricity one of his campaign priorities during his successful run for governor of New York in 1928. Once elected to the presidency and empowered by the crisis of the Great Depression to expand the role of the state, he pioneered several New Deal programs that enhanced access to electricity among the nation's poor and farmers, including the Tennessee Valley Authority (1933) and the Rural Electrification Act (1935), both programs based largely on Giant Power principles. Through such measures, the state began to play an increasingly active role in the nation's energy practices.[33]

Networking the Lower Susquehanna River

Despite the positive attention given to interconnection in trade journals and government reports, most private utilities in the mid-Atlantic continued to take a conservative approach to transmission wire investments in the years after World War I. Focusing on their own service areas allowed them to maintain control over operations and justify rate increases when they invested in new generating stations. Developments along the lower Susquehanna River were a notable exception to this pattern. Nature's variability proved to be a more compelling framework for interconnection than technocratic dreams.

From 1926 to 1931, two new dams and sets of transmission wires were built along the Susquehanna River. As was the case with Holtwood, boosters chose to complement the inconstant river flows by integrating hydroelectric facilities into a network of coal-fired power plants. These transmission wires offered some of the technical benefits envisioned by government officials but also exhibited their own logic. Instead of the straight and direct transmission lines that were to connect the most systems with the shortest length, as proposed by Murray and Pinchot, the wires built from new dams along the Susquehanna were a patchwork system in which financial interrelationships were more consequential than engineering efficiency. If Superpower and Giant Power represented the ordering gaze of the technocrat, the Pennsylvania–New Jersey (PNJ) Interconnection and extension of the Aldred systems represented the messy opportunism of the financier.

The first new hydroelectric development along the Susquehanna River gave rise to the world's largest power-sharing pool at the time: the PNJ Interconnection.[34] After the waters of the Susquehanna exited the powerhouse of Holtwood Dam, they continued their rapid descent into the Chesapeake Bay. Electrical boosters had long been interested in capturing this energy a second time. While surveys were made for Holtwood at the beginning of the twentieth century, others were investigating the possibility for a dam near Conowingo Falls, about ten miles from the river's mouth in Maryland.[35] The Susquehanna Power Company was the main force behind these efforts and it owned many of the necessary property rights. But it would take more than two decades for booster dreams to become reality, largely because of the difficulty of finding markets. Baltimore was already well supplied with hydroelectric power and other nearby cities such as Harrisburg, Reading, and Wilmington did not have enough demand to justify building a large dam.

Philadelphia was the only other regional market of suitable size. During the first two decades of the twentieth century, there were several rounds of negotiations between the Philadelphia Electric Company (PECO) and the Susquehanna Power Company, but no agreement was reached. In the mid-1920s, the Philadelphia financial firm of Drexel and Company acquired the property rights of the Susquehanna Power Company and brokered a deal with PECO to get the project going. In 1926, PECO began constructing a 378,000 hp dam at Conowingo—larger than any American hydroelectric facility at the time other than Niagara. Over the next two years, thousands of men labored to construct the dam. As with Holtwood, contemporaries enjoyed crafting comparisons for the amount of concrete needed. In this case, it was reported that it would make a block ten stories high that was the width of Pennsylvania Avenue and the distance from the U.S. Capitol building grounds to the Raleigh Hotel, nearly a mile away. The powerhouse and turbines were the largest ever built. Construction was completed in early 1928 and the first power transmission occurred on March 1.[36]

Part of the reason PECO had delayed so many years in participating in the development of Conowingo was that it had not developed sufficient markets for such a large quantity of power: at times of high river flow, the dam was capable of producing more electricity than PECO's customers could absorb.[37] Even the company's official historian noted that during the 1910s and 1920s, PECO was a "high rate, low use" utility that was not particularly aggressive in finding new customers. But with the construction of Conowingo Dam and its transmission wires to Philadelphia, the company suddenly found itself in a position where excess supply needed to drive demand. Conowingo, like Holtwood, created a landscape of intensification that stimulated PECO and its employees to find ways to increase consumption. Between 1928 and 1934, PECO transformed itself into a "high use, low rate" utility.[38]

The Susquehanna's shifting water flows exacerbated the challenge of integrating Conowingo. Particularly since PECO knew it would take time to build demand within its own network, it looked to surrounding utilities to help it absorb the river's peak capacity. But not all parties were welcome. In 1923, Aldred reportedly approached PECO offering to finance half the cost of Conowingo in exchange for delivering half the power to Baltimore. His offer was rejected, partly because PECO wanted to retain control over the project and partly because the companies were competitors for new territories, as evidenced by the "battle for Havre de Grace" that erupted a few years later.[39]

Financial interrelationships proved to be more decisive than geographic proximity. In 1927, PECO was acquired by a holding company, United Gas Improvement, in which Drexel and Company was a major shareholder. United Gas Improvement also controlled Public Service Electric & Gas, a utility that operated throughout New Jersey. The Pennsylvania Power & Light Company operated in the anthracite regions and was owned by the Electric Bond and Share Company, an organization that had good relations with United Gas Improvement. Just as Aldred's combined management of Holtwood and Consolidated had smoothed over potential obstacles to their integration, Drexel and Company's coordinating role facilitated a complex power-sharing agreement between the three utilities to divide the power of Conowingo.

The result was the PNJ Interconnection, an innovative power-sharing pool in which three utilities coordinated their power supply. This arrangement raised substantial management challenges as it forced the companies to negotiate regularly to determine payments, anticipate demand, and determine when and where to build new capacity. The material basis of the PNJ was 210 miles of 220,000-volt transmission lines extending from Conowingo to major substations serving each utility: Plymouth Meeting for PECO, Roseland for Public Service Electric & Gas, and Siegfried for Pennsylvania Power & Light. These wires allowed power to be shared between the utilities, thereby maximizing the energy of the Susquehanna River and the existing steam plants of each company. The transmission lines held the system together, enabling the Susquehanna's energy to power homes and factories as far away as Newark, New Jersey.[40]

The completion of Safe Harbor Dam in 1931 resulted in the other significant expansion of hydroelectric capacity and transmission wires along the lower Susquehanna River. Aldred once again played a pioneering role. Under

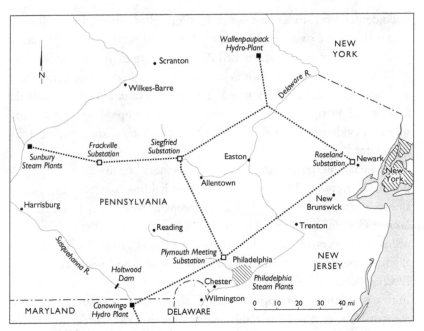

MAP 6.1. PNJ Interconnection, 1928.

his leadership, PWP and Consolidated actively sought to expand their regional networks. The companies were proponents of the Superpower survey, providing Murray with information, assigning the engineer J. A. Walls to be one of the project's advisors, and proclaiming Holtwood to be ideally located for such a system in promotional literature.[41] Their interest in Superpower reflected the realities of tapping the Susquehanna: the broader the markets that the company could access, the easier it would be to absorb the peaks and valleys of Holtwood's production. As he realized that the Superpower proposal was unlikely to be implemented, Aldred took matters into his own hands and expanded PWP's network in 1923 by signing new contracts with the Edison Light & Power Company in York, Pennsylvania, and the Chester Valley Electric Company in Coatesville, Pennsylvania, and building 70,000-volt transmission lines to each of the cities.[42]

After his pitch to participate in the construction of Conowingo was rejected, Aldred turned his attention to the creation of a new dam eight miles north of Holtwood near Safe Harbor. PWP executives had been considering a second dam since at least the 1910s; surveys were carried out with absolute secrecy—one of the engineers was even told to withhold his activities from his immediate supervisor.[43] By the late 1920s, company officials believed there was sufficient demand to justify the construction of a dam with nearly twice the capacity of Holtwood. PWP and Consolidated financed the project jointly and established a third corporation to manage the dam: the Safe Harbor Water Power Corporation. Aldred headed all three companies and operated them collaboratively. Workers broke ground in April 1930, and with a fortuitous combination of cheap labor due to the start of the Great Depression and a year of low river flow, the dam was completed ahead of schedule in December 1931. Most of the power was absorbed by Consolidated while the Pennsylvania Railroad, which was in the process of electrifying its railroad lines between Washington, D.C. and New York, consumed much of the rest.[44]

As with the construction of Holtwood and Conowingo, the creation of Safe Harbor Dam required a new set of transmission wires to distribute its power. These included a 70-mile set of 220,000-volt wires to Baltimore, a 32-mile, 132,000-volt transmission wire from Safe Harbor to Perryville, Maryland (near Havre de Grace), to supply the Pennsylvania Railroad, and a 70,000-volt line connecting the Safe Harbor and Holtwood Dams. Consolidated also built a 60-mile, 220,000-volt line from Baltimore to Washington D.C. to provide an interconnection with the Potomac Electric Power Company.[45]

The transmission wires of the Aldred companies were similar to the PNJ Interconnection in that they reflected the primacy of financial interrelationships. They served the regions and utilities with which Aldred had created working relationships and bypassed all others. The Safe Harbor and Holtwood Dams were not integrated into the PNJ Interconnection, nor did they supply energy to surrounding towns or communities that were not already served by PWP and Consolidated.[46] The benefits of interconnection were limited in geographic scope.

The histories of Superpower, Giant Power, PNJ, and the Aldred systems reveal that wires were more than simple conduits for moving energy from one place to another. They reflected distinctive visions and priorities for who would have access to electricity and who would receive its benefits. Though all shared the idea that interconnection could produce efficiencies, there were notable differences in how these gains were to be distributed.

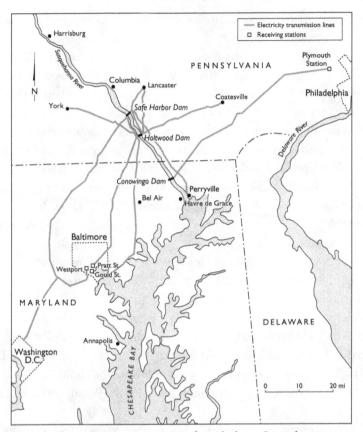

MAP 6.2. Electricity transmission wires from the lower Susquehanna
River, ca. 1933.

Superpower and Giant Power proposed interconnections that integrated all
utilities, not simply pairings of financial convenience. Including each utility was not simply an egalitarian gesture; it was necessary to achieve optimal efficiency. Only when every system was involved could technocrats
design the shortest transmission wires that would serve the broadest area.
Superpower contended such cost savings would propel industrial growth
while Giant Power aimed to translate these efficiencies into greater access
for Pennsylvania's citizens.

The PNJ Interconnection and Aldred networks took a much more limited view. Farley Osgood, former head of the American Institute for Electri-

cal Engineers and an executive with Public Service Electric & Gas in New Jersey, no doubt summarized the thoughts of many company engineers when he wrote of interconnection in 1928: "There is no such thing as super power, or giant power; that isn't what it is. It is just the everyday work of the electrical fellow connecting together his physical links. That is all there is to it."[47] But such a statement masked the deep interconnections between technology and politics. The choice to build transmission wire networks based on engineering efficiency and preexisting financial relationships benefited some parties far more than others.

In the end, the variable flows of the lower Susquehanna River proved a more powerful impetus to transmission wire development in the mid-Atlantic than technocratic ideals. Though experts devoted significant effort to mapping the possible gains of interconnection, most private utilities were reticent to invest in such systems because of their financial incentives, competitive threats, and desire for control. But as Aldred knew from operating Holtwood Dam, the annual fluctuations of the river could best be maximized by linking dams to several markets and a series of coal-fired power plants. Overcoming the capricious lower Susquehanna River proved to be central to extending the mid-Atlantic's transmission network.

Electricity and the Mineral Energy Regime

The overall growth of electrification between 1900 and 1930 was remarkable. Whereas total American energy consumption grew two and a half times over these decades, the use of electricity increased more than twenty-fold.[48] Yet because the mid-Atlantic's transmission wires were built to serve the financial interests of utility companies, access to electricity was based on considerations of profit rather than equity. Like coal and oil, electricity deepened the hold of the mineral energy regime in the mid-Atlantic, but it did so inequitably.

Industries gained the greatest share of the benefits of electricity. By the dawn of the Great Depression, electricity provided more than 80 percent of industrial power across the nation, and industrial consumers used over four times as much electricity as homes or stores.[49] Factories not only had nearly universal access to electricity, they were also charged the lowest rates by utilities. While most urbanites had the opportunity to purchase electricity, their prices were typically much higher: in 1927, residential rates averaged 6.8 cents per kilowatt-hour (kwh) while industrial rates averaged 1.4 cents per kwh. The disparity was even more extreme in the mid-Atlantic: 7.4 cents per kwh for residential consumers and 1.2 cents per kwh for factories.[50] In rural areas, electrification was rare, both in the mid-Atlantic and in the rest of the nation: in 1930 only about 10 percent of American farmers had access to electricity. This paled in comparison to many European nations: almost all farmers in the Netherlands had access to electricity, as did 90 percent of German farmers and half of Swedish farmers.[51] As Pinchot had feared, utilities prioritized the most profitable customers and performed less work to bring electrical service to homes and farms. The politics of wires favored urban and industrial consumers at the expense of residential and rural ones.

As a source of industrial power, electricity furthered the growth and reliance of the region on mineral energy sources. In large factories such as automobile plants, assembly lines led to dramatic increases in the efficiency of production. But the benefits of electricity were not restricted to mass producers. For many small enterprises, operating a steam engine was a costly and inefficient proposition. By purchasing electricity from a utility and using small motors, a much broader range of enterprises could take advantage of mineral energy sources. The ready-made clothing industry, for example, employed over 20,000 workers in Philadelphia in 1929 using sewing machines that together consumed only a few thousand horsepower of energy.[52] Even though a sewing machine did not require a great deal of power, replacing a foot-powered model with an electric one could increase output significantly. Therefore, electricity brought mechanical power to a range of operations for which steam engines or waterwheels were impractical. Collectively, these uses of electricity had a dramatic effect on the nation's output as the price-adjusted Gross National Product grew by more than 40 percent during the Roaring Twenties.[53]

Electricity also deepened the hold of the mineral energy regime by helping manufacture a whole host of goods that increased consumers' demands for mineral energy. The mass production of inexpensive automobiles on assembly lines, for example, led to significant expansions in the consumption of oil during this period: gasoline use in 1930 was thirty-three times higher than it was in 1909.[54] Companies sold electrical appliances to homes and factories that required significant quantities of electricity to operate. New materials made with electricity, like aluminum, were important inputs for other energy-intensive innovations like airplanes. Thus, the products of electrified factories reinforced patterns of ever-increasing energy consumption.

The expansion of electricity use in industry occurred across the nation, though the mid-Atlantic's extensive industrial base meant that the region consumed a disproportionate share. With 20 percent of the nation's population, mid-Atlantic industries consumed at least 30 percent of the total electricity used by industries in 1927.[55] In Pennsylvania, electric power supported the continued growth of established industries like iron and steel, coke, cement, paper, and glass.[56] It also gave rise to new businesses focused on manufacturing electrical products, such as Philadelphia's Electric Storage Battery Company and the radio producer Atwater Kent Manufacturing Company. In Baltimore, manufacturers using large blocks of electricity included metal industries, railroads, and shipbuilders.[57]

For those working in factories, electrification brought a number of gains and losses. Compared with plants with millwork systems, electrified factories generally offered a more pleasant work environment. Eliminating the shafts and belts reduced the noise and dirt within the factory, and electric lights lowered eyestrain. Electric power was also significantly safer, as the spinning belts in line-drive systems were responsible for many industrial accidents. Some of the profits from increased productivity were returned to workers, as wages in many electrified factories rose more than 30 percent between 1919 and 1929. And by substituting the power of machines for the power of muscles, electrified factories made it easier for women to enter the industrial workforce.[58]

But working on assembly lines could be a great challenge. While some workers felt pride in being part of a production team, many felt the rapid pace of the labor to be exhausting. Instead of spurts of intense activity followed by slowdowns that had been common in craft production, assembly lines left almost no time for catching one's breath; even bathroom breaks were often scheduled in advance. The labor itself could be very dull and repetitive: much skill was transferred from the body of the laborer to the flow of parts. Many workers feared new production techniques would decrease the number of available jobs, and they may have been right: in a time of rapid growth in output from 1919 to 1929, the number of factory workers actually declined. For laborers, better wages and safer conditions were often counteracted by fewer opportunities and less satisfaction.[59]

Industrial uses of electricity contributed significantly to the entrenchment of the mineral energy regime in the mid-Atlantic and the rest of the nation. While the region already had a mature industrial base by the turn of the twentieth century, electricity reinforced the centrality of manufacturing by providing a safe and flexible form of energy that could be used to rearrange production processes and increase output. Industrial electrification further committed the mid-Atlantic to a development path requiring ever-increasing supplies of mineral energy to maintain.

Powering the Home

The use of electricity in domestic settings further extended the mineral energy regime by providing the first source of inanimate power in the home. Though residential heating and lighting markets were key drivers for the rising use of anthracite coal and petroleum, most of the labor in the home before 1920 remained the province of the organic energy regime. Coal stoves, kerosene lamps, and electric lights provided heat and light, but muscles supplied power. The ability of electricity to power small motors changed this situation. Beginning in the 1910s and accelerating in the 1920s, many residential consumers adopted new devices like irons, fans, vacuum cleaners, and washing machines. While these appliances consumed only a small percentage of overall electrical production, they were similar to petroleum-based lubricants in that their importance went beyond the absolute amount of electricity they used.[60]

Domestic appliances captured the imagination of visionaries like Pinchot who celebrated the potential of electricity to alleviate "the drudgery of human life."[61] Yet despite the wide interest in labor-saving technologies for the home, the adoption of domestic appliances occurred far more slowly than markets for urban lighting, street railways, and industrial power. In 1923, for example, lighting accounted for more than three-quarters of residential electrical consumption in Chicago, one of the nation's most electri-

fied cities. Only 5 percent of the outlets in the city's homes powered appliances.[62] This was, in large part, why Pinchot felt the Giant Power initiative
was so important. Led by private utilities, electricity boosters had furthered
the interests of industrial and commercial establishments more than those
of residential consumers.

The slower adoption of domestic appliances reflected the gradual electrification of American homes. In 1907, only 8 percent of American homes were
electrified; this increased to 35 percent of homes by 1920 and 68 percent by
1930.[63] The degree to which homes had access to electricity depended both
on their location and how aggressive local boosters had been. For example,
in 1919, only about 35 percent of homes in PECO's service area were electrified. Consolidated made a bigger push in Baltimore, promoting electricity in
a 1923 advertisement as a "convenience outlet" users could "command" to
"cook your breakfast, to clean your rugs, to wash or iron your clothes."[64] By
1927, 80 percent of Baltimore homes had electrical service.[65] However, even
when homes had access, some had only thin wires with a couple of outlets
incapable of safely handling more than a few lights and perhaps an iron. To
run power-intensive devices like washing machines and refrigerators, homeowners had to invest in thicker wires with better insulation.[66]

After World War I, these barriers began to drop. In 1922, about a third of
electrified households had electric washing machines and nearly two-fifths
did by 1929.[67] Between 1922 and 1927, PECO sold approximately $9 million
worth of appliances, roughly 40 percent of the total sales in the Philadelphia
area. Consumers there purchased more than 95,000 irons, 54,000 vacuum
cleaners, 21,000 washing machines, 2,000 sewing machines, and 500 refrigerators.[68] By 1935, the adoption of electric irons was nearly universal, while
about half of American households had vacuum cleaners, washing machines, toasters, and clocks. Roughly a third of Americans had refrigerators,
and many owned waffle irons, ranges, hot plates, and heaters.[69]

Aggressive sales campaigns by electricity boosters were an essential un-
derpinning for consumer choices. Utilities maintained display rooms to
educate people about new devices and hired salesmen to go door to door.
Consolidated promised prospective consumers that "electricity will transform night into day for you, and a house of drudgery into a house of ease."[70]
In addition, the manufacturers of appliances spent lavishly on advertisements touting the benefits of a modern home. These efforts were important

in helping consumers overcome concerns about the cost, safety, and reliability of electricity. The state also played a critical role. New Deal programs such as Title I of the National Housing Act provided cheap financing that allowed homeowners to obtain credit for installing wires and purchasing appliances. It was only after seeing the success of these government programs that many private utilities began to offer consumers credit and implemented similar financing programs that led to increased residential adoption of appliances.[71]

Supplying electricity to the home had significant consequences for domestic labor, though it was not as revolutionary as advocates like Pinchot had hoped. Similar to the utopian dreams associated with streetcar systems and rural revival, the reality of the mineral energy regime was more mixed. To be sure, home appliances relieved some of the demands for physical labor around the home. Electric irons made it easier to maintain the right temperature for pressing clothes. Electric washing machines relieved some of the difficult work of laundry. Refrigerators made it possible to buy several days' worth of groceries on a single shopping trip. Vacuum cleaners eased the task of home cleaning. But these benefits were offset by other developments. Households that could afford electric appliances often were in a position to retain domestic servants. However, appliances often replaced domestic servants, leaving housewives in charge of tasks that had previously occupied several workers. And improvements in household appliances frequently led to increased expectations for how often a house was cleaned or clothes washed. Mineral power sources may have made household work more productive, but they did not necessarily reduce the amount of time needed to maintain a home. The nature of housework had changed, but much of the drudgery still existed.[72]

Once consumers obtained access to better wiring and credit to purchase domestic appliances, it began a cycle of ever-increasing demand for electricity in homes. In 1919, the average residential consumer in Baltimore used 391 kwh of electricity per year, but this grew to 902 kwh by 1937—about 15 percent more than the national average.[73] By 1960, the average domestic electrical consumption in the nation had skyrocketed to 3,854 kwh per year.[74] At midcentury, residential consumption had reached a quarter of the nation's electrical use, and by 1986 as much electricity was being used in the home as in industries.[75] Characteristic of the mineral energy regime, as the use of electric appliances increased, so too did consumers' demands for more energy.

The Power of Leisure

The use of electricity to provide leisure and entertainment marked a new wrinkle in the spread of the mineral energy regime. Because energy was correlated with personal exertion in the organic energy regime, leisure was often characterized by the avoidance of energy expenditure. But as energy was transformed into a cheap and abundant commodity, leisure time increasingly involved the consumption of energy rather than its avoidance.

Streetcar companies developed one of the early forms of electrified leisure: the amusement park. As in several other cases, abundant supply encouraged new consumption patterns. These companies had invested large amounts of capital in generating capacity to operate their streetcars. Most of the traffic occurred during the day, meaning that in the evenings and on weekends there was surplus capacity. One way to take advantage of this cheap energy was to build amusement parks at the end of a transit line with rides, attractions, and extravagant lighting displays. This increased ridership and took advantage of sunk costs. For attendees, these parks offered a safe and attractive place for social gatherings and became a common form of recreation.[76]

Radio became the most widely dispersed form of electrified entertainment in the 1920s. After Guglielmo Marconi's pioneering work in 1899 to demonstrate the feasibility of point-to-point communication without wires, groups of amateurs, corporations, and military personnel began experimenting with radio technology. By the early 1920s, a combination of advancement in receiver sets and expanding broadcast options helped radio become a national craze. Sales of radios and parts increased from $60 million in 1922 to $136 million a year later and $358 million in 1924.[77] Within a few years, the radio became "a substitute hearth" in homes as families gathered around it to hear broadcasts of sporting events, concerts, and news programs.[78] By the late 1920s, Americans had purchased more radio sets than any other electrical device besides lights or an iron; over 24 million sets had been sold by 1933.[79] Investing in leisure appliances seemed a better idea to most Americans than purchasing domestic appliances to save labor.

Movies became another form of energy-consuming leisure activity during this era. In 1891, Thomas Edison invented a kinetographic camera that captured moving images, helping give rise to the film industry. In the first decades of the twentieth century, nickelodeons charged viewers five cents to view a film that was sometimes supplemented by music and a vaudeville act. By the 1920s, studios began to create more elaborate feature-length films that were shown in over twenty thousand movie theaters across the country. When "talkies" were introduced in the late 1920s by linking electronic sound-recording equipment to the films, movies began to draw even broader audiences. Fifty million Americans went to the cinema each week in 1925, and twice as many attended in 1930. Not only did movie theaters depend on electricity for lighting and operating the projector, they used energy extensively for temperature control to draw in consumers hoping to be warm in the winter or cool in the summer.[80]

Along with devices like phonographs, these new practices marked a significant advance of the mineral energy regime into the ways Americans played. The application of electricity shifted the relationships between energy and leisure that had characterized the organic energy regime. It did not require personal exertion and therefore encouraged the expansion of energy-consuming leisure technologies. Like domestic appliances, amusement parks, radios, and motion pictures expanded how and where Americans used energy: even the logic of recreation was different in the mineral energy regime.

A Modern Nation

By 1930, cheap and abundant energy had transformed the ways millions lived, worked, and played. Energy consumption had increased 250 percent over the first three decades of the twentieth century, more than twice the rate of population growth.[81] Urban homes were heated with coal and lit with kerosene or electricity. City dwellers commuted to work on electric streetcars or in gasoline-powered automobiles. In factories, laborers produced goods using machines powered by coal and electricity. Stores attracted customers with electric elevators, lights, and fans. Leisure practices reflected a world of mineral energy abundance as well: many relaxed by plugging in radios, taking drives in the country, or going to movie theaters. The mineral energy regime had become integrated into nearly every aspect of life.

Electricity was at the heart of these changes. The production of electricity grew nearly twenty-fold from 1902 to 1930, supporting a tripling of American industrial output.[82] While the mechanical energy available to each industrial worker doubled from 1899 to 1925, the amount supplied by electricity increased more than thirty times.[83] Additionally, electrification furthered the gap between America and the rest of the world: in 1929, U.S. electrical production exceeded the combined total of all other countries.[84]

Within America, the mid-Atlantic continued to reap disproportionate benefits from the mineral energy regime. In 1925, New York and Pennsylvania were ranked first and second in terms of electricity production, as well as population, wealth, and manufacturing output.[85] Yet the mid-Atlantic's advantages were not as extreme as in the case of coal and oil. Much of the rest of the nation electrified quickly as well, although there were salient differences. On the West Coast, hydroelectricity was more common than steam plants, and a greater percentage of electricity was used in agriculture for powering irrigation pumps than in other regions.[86] Southern states continued to lag behind: with more than three-tenths of the nation's population, they consumed less than two-tenths of the nation's electricity.[87] But while comparatively fewer in the rural South had access to electricity, those who adopted it consumed similar per capita quantities as those in other regions.[88] In many ways, electrification was a national trend.

The differences within regions were often more significant than the differences between them. As with coal and oil, urbanites had much easier access to electricity than farmers. Industrial users gained the greatest advantages because they paid the lowest rates for electricity and could use it in the widest range of applications. This led to large profits for factory owners and ambivalent gains for workers. Wages increased fastest in industries adopting electricity, but the pace of work was frantic and the labor was often agonizingly repetitive. For residential consumers, electricity offered a superior source of light and an opportunity to replace muscle power in the home with appliances. Yet it took boosters a surprisingly long time to develop this market: the adoption of appliances such as vacuum cleaners and washing machines began in earnest in the late 1910s, more than three decades after Edison's first utility station was opened. About a third of American homes still remained unwired at the dawn of the Great Depression. Given the nearly universal electrification in many European countries, it is clear that these inequalities were not inevitable.

These energy changes were not simply about how people got and used power: they transformed the course of the nation's development. By 1930, America was a modern nation characterized by large cities, an industrial economy, giant corporations, a powerful government, faith in science and technology, and new conceptions of space and time. More Americans lived in cities than in rural areas; in New York and Pennsylvania the ratio was greater than two to one.[89] Despite Americans maintaining an impressive output of agricultural goods, manufacturing had become the lifeblood of the economy, producing three times as much wealth as the fruits of the organic energy regime.[90] Companies providing coal, oil, and electricity were among the nation's largest corporations, and their products underpinned the rise of other industrial behemoths including U.S. Steel and the railroad companies. Progressive reformers targeted many of the abuses of these companies and believed that a combination of rational management and expanded state power could achieve better outcomes than a laissez-faire system; their efforts led to a considerable growth in the size and strength of government bodies in the first decades of the twentieth century. Railroads, steamboats, streetcars, and automobiles whisked Americans through cities and across countrysides at speeds that were unattainable without mineral energy sources. The rural, agricultural, and decentralized nation of a hundred years before would hardly be recognizable to most Americans in 1930.

Turning back the clock was not a realistic option. By this time, the mineral energy regime was firmly established and required abundant supplies of coal, oil, and electricity to maintain itself. Wood and water simply could not provide enough energy to heat the homes of millions of urban residents, power thousands of factories in a metropolitan region, or transport people and goods across expanding cities and overland trade routes. While individual homeowners or factory managers could choose to do without a coal stove or electric motor, a collective decision to forgo mineral energy sources would have brought the nation's industrial economy and bustling cities to a grinding halt. Even the modest reductions in coal and electricity available for non-war purposes in World War I were sufficient to provide serious disruptions in everyday life for those who were affected. Mineral energy sources were not a luxury for Americans in 1930: they were a necessity.

Conclusion

Since 1930, the radical transformations in energy practices ushered in during the preceding century have been deepened and extended. Electricity production in America grew more than ten-fold between 1950 and 2000 while oil consumption practically tripled in the same period. Even though most people associate coal with the nineteenth century, its use nearly doubled in the second half of the twentieth century as well.[1] In America, as in the rest of the industrialized world, coal, oil, and electricity heat and cool our homes, transport us in cars and planes, and power the devices we use for work and play. We drive to supermarkets to purchase food that is grown in fertilized fields, harvested with tractors, and delivered in refrigerated trucks. Nearly every good we buy is manufactured using fossil fuel energy and shipped around the globe by trains, freighters, and delivery vans. Between the alarm clock that wakes us up in the morning and the bedside light that we turn off before going to sleep, residents of the global north rely on mineral energy sources hundreds of times a day. Yet an irony of the mineral energy regime is that higher levels of use are often correlated with lower levels of awareness. Whereas direct links between energy and personal exertion in the organic energy regime forced Americans to be physically conscious of their choices, the mineral energy regime introduced a different logic. As long as these energy sources are available, we have little reason to pay attention. The more we use, the less we notice.

These practices had their roots in the material transformations of the mid-Atlantic region between 1820 and 1930. The building of coal canals, oil pipelines, and electricity transmission wires pioneered the energy transitions that remade the nation. They created landscapes of intensification in which the continual growth of energy consumption became a logical pattern. These technological alterations of the environment made it possible, for the first time, to ship mineral energy sources cheaply, abundantly, and reliably. The financial systems of the mid-Atlantic encouraged growth because large capital investments established strong incentives for the owners and operators of these networks to become boosters dedicated to building demand for coal, oil, and electricity. As consumers experienced the benefits of substituting mineral energy sources for their own exertions, they began to change their behaviors and desire ever-greater supplies of energy. In response to increasing demand, transport networks were further expanded, thereby enabling energy to be shipped at lower costs and in greater quantities. These positive feedback loops lay at the heart of the mineral energy regime.

At first, mid-Atlantic residents experienced new energy sources as an open choice; they could decide whether or not they wanted to adopt coal, oil, or electricity. But as people reconstructed their built environments around these energy landscapes, they began to depend on continuous supplies of mineral energy. By the turn of the twentieth century, dense clusters of homes and factories in cities like Philadelphia and New York could no longer be supported with organic energy sources. Industrialists had opened iron furnaces and aluminum smelters that could only operate with huge inputs of coal and electricity. Merchants had established new patterns of trade that depended on rapid and reliable transit from steamboats, railroads, and streetcars. The logic of these landscapes ran one-way: toward the ever-increasing consumption of energy.

What began in the mid-Atlantic soon spread beyond its borders to reshape the energy practices of the entire nation. Iron forged in the mid-Atlantic became the tracks and locomotives of the transcontinental railroads, thereby spreading the mineral energy regime to the Pacific Ocean.[2] Prospectors in Pennsylvania's petroleum regions gained valuable experience that they used to discover oil in places like Kansas, Texas, and California.[3] And the electrification of America depended on crucial innovations made in the mid-Atlantic at sites like Thomas Edison's New Jersey laboratory and by New York-based inventors such as Nikola Telsa. Though regional resource endowments, histories, and cultures mean that there continue to be relevant energy differences between areas like New England, the Pacific Northwest, and the South, all have come to replicate key patterns of the mineral energy regime first established in the mid-Atlantic.

From one perspective, the rise of the mineral energy regime has been one of humanity's greatest accomplishments. This shift has created enormous wealth by replacing the limits of the organic energy regime with the positive feedback loops of constant growth. Countless tasks of physical labor have been eased by the introduction of industrial machinery, mechanized vehicles, and domestic appliances. Abundant supplies of coal, oil, and electricity have underpinned advances in food production, housing, and medicine that have extended the average lifespan. The mineral energy regime has enabled the manufacture and distribution of millions of products that have been eagerly procured by global consumers. Any member of the middle class in an industrialized nation now has access to luxuries once restricted to ruling elites.

Yet these undeniable benefits are not the complete story. This narrative of progress contains many darker sides. The introduction of coal, oil, and electricity was not a rising tide that raised all boats: it was a dead-end for some people, a modest boost for many, and an express elevator to enormous riches for a lucky few. Owners and operators of energy transport systems often gained the largest profits from these systems while miners and oil drillers received much lower wages. A lucky driller might make a fortune upon striking a gusher, but the vast majority left the oil regions broke and dispirited. Because transport networks privileged urban locations over rural ones, city dwellers gained access to cheap sources of home heating and lighting while most farming communities were bypassed. Within cities, the use of coal, oil, and electricity in factories produced enormous wealth for capitalists. Workers, by contrast, rarely shared the profits. The benefits of the mineral energy regime were not distributed equally.

The sacrifice of energy-producing zones was another unfortunate and preventable aspect of the emergence of the mineral energy regime. There were few social mores, and even fewer laws, against the exploitation of environments in which coal, oil, and electricity could be produced. The anthracite coal regions were littered with coal dust, culm banks, and abandoned mines. Large swaths of western Pennsylvania were drenched in oil by petroleum drillers. And the Susquehanna River was dammed across its entire length, creating reservoirs filled with coal dust and cutting fish off from their breeding grounds. Both the inequalities and environmental degradation accompanying the rising use of coal, oil, and electricity were apparent to many. It was possible, as advocates at the time noted, to pass laws and policies that would have lessened these costs. But few of these measures were enacted, and those that were ratified often lacked enforcement mechanisms necessary to make a substantial impact.

Yet the graver threats to the mineral energy regime were not necessarily clear to historical actors. From today's vantage point, we face the odd challenge that we have both too little *and* too much fossil fuel energy. We have too little because mineral energy stocks are being drawn down much more rapidly than they are being replaced. While there are widespread disagreements about the size of fossil fuel reserves and whether we have reached peak oil, it is clear that we will eventually cease to be able to access ever-increasing stocks of coal, oil, and natural gas. The question is when, not if, these limits will be reached.[4] On the other hand, overwhelming scientific evidence demonstrates that consuming our remaining mineral energy reserves will lead to climatic changes that will heavily disrupt the ecosystems on which human life depends. If we persist in burning fossil fuels, we will no longer simply pollute sites of production; instead, we risk turning the entire earth into a sacrifice zone. One of the great challenges of the twenty-first century will be navigating between the Scylla of too little mineral energy to sustain current energy practices long into the future and the Charybdis of releasing too much trapped carbon to maintain a stable climate.[5]

With these considerations in mind, the mineral energy regime looks to be as much of a Faustian bargain as it is a story of progress. Like Faust, who offers his soul to the devil in exchange for unlimited knowledge, we have chosen a better quality of life in the present at the expense of our future. We have reveled in the immediacy of economic growth and personal comfort while downplaying the importance of the long-term health of ecosystems that sustain life. Though we may not have known the terms of the bargain in advance, the consequences of maintaining our current patterns are becoming increasingly dire.

Patterns of Energy Transitions

The twin challenges of finite resources and climate change suggest the importance of pioneering new energy transitions away from fossil fuel stocks. The story of America's first energy transitions suggests several patterns that can inform contemporary debates.

Transport matters. Most analyses of energy transitions focus on the production of new sources. This history shows that transporting energy cheaply, reliably, and abundantly has been an equal or greater challenge in stimulating energy transitions. People knew about the potential energy from the anthracite coal regions, western Pennsylvania's oil seeps, and the falling waters of the Susquehanna River decades before they began to use them intensively. But these resources were of relatively little use because it was prohibitively costly and difficult to transport them to places where consumers lived. It was only when entrepreneurs built transport systems tailored to each particular form of energy that consumption grew rapidly. These systems were important not only because they performed the necessary, albeit mundane, task of moving energy from point a to point b. They also mattered because the high capital costs of building these technologies created a set of actors with a vested financial interest in ensuring that as much energy was shipped as possible. As a result, the companies that built transport infrastructure were often among the most active agents seeking to convince consumers to alter their energy behaviors. Canals, pipelines, and wires gave rise to landscapes of intensification that both pioneered and sustained the rising use of coal, oil, and electricity. Today, it stands to reason that transmission wires connecting sites of abundant wind and sun might have a similarly positive impact on encouraging the use of renewable energy sources.

Supply drives demand. In the energy transitions to coal, oil, and electricity, new energy supplies were developed in advance of consumer demand. Our seemingly insatiable demand for energy is neither a historical constant nor an inherent feature of human nature. It has been actively created, in large part by energy boosters involved in the transport of coal, oil, and electricity. When first introduced to anthracite coal, most consumers found it difficult to use. They resisted investing in special stoves and grates to burn it until concerted efforts by anthracite coal merchants eventually convinced them it was superior to firewood. Though large markets for kerosene existed, boosters had to work for decades in order to create demand for petroleum as a source of heat and power. When completed in 1910, Holtwood Dam was capable of producing more electricity than local markets could absorb. This encouraged utility executives to work with homeowners and factory operators to increase their consumption. Users did not simply line up to adopt new energy sources. Rising demand for coal, oil, and electricity was a response to the actions of boosters, rather than a preexisting condition energy entrepreneurs could rely on.

Energy transitions are overlapping and reinforcing. Energy transitions do not happen in isolation. The adoption of a new energy source can result in social changes that alter the trajectory of future energy transitions. The timing and patterns of nineteenth-century oil developments, for example, were influenced by urban and industrial growth due to the use of anthracite coal in the preceding decades. As greater numbers of people lived and worked indoors, they began to desire larger quantities of artificial illuminants. This encouraged a group of entrepreneurs to reconsider the value of oil seeps that naturally rose to the surface of some streams in western Pennsylvania. If they could acquire oil in significant amounts, they believed they could profit from the burgeoning lighting market. The transition to anthracite coal was therefore a crucial motivation for oil pioneers. Moreover, anthracite coal provided the means for extracting oil. Oilmen relied on steam engines, cheap iron, and railroads made possible by abundant anthracite. The transformation of crude oil into a reliable illuminating liquid and a high-performing lubricant, in turn, further encouraged the rising use of anthracite coal because cheap light and reduced friction helped accelerate urban and industrial growth. Similarly, the most significant initial applications of electricity were for street lighting and streetcars, both of which were a response to urbanization stimulated by coal and oil. In other words, while one energy transition does not determine the next one, it alters the world in ways that reconfigure how and why people undertake the next energy transition.

Energy transitions create unequal geographies. Energy transport systems actively shape spatial politics. The construction of canals, pipelines, and wires introduced at least two major shifts in the geographic consequences of energy transitions. First, they privileged certain people and places over others. Some regions, such as the mid-Atlantic, benefited disproportionately from the energy abundance provided by these systems. Other regions with less access to mineral energy sources, such as the southern states, found their economies falling far behind the mid-Atlantic. But even within the mid-Atlantic, there were vast disparities. Most of the energy was shipped to large eastern seaboard cities. Many rural communities located but a few miles from canals, pipelines, or wires were bypassed completely, and did not garner the same benefits as their urban counterparts. Within cities, there were further inequalities as factory owners used control over energy supplies to increase output and profitability while workers obtained only a fraction of these gains and often faced dangerous working conditions.

Canals, pipelines, and wires also augmented the unequal spatial distribution of environmental harms accompanying energy transitions. Much of the environmental degradation associated with the use of coal, oil, and electricity has been centered at sites of production. In the organic energy regime, consumers had a significant incentive to limit the environmental costs of obtaining energy because it usually occurred near their homes. But the creation of canals, pipelines, and wires altered this logic. By shipping energy long distances, most consumers no longer had to live with the negative consequences of energy production. The users of coal, oil, and electricity were rarely exposed to ever-present coal dust, oil spills, or the loss of river fishing opportunities. As a result, they had little reason to push for environmental protections. The ability to separate sites of consumption and production helped turn the anthracite regions, oil fields, and Susquehanna River into environmental sacrifice zones.

Differences between transport systems matter. Canals, pipelines, and wires built between 1820 and 1930 were similar in that they all helped stimulate and sustain energy transitions. But there were important material differences between these systems that structured the allocation of benefits. Canals, for example, were multi-product, bidirectional systems: they could carry a wide variety of goods up and down rivers. As a result, their construction led to widespread regional development between their origins and termini because they could deliver goods to intermediate points. Thriving ironworks at towns along the canal banks including Reading, Allentown, and Bethlehem typified these developments, as these factories received coal from upriver and ore and lime from downriver, and could cheaply ship their finished goods to markets. Oil pipelines, by contrast, were designed to carry one product in one direction to one location. This meant that a valuable natural resource could be transported away from western Pennsylvania without anything material being returned in its wake. Even the capital that paid for oil was often rerouted. Because Standard Oil dominated the pipeline network, most of the profits were sent to its New York City headquarters, not the oil regions. As unidirectional, uni-product systems, pipelines did not serve intermediate points, thereby contributing to the absence of amplifier effects along their paths or in the oil-producing cities like Titusville and Oil City. The greater flexibility and adaptability of canals compared with pipelines fostered different geographies of regional growth.[6]

Energy transitions reconfigure social power as well as mechanical power. Energy systems do not simply supply heat, light, and power; they also deliver social, political, and economic power to some at the expense of others. The ability to control the production, transport, or sale of energy sources has given certain companies monopoly powers and profits. The meteoric rise of the Standard Oil Trust is one example among many of an energy company growing to dominate its industry. Furthermore, everyone may not have the option to be a consumer. Preferential access to cheap energy enabled urban residents of the mid-Atlantic to benefit far more than their rural counterparts. The effects of new energy sources shaped power relations outside of the energy industries as well. The Union Army had a decided advantage over the forces of the Confederacy in the Civil War because America's first mineral energy transition occurred in the northern states in the preceding decades. The industrialization of many parts of America throughout the nineteenth and early twentieth century, based on the consumption of coal, oil, and electricity, was essential to the rise of the United States as a global superpower that could influence the destinies of other nations. When talking about energy transitions, we should be conscientious in noting that they are not simply changes in the type of energy we use. They are also shifts that give power to some groups and take it away from others.[7]

Energy transitions are shaped by public and private actors. We cannot understand the rising use of coal, oil, and electricity without paying attention to both the actions of private capital and government policy. Entrepreneurial individuals were essential to these energy transitions because they raised money, directed the building of infrastructure, and created markets for these energy sources. But they did so in a world that was shaped by the actions, and just as importantly the inactions, of government bodies. State authorities gave canal and dam builders extensive rights to alter natural waterways, ceded ownership of underground mineral rights to corporations, kept taxes low, and defended the rights of private property owners to pollute. Government authorities often helped to stimulate new markets by paying for geological surveys and performing experiments that helped pioneer new uses of energy. Moreover, states rarely required energy companies to minimize their environmental impacts or adhere to strict labor safety laws. Histories of energy industries often celebrate heroic inventors and financiers, but it is critical to recognize that public actions were just as necessary to create these energy transitions.

Paying attention to these patterns of historical energy transitions suggests alternative policies to consider in the present. We might want to pay greater attention to transport systems than we currently do. Given that places where the sun shines the brightest and wind blows the hardest are often far removed from areas where people live, new transmission wires seem particularly important for the development of renewable energy sources. But because transport systems are not egalitarian, we should institute policies that insist they provide fair access to all and seek to balance the environmental costs between producers and consumers. Recognizing that energy demand is shaped by boosters can encourage us to undertake long-term projects to alter behaviors so that people use less energy and are more flexible in their consumption. We can maximize the use of renewable energy sources if people are capable of increasing energy use when the sun shines and wind blows and decreasing their consumption when they do not. Finally, by recognizing that public policy has always shaped energy transitions, we can eliminate some of the conditions that have favored mineral energy sources such as low taxes, private ownership of mineral rights, and minimal environmental safeguards. At the same time, we can initiate practices that support renewable energy sources such as production credits and eminent domain rights for transmission projects.

Toward a More Sustainable Energy Future

If we desire to craft a more sustainable energy future, it is clear that we must abandon many practices of the mineral energy regime. We cannot continue to draw the vast majority of our energy from nonrenewable stocks.[8] Instead, we must return our attention to the flows of the organic energy regime. This does not necessarily mean a simplistic return to the practices of 1820 when Americans relied on photosynthesis and metabolism for their energy needs. Technological developments such as photovoltaic cells, hydroelectric dams, and wind turbines have provided new mechanisms for capturing and utilizing solar energy. Like the dams along the Susquehanna River, these are hybrid systems that combine features of the organic and mineral energy regimes: they are derived from renewable flows but can be densely concentrated and transported long distances.[9]

Coming to terms with the possibilities and limitations of these hybrid systems is essential to creating a sustainable future. One thing we must remember is that the organic energy regime has never gone away. Though organic energy sources have been eclipsed in absolute terms by exponential increases in the consumption of mineral energy sources over the past two centuries, they have remained essential to sustaining human life. At the most basic level, our bodies require food from plants or animals, and our muscles provide indispensible power. The processes of photosynthesis and metabolism sustain human life. Large dams and arrays of wind turbines will do little for us without a sufficient quantity of organic energy sources.

Our ability to maintain the output of organic energy sources, however, will be challenged by the decline of mineral energy stocks. Though we cannot literally eat mineral energy sources, we have used them to increase harvests. Mechanized farm equipment has expanded the amount of land under cultivation and large transport systems have allowed us to ship agricultural goods around the globe. Moreover, the extensive use of fossil fuel–based fertilizers has greatly enhanced agricultural productivity. This suggests that the decline of mineral energy stocks will not only increase our demand for organic energy sources, it will also decrease our ability to produce them. One of the first grand challenges of the new energy regime, therefore, will be to maintain the production of organic energy sources in the absence of fossil fuels.

A related observation is that the carrying capacity of the land is likely to become a topic of greater concern. During the past two hundred years, mineral energy sources have acted as virtual land. They have allowed Americans to produce goods without requiring land to be put aside for their provision. Coal, for example, enabled the smelting of iron without dedicated forests for charcoal, and farm tractors replaced horses that required pastures. But in a world with less mineral energy, virtual land may have to be replaced with real land. This suggests that the spatial requirements of renewable energy technologies must be weighed against alternative uses of the same territory. It would make sense, therefore, to prioritize those that can be deployed without occupying a great deal of area, such as photovoltaic cells that can be added to the roofs of houses or windmills that can be erected in fields that can also be planted with crops. Biofuels, by contrast, often require large tracts of land. Expanding their development might threaten food production and, as a result, they may prove to be less attractive. As in the organic energy regime, we will need to account for the carrying capacity of land as part of our decision-making calculus when considering renewable energy systems.

We can also learn from our forebears' adaptations to a world where energy availability varied throughout the day and across seasons. Behaviors and living patterns in the mineral energy regime have been built around the expectation that stocks of energy will always be available. This may not always be the case in a world of renewable energy. In the organic energy regime, traders waited to ship goods until favorable winds were blowing or rivers had sufficient levels of water. People did laundry on days where the sun was shining so that the wash would dry more quickly. They moved kitchen stoves onto back porches during the summer to avoid overheating homes. Manufacturers developed techniques to produce goods that saved labor. Builders adjusted the designs of structures to local environmental conditions to make them easier to heat and cool. These personal behaviors were reflected in the patterns of human settlements. In the organic energy regime, people congregated in places where energy was easily available or there were ways to avoid energy expenditure, such as the banks of rivers that made it easier to transport goods to market and provided a source of power.[10]

If we can find modern equivalents to some of these behaviors, it will ease the transition to renewable sources. For example, if we can run major appliances like washing machines at times when renewable energy production is high, it will reduce demand when it is dark or the wind is calm. It is possible to design buildings so that they are more efficiently heated by the sun rather than furnaces and cooled by wind rather than air conditioners. Cities can be built to enhance walkability by integrating residential and commercial areas and providing public transportation options. Such measures will lower overall energy demand and increase its flexibility, both of which will facilitate the use of renewable energy sources.

The story of Faust does not necessarily have a determinative ending. In many early versions of the fable, the terms of the bargain were indeed nonnegotiable: upon the end of his life, the doctor's soul was claimed by the devil and he was consigned to eternal damnation. In other versions, however, God steps in to save Faust's soul because he is moved by the doctor's spirit of continual striving and the pleadings of his pious friends. Similarly, the path of our energy future is not foreordained. Unlike Faust, we are not dependent on divine intervention to rescue us from our present challenges. But we would be served well by taking note of his interest in earthly knowledge. Our ability to pioneer a sustainable energy regime will depend on creating a better fit between our technologies, desires, and environmental resources. While it will not be easy, we also share with Faust an advantage. Just as the devil's grant of unlimited knowledge allowed Faust to advance his studies, the prodigious material and financial surpluses we have accumulated from the abundance of the mineral energy regime are an invaluable resource we can draw on to facilitate new energy transitions. We already have enough knowledge, resources, and technologies to initiate change. Whether we take advantage of this opportunity will be one of the great questions of the twenty-first century.

Notes

Introduction

1 David E. Nye, *When the Lights Went Out: A History of Blackouts in America* (Cambridge, MA: MIT Press, 2010).

2 In focusing on the role of infrastructure and transport, this study has been inspired by Thomas Hughes's analysis of electrical networks and William Cronon's study of commodity flows and the Chicago hinterland. Thomas Parke Hughes, *Networks of Power: Electrification in Western Society, 1880–1930* (Baltimore: Johns Hopkins University Press, 1983); William Cronon, *Nature's Metropolis: Chicago and the Great West* (New York: W. W. Norton, 1991). Within the historical literature on energy systems, most of the focus is on the production of new energy sources, and there has been relatively little attention to transport. Notable exceptions of works studying the role of transport in energy systems between 1820 and 1930 include Hughes, *Networks of Power;* Arthur Menzies Johnson, "The Development of American Petroleum Pipelines: A Study in Private Enterprise and Public Policy, 1862–1906" (Ph.D diss., Vanderbilt University, published for the American Historical Association by Cornell University Press, 1956);

Chester Lloyd Jones, *The Economic History of the Anthracite-Tidewater Canals* (Philadelphia: University of Pennsylvania Press, 1908).

3 E. A. Wrigley, *Continuity, Chance and Change: The Character of the Industrial Revolution in England* (Cambridge: Cambridge University Press, 1988); Rolf Peter Sieferle, *The Subterranean Forest: Energy Systems and the Industrial Revolution* (Cambridge: White Horse Press, 2001).

4 In this work, I understand the mid-Atlantic to be primarily composed of the states of Pennsylvania, New Jersey, and New York, along with Delaware and Maryland. However, energy flows did not always respect political boundaries or conventional definitions of the mid-Atlantic. When there is a tension between state borders and the paths of canals, pipelines, or wires, I follow the latter. As a result, this is an analysis of energy landscapes largely contained within the conventional boundaries of the mid-Atlantic while occasionally transgressing these borders.

5 Wrigley, *Continuity, Chance, and Change;* Sieferle, *Subterranean Forest.*

6 Clark A. Miller, Alastair Iles, and Christopher F. Jones, "The Social Dimensions of Energy Transitions," *Science as Culture* 22, no. 2 (2013): 135–48.

7 The energy transitions literature is vast and incorporates numerous works in science and engineering as well as the humanities and social sciences. Some of the key historical works on the topic include Martin V. Melosi, *Coping with Abundance: Energy and Environment in Industrial America* (New York: Knopf, 1985); David E. Nye, *Consuming Power: A Social History of American Energies* (Cambridge, MA: MIT Press, 1998); Vaclav Smil, *Energy Transitions: History, Requirements, Prospects* (Santa Barbara, CA: Praeger, 2010).

8 George Rogers Taylor, *The Transportation Revolution, 1815–1860* (New York: Rinehart, 1951), 132–33.

9 Cronon, *Nature's Metropolis,* chap. 2.

10 Hughes, *Networks of Power;* Paul N. Edwards, "Infrastructure and Modernity: Force, Time, and Social Organization in the History of Sociotechnical Systems," in *Modernity and Technology,* ed. Thomas J. Misa, Philip Brey, and Andrew Feenberg (Cambridge, MA: MIT Press, 2003); Arne Kaijser and Erik van der Vleuten, eds., *Networking Europe: Transnational Infrastructures and the Shaping of Europe, 1850–2000* (Sagamore Beach, MA: Science History Publications, 2006).

11 Sheila Jasanoff, *States of Knowledge: The Co-Production of Science and Social Order* (London; New York: Routledge, 2004); Merritt Roe Smith and Leo Marx, eds., *Does Technology Drive History?: The Dilemma of Technological Determinism* (Cambridge, MA: MIT Press, 1994).

12 This is similar to the "logic of capital" that animated the actions of many boosters in Chicago and its hinterlands during the nineteenth century. Cronon, *Nature's Metropolis*.

13 On the role of "agents of diffusion" in introducing new energy practices, see Mark H. Rose, *Cities of Light and Heat: Domesticating Gas and Electricity in Urban America* (University Park, PA: Penn State University Press, 1995).

14 On the politics of energy flows, see Timothy Mitchell, *Carbon Democracy: Political Power in the Age of Oil* (London: Verso, 2011).

15 Richard Bensel, *The Political Economy of American Industrialization, 1877–1900* (Cambridge: Cambridge University Press, 2000).

16 Carolyn Merchant, *The Death of Nature: Women, Ecology, and the Scientific Revolution* (San Francisco: Harper & Row, 1980); David E. Nye, *America as Second Creation: Technology and Narratives of New Beginnings* (Cambridge, MA: MIT Press, 2003).

17 John F. Kasson, *Civilizing the Machine: Technology and Republican Values in America, 1776–1900* (New York: Grossman Publishers, 1976); Daniel T. Rodgers, "Republicanism: The Career of a Concept," *Journal of American History* (1992); Thomas Jefferson, *Notes on the State of Virginia* (New York: Penguin, 1999 [1785]).

18 The phrase "sacrifice zone" first came into popular use following a 1988 *New York Times* article in which Department of Energy officials reportedly described nuclear laboratories in Superfund sites that were too expensive to clean up as "national sacrifice zones." Keith Schneider, "Dying Nuclear Plants Give Birth to New Problems," *The New York Times,* October 31, 1988. See also Steve Lerner, *Sacrifice Zones: The Front Lines of Toxic Chemcial Exposure in the United States* (Cambridge, MA: MIT Press, 2010). On the environmental impacts of separating sites of consumption and production, see William Cronon, "Kennecott Journey: The Paths out of Town," in *Under an Open Sky: Rethinking America's Western Past,* ed. William Cronon, George Miles, and Jay Gitlin (New York: W. W. Norton, 1992).

19 Economic historians describe this as path dependence. The historian of technology Thomas Hughes has analyzed this phenomenon as technological momentum. The environmental historian Donald Worster has suggested that technological systems can operate as an "infrastructure trap" that limits the ways societies think about addressing problems. Hughes, *Networks of Power;* Donald Worster, *Under Western Skies: Nature and History in the American West* (Oxford: Oxford University Press, 1992), chap. 4; Paul David, "Clio and the Economics of QWERTY," *The American Economic Review* 75, no. 2 (1985).

20 Different scholars have introduced a number of similar concepts to
describe the differences between societies with and without fossil fuel
energy: organic and mineral economies (E. A. Wrigley), the solar-agrarian
regime (Rolf Peter Sieferle), the somatic energy regime (John McNeill), and
the biological old regime (Robert Marks). Wrigley, *Continuity, Chance, and
Change;* Sieferle, *Subterranean Forest;* John Robert McNeill, *Something
New under the Sun: An Environmental History of the Twentieth-Century
World* (New York: W. W. Norton, 2000); Robert Marks, *The Origins of the
Modern World: A Global and Ecological Narrative* (Lanham, MD: Rowman
& Littlefield, 2002). This book furthers our understanding of organic and
mineral energy regimes in three ways. First, it provides a new explanation
for how the mineral energy regime was created by privileging the role of
transport systems. Second, it offers a detailed account of this transition in
America, which became the world's largest consumer of mineral energy
sources during this period. Third, it explores the contingent and uneven
nature of this shift. While the broad trend was a move away from the
organic energy regime, this did not happen everywhere at once. Certain
people and places experienced the mineral energy regime before others,
and the costs and benefits of new energy practices were highly unequal.
To the wide brushstrokes of changes in energy regimes, this book adds
finer-grained detail about how, when, where, for whom, and in what ways
this transition occurred.

21 Heat from decaying isotopes such as uranium and tidal energy from the
moon are the other main planetary energy sources. The decay of uranium
isotopes can be captured to provide nuclear energy, and it also generates
much of the heat in the center of the earth, thereby giving rise to geothermal energy. In historical terms, tidal and geothermal energy have been
used very rarely by human societies, and nuclear energy has only made a
meaningful contribution to human energy needs over the last fifty years.

22 Vaclav Smil calculates that people and animals provided over 98 percent of
the capacity of prime movers in world history before the intensive use of
fossil fuels, with waterwheels and windmills supplying only a small amount
of additional energy. Vaclav Smil, *Energy in World History* (Boulder, CO:
Westview Press, 1994), 230. Paul Warde calculates that wind and waterpower represented at most 1.5 percent of the total energy supply in
England and Wales circa 1600. Paul Warde, *Energy Consumption in
England and Wales, 1560–2000* (Consiglio Nazionale delle Ricerche
[CNR], Istituto di Studi sulle Società del Mediterraneo [ISSM], 2007),
60, 69.

23 There are great variations in the carrying capacity of land areas based on climate and how humans interact with their environments. For example, a hunter-gatherer society can require as much as 50,000 times more land per person to meet subsistence needs as compared with highly productive, multi-cropped Chinese rice production. Sieferle, *Subterranean Forest*, 19. Wrigley argues that between 1600 and 1800 English farmers greatly increased the output of croplands through the more intensive use of animals. Work animals increased the amount of labor at the disposal of workers (for example, making it practical to transport and use marl) and produced manure that increased yields. Wrigley describes this system as an "advanced organic economy." Wrigley, *Continuity, Chance, and Change*, chap. 2.

24 Sieferle, *Subterranean Forest*, 59. Even in contemporary timber operations, paved roads are a rarity because trees require so much land that it is not profitable to invest heavily in infrastructure for their transport.

25 E. A. Wrigley, "The Limits to Growth: Malthus and the Classical Economists," *Population and Development Review* 14 (1988): 30–48.

26 Sieferle, *Subterranean Forest*, 124–25.

27 Ibid., 45.

28 Over the course of industrialization in the nineteenth century, for example, Americans steadily increased their use of horses, and mechanized factories often demanded greater muscle power from workers. Ann Norton Greene, *Horses at Work: Harnessing Power in Industrial America* (Cambridge, MA: Harvard University Press, 2008); Dolores Greenberg, "Reassessing the Power Patterns of the Industrial Revolution: An Anglo-American Comparison," *American Historical Review* 87, no. 5 (1982): 1237–61.

29 Methodologically, it can be thought of as a middle-level (or "meso-level") analytical framework that connects microanalysis with macro trends. Thomas J. Misa, "Retrieving Sociotechnical Change from Technological Determinism," in *Does Technology Drive History?: The Dilemma of Technological Determinism*, ed. Leo Marx and Merritt Roe Smith (Cambridge, MA: MIT Press, 1994).

1 · Coal's Liquid Pathways

1 Donald L. Miller and Richard E. Sharpless, *The Kingdom of Coal: Work, Enterprise, and Ethnic Communities in the Mine Fields* (Philadelphia: University of Pennsylvania Press, 1985).

2 Martin V. Melosi, *Coping with Abundance: Energy and Environment in Industrial America* (New York: Knopf, 1985), 19.

3 Philadelphia's population was 28,522 in 1790, 41,220 in 1800, and 53,722 in 1810, according to the Census. Michael Knies, *Coal on the Lehigh, 1790–1827: Beginnings and Growth of the Anthracite Industry in Carbon County, Pennsylvania* (Easton, PA: Canal History and Technology Press, 2001), chap. 1; Howard Benjamin Powell, *Philadelphia's First Fuel Crisis: Jacob Cist and the Developing Market for Pennsylvania Anthracite* (University Park, PA: Penn State University Press, 1978), 9, 16, 24–25.

4 Thomas Cooper, "Statement on Coal" from early nineteenth century, as cited in Powell, *Philadelphia's First Fuel Crisis,* 1. On coal and British industrialization, see E. A. Wrigley, *Continuity, Chance and Change: The Character of the Industrial Revolution in England* (Cambridge: Cambridge University Press, 1988); Richard Wilkinson, "The English Industrial Revolution," in *Ends of the Earth,* ed. Donald Worster (Cambridge: Cambridge University Press, 1988); Robert C. Allen, *The British Industrial Revolution in Global Perspective* (Cambridge: Cambridge University Press, 2009).

5 George Rogers Taylor, *The Transportation Revolution, 1815–1860* (New York: Rinehart, 1951), 132–33.

6 Vaclav Smil, *Energy in Nature and Society: General Energetics of Complex Systems* (Cambridge, MA: MIT Press, 2008), 197–200; Miller and Sharpless, *Kingdom of Coal,* chap. 2.

7 *Comparative Calculations, and Remarks on Internal Improvements by Roads, Canal, and River Navigation; Illustrative of the Advantages to Be Derived from the Improvement of the River Lehigh* (Philadelphia: William Brown, printer, 1821), 7, 9.

8 Josiah White, "English Industry," *The Democratic Press,* March 20, 1821, as cited in Norris Hansell, *Josiah White: Quaker Entrepreneur* (Easton, PA: Canal History and Technology Press, 1992), 56.

9 Christof Mauch and Thomas Zeller, eds., *Rivers in History: Perspectives of Waterways in Europe and North America* (Pittsburgh: University of Pittsburgh Press, 2008); David Blackbourn, *The Conquest of Nature: Water, Landscape, and the Making of Modern Germany* (New York: W. W. Norton, 2007).

10 W. Bernard Carlson, "The Pennsylvania Society for the Promotion of Internal Improvements," *Proceedings of the Canal History and Technology Symposium* 7 (1988); Thomas Childs Cochran, "Early Industrialization in the Delaware and Susquehanna River Areas: A Regional Analysis," *Social*

Science History 1, no. 3 (1977): 291; William J. Duane, *Letters, Addressed to the People of Pennsylvania Respecting the Internal Improvement of the Commonwealth; by Means of Roads and Canals* (Philadelphia: Jane Aitken, printer, 1811); John Larson, *Internal Improvement: National Public Works and the Promise of Popular Government in the Early United States* (Chapel Hill: University of North Carolina Press, 2001).

11 United States Department of the Treasury, *Report of the Secretary of the Treasury, on the Subject of Public Roads and Canals* (Philadelphia: William Duane, 1808), 56; *Memorial of the Commissioners of the State of New York, in Behalf of Said State; Praying the Aid of the General Government in Opening a Communication between the Navigable Waters of Hudson River and the Lakes* (Washington, D.C.: William A. Davis, printer, 1816).

12 In 1800, most American observers assumed the bituminous coalfields near the James River were the most promising source of domestic coal. But while the James River could support small coal arks during certain parts of the year, it did not have the necessary depth to support large boats, and the shipping season was limited. The lack of canal development constrained the development of Virginia coal. Sean P. Adams, *Old Dominion, Industrial Commonwealth: Coal, Politics, and Economy in Antebellum America* (Baltimore: Johns Hopkins University Press, 2004).

13 Drew McCoy, *The Elusive Republic: Political Economy in Jeffersonian America* (New York: W. W. Norton, 1982); Larson, *Internal Improvement*.

14 *Memorial of the Commissioners of New York*, 8.

15 Canals drew a broad base of support from a wide variety of Americans. Those favoring the development of an industrial society, like Tench Coxe, as well as advocates of rural farmers, such as Thomas Jefferson, agreed that canals supported their view of a good society. Ronald E. Shaw, *Canals for a Nation: The Canal Era in the United States, 1790–1860* (Lexington: University Press of Kentucky, 1990), 19–29.

16 Carlson, "Pennsylvania Society for Internal Improvements."

17 Sources on the early history of coal in the Lehigh region include Knies, *Coal on the Lehigh;* Anthony Brzyski, "The Lehigh Canal and Its Economic Impact on the Region through Which It Passed, 1818–1873" (Ph.D. diss., New York University, 1957); Josiah White, *Josiah White's History, Given by Himself* (Philadelphia: Press of G. H. Buchanan Company, 1909); Chester Lloyd Jones, *The Economic History of the Anthracite-Tidewater Canals* (Philadelphia: University of Pennsylvania Press, 1908), chap. 1; Powell, *Philadelphia's First Fuel Crisis*.

18 Donald Sayenga, "The Untryed Business: An Appreciation of White and Hazard," *Proceedings of the Canal History and Technology Symposium* 2 (1983): 114.

19 A ton of coal offers the heating equivalent of at least 1.25 cords of wood. An acre of forest contains roughly 30 cords of wood if clearcut. Therefore, 250 million tons of coal offer the heating value of 312,500,000 cords of wood or more than 10 million acres of land. As there are 640 acres in a square mile, this is more than 16,000 square miles. New Jersey's area is 8,729 square miles. Forest wood yield estimate from Michael Williams, *Americans and Their Forests: A Historical Geography* (Cambridge: Cambridge University Press, 1989), 106.

20 Knies, *Coal on the Lehigh,* 12.

21 Their economic misfortunes were aggravated by the failure of the Lehigh Coal Mine Company but not caused by them. The general loss of trade to New York was a much bigger factor in the declining fortunes of the company's founders. Ibid., 13–16.

22 Powell, *Philadelphia's First Fuel Crisis,* 24. A bushel is a volumetric measure corresponding to about 80 pounds for coal. There are about 28 bushels in a long ton of 2,240 pounds, the usual weight for anthracite shipments. Knies, *Coal on the Lehigh,* 18.

23 Cist hoped to achieve costs of $7.50 per ton shipped along the river, but his actual expenses ended up being $10.50, 90 percent of which were transport-related ($1 for mining, $3 for hauling, $5.50 for arking, $1 for provisions for the boatmen). Powell, *Philadelphia's First Fuel Crisis,* 33.

24 Taylor, *Transportation Revolution,* 132–33.

25 John P. Miller, *The Lehigh Canal: A Thumbnail History* (Allentown, PA: printed for the Sesquicentennial of the Opening of the Lehigh Canal by Jibby Printing, 1979), 3; White, *Josiah White's History,* 15.

26 Powell, *Philadelphia's First Fuel Crisis,* chap. 3.

27 Richard Richardson, *Memoir of Josiah White. Showing His Connection with the Introduction and Use of Anthracite Coal and Iron, and the Construction of Some of the Canals and Railroads of Pennsylvania, Etc* (Philadelphia: J. B. Lippincott & Co., 1873), 23–24.

28 White, *Josiah White's History,* 12–13.

29 The men met at the house of Ebenezer Hazard, Erskine's father. Ebenezer Hazard was a postmaster general of the United States and hosted many gatherings of Quakers. Seven years younger than Josiah, Erskine shared his mechanical aptitude and business interests and also had the benefit of

formal education. Erskine attended Princeton and had published original scientific research on electricity in 1809. Erskine's brother Samuel was the editor of the widely circulated journal *Hazard's Register.*

30 These savings are described in a testimonial White and Hazard gave to Jacob Cist in November of 1814, in which White cited a cost of $17 per ton with anthracite compared with $52 per ton with bituminous. Testimonial cited in Hansell, *Josiah White,* 33. See also Powell, *Philadelphia's First Fuel Crisis,* 50–51.

31 White, *Josiah White's History,* 15; Ronald Filippelli, "The Schuylkill Navigation Company and Its Role in the Development of the Anthracite Coal Trade and Schuylkill County, 1815–1845" (M.A. thesis, Penn State University, 1966).

32 Miller, *Thumbnail History,* 6.

33 Knies, *Coal on the Lehigh,* 13, 31, 38.

34 White, *Josiah White's History,* 24–27, 42–45; Knies, *Coal on the Lehigh,* 38–40.

35 As John Majewski has shown, Pennsylvania farmers were large investors in transport improvements. These investments were driven more by a desire to improve the value of their land and their access to market, not because they expected the company to return dividends. John D. Majewski, *A House Dividing: Economic Development in Pennsylvania and Virginia before the Civil War* (Cambridge: Cambridge University Press, 2000), 13; Jones, *Economic History of the Anthracite Canals,* 127; Knies, *Coal on the Lehigh,* 39.

36 Knies, *Coal on the Lehigh,* 40–41; Eleanor Morton, *Josiah White, Prince of Pioneers* (New York: Stephen Daye Press, 1946), 118.

37 *History of the Lehigh Coal and Navigation Company, Published by Order of the Board of Managers* (Philadelphia: William S. Young, 1840), 10; White, *Josiah White's History,* 36.

38 White, *Josiah White's History,* 35.

39 Knies, *Coal on the Lehigh,* 53.

40 Richardson, *Memoir of Josiah White,* 58.

41 White, *Josiah White's History,* 28.

42 As cited in Miller and Sharpless, *Kingdom of Coal,* 27.

43 Peter Way, *Common Labour: Workers and the Digging of North American Canals, 1780–1860* (Cambridge: Cambridge University Press, 1993), 10, 132.

44 James Weston Livingood, *The Philadelphia-Baltimore Trade Rivalry, 1780–1860* (Harrisburg: Pennsylvania Historical and Museum Commission, 1947).

45 William Cronon, *Nature's Metropolis: Chicago and the Great West* (New York: W. W. Norton, 1991).

46 Jones, *Economic History of the Anthracite Canals*, 99; John Majewski, "Toward a Social History of the Corporation: Shareholding in Pennsylvania, 1800–1840," in *The Economy of Early America: Historical Perspectives & New Directions*, ed. Cathy Matson (University Park, PA: Penn State University Press, 2006).

47 Jones, *Economic History of the Anthracite Canals*, 127.

48 Filippelli, "Schuylkill Navigation Company," 34.

49 Jones, *Economic History of the Anthracite Canals*, 127–28.

50 Thomas Dublin and Walter Licht, *The Face of Decline: The Pennsylvania Anthracite Region in the Twentieth Century* (Ithaca, NY: Cornell University Press, 2005), 13.

51 Jones, *Economic History of the Anthracite Canals*, 149, 151.

52 *History of the Lehigh Coal and Navigation Company*, 11.

53 White, *Josiah White's History*, 49.

54 R. C. Taylor, *Statistics of Coal* (Philadelphia: J. W. Moore, 1855), 455.

55 "Coal and Wood," *Hazard's Register*, October 10, 1829; "Anthracite Coal, Versus Wood," *Hazard's Register*, November 15, 1834. The Fuel Savings Society was a philanthropic organization helping poor people offset the high costs of wood during the winter. "Fuel Savings Society," *Hazard's Register*, August 20, 1831. According to the 1860 Census, the average number of persons per dwelling was 5.98 in 1850 and 5.64 in 1860. United States Bureau of the Census, *Census of Population, 1860* (Washington, D.C.: Government Printing Office, 1862), xxvii.

56 *Comparative Calculations on Internal Improvements*, 11.

57 Sean P. Adams, "Warming the Poor and Growing Consumers: Fuel Philanthropy in the Early Republic's Urban North," *Journal of American History* 95, no. 1 (2008): 69; "Exposition," *Miners' Journal*, April 2, 1831.

58 "The Economy of Heat," *Hazard's Register*, February 23, 1833; *Comparative Calculations on Internal Improvements*, 11.

59 Robert Roberts, *The House Servant's Directory: Or a Monitor for Private Families . . .* (Boston: Munroe and Francis, 1827), 159–73.

60 Knies, *Coal on the Lehigh*, 52.

61 Marcus Bull, *Experiments to Determine the Comparative Value of the Principal Varieties of Fuel Used in the United States, and Also in Europe and on the Ordinary Apparatus Used for Their Combustion* (Philadelphia: Judah Dobson, 1827). In addition to being a scientist, Bull was also an officer of the North American Coal Company, active in the Schuylkill region.

62 "Fuel Savings Society," *Hazard's Register,* August 20, 1831.

63 Priscilla J. Brewer, *From Fireplace to Cookstove: Technology and the Domestic Ideal in America* (Syracuse, NY: Syracuse University Press, 2000), 64; Howell Harris, "Inventing the U.S. Stove Industry, c. 1815–1875: Making and Selling the First Universal Consumer Durable," *Business History Review* 82, no. 4 (2008).

64 On the simplifying of the natural world to suit the needs of commerce, see Cronon, *Nature's Metropolis,* chap. 3–5.

65 Richard G. Healey, *The Pennsylvania Anthracite Coal Industry, 1860–1902: Economic Cycles, Business Decision-Making and Regional Dynamics* (Scranton, PA: University of Scranton Press, 2007), 36–40. These various differences suggest several reasons why early anthracite pioneers may have had difficulty getting the coal to burn. If the coal was exposed to the elements, broken into different-size pieces, or taken from the northwest edge, this may have explained why it was tossed into the streets. The fact that some of the coal in the Wyoming field had a higher percentage of volatile gases, and was easier to burn, also helps explain why anthracite use in the eighteenth century was more common in that region.

66 The totals were 34,893 in 1825, 174,734 in 1830, and 560,758 in 1835. *Statistics of the Coal Trade of the United States, Moved toward the Seaboard, for 1866* (Pottsville, PA: Miners' Journal Office, 1867), Insert: "Anthracite Coal Trade of the United States."

67 Anthracite was selling at $6.50 per ton wholesale in Philadelphia during these years, meaning that a maximum of 47,446 tons of coal were sold in the marketplace. Since most coal was not purchased wholesale and there were likely a few thousand tons of imported bituminous included in this total, I estimate that these sales represented approximately 35,000 tons of anthracite. If we assume 20,000 tons were used for home heating and the remainder by businesses, this gives us an adoption rate of roughly 10 percent (assuming one ton of coal per person or six per family), as the population of Philadelphia City and County was 188,797 in 1830. Coal sales information from "Report of the Committee of the Senate of Pennsylvania Upon the Subject of the Coal Trade" (Harrisburg, PA: Henry Welsh, 1834), 43.

68 Frederick Moore Binder, *Coal Age Empire: Pennsylvania Coal and Its Utilization to 1860* (Harrisburg, PA: Commonwealth of Pennsylvania, Pennsylvania Historical and Museum Commission, 1974), 17.

69 "Coal Trade," *Hazard's Register,* March 7, 1835; "Fuel," *Hazard's Register,* May 4, 1833.

70 "The Coal Trade," *Hazard's Register,* February 23, 1833.

71 "Lowell Factories," *Niles Weekly Register,* November 8, 1833.

72 "Anthracite Coal," *Hazard's Register,* December 24, 1831.

73 Jeremy Atack, Fred Bateman, and Thomas Weiss, "The Regional Diffusion and Adoption of the Steam Engine in American Manufacturing," *Journal of Economic History* 40, no. 2 (1980): 282. The authors document the presence of 43 American steam engines in 1820.

74 Binder, *Coal Age Empire,* 50.

75 "Anthracite Coal Trade of the United States," *Hazard's Register,* July 16, 1831.

76 "To the Editor of the NY Post," *Miners' Journal,* February 5, 1831.

77 Secretary of the Treasury, *Report on Steam Engines* (Washington, D.C.: Thomas Allen, printer, 1838), 156–67, 379.

78 Miller and Sharpless, *Kingdom of Coal.*

79 *Comparative Calculations on Internal Improvements,* 10.

80 Knies, *Coal on the Lehigh,* 58–60; William H. Shank, *The Amazing Pennsylvania Canals* (York, PA: American Canal & Transportation Center, 1973), 63; Jones, *Economic History of the Anthracite Canals,* 29.

81 White, *Josiah White's History,* 51; Knies, *Coal on the Lehigh,* 51; Jones, *Economic History of the Anthracite Canals,* 17.

82 Lehigh Coal and Navigation Company, *Report of the Engineers of the Lehigh Coal & Navigation Company, Who Were Appointed, on the Nineteenth Instant, a Committee on the Subject of an Expose of the Property of the Company* (Philadelphia: S. W. Conrad, 1826), 5.

83 By 1862, the Reading Railroad's shipments exceeded this number, and the Lehigh Valley Railroad was shipping more than three million tons by 1870. Miners' Journal, *Coal Statistical Register for 1870* (Pottsville, PA: Miners' Journal Office, 1870), Insert: "Anthracite Coal Trade of the United States."

84 Miller and Sharpless, *Kingdom of Coal,* 36.

85 Jones, *Economic History of the Anthracite Canals,* 76–78.

86 Ibid., 109–12.

87 Shaw, *Canals for a Nation,* 94–97.

88 Jones, *Economic History of the Anthracite Canals,* chap. 2; Shaw, *Canals for a Nation,* chap. 3.

89 On the experience of coal boat operators, see Miller and Sharpless, *Kingdom of Coal,* chap. 2.

90 "Report of the Senate Upon the Coal Trade," 31.

2 · The Anthracite Energy Transition

1 Brooke Hindle and Steven Lubar, *Engines of Change: The American Industrial Revolution, 1790–1860* (Washington, D.C.: Smithsonian Institution Press, 1986), chap. 15.

2 Total anthracite shipments increased geometrically: 365 tons in 1820; 174,734 in 1830; 826,079 in 1840; 3,230,286 in 1850; 8,034,007 in 1860. This data includes shipments on all carriers (canals and railroads) operating in the Schuylkill, Lehigh, and Wyoming Valleys. Small amounts of additional anthracite coal were shipped by canals and railroads from the Pinegrove, Little Schuylkill, and Shamokin regions but are not included in the totals. *Statistics of the Coal Trade of the United States, Moved toward the Seaboard, for 1866* (Pottsville, PA: Miners' Journal Office, 1867), Insert: "Anthracite Coal Trade of the United States." The population of the region and nation roughly tripled during this period. United States Bureau of the Census, *Historical Statistics of the United States, Colonial Times to 1970* (Washington, D.C.: Government Printing Office, 1975), part 1: 8, 32, 33.

3 Christopher F. Jones, "The Carbon-Consuming Home: Residential Markets and Energy Transitions," *Enterprise & Society* 12, no. 4 (2011).

4 R. C. Taylor, *Statistics of Coal* (Philadelphia: J. W. Moore, 1855), 455.

5 Firewood consistently sold at prices that were much higher than anthracite coal per heating value. In 1815, Jacob Cist argued that the average winter price of cordwood in Philadelphia was $7.00 per cord. In 1835, the Fuel Savings Society was selling wood at a discount cost of $4.40 per cord to Philadelphia's poor, which was considered half of the market price. Sean P. Adams, "Warming the Poor and Growing Consumers: Fuel Philanthropy in the Early Republic's Urban North," *Journal of American History* 95, no. 1 (2008): 80–81. Moreover, assuming that firewood prices followed the general trajectory of the lumber market, there is clear evidence that coal steadily became more cost-competitive than firewood. Between 1820 and 1860, the price of coal fell dramatically, from an index price of 100 to 42, a nearly 60 percent drop. Lumber markets, by contrast, fell only 10 percent during the same time period. White pine went from an index price of 91 to 81 and wooden staves for barrels went from 120 to 109. As the price of anthracite in 1820 ($8.20 per ton) was competitive with other heating materials, over the course of the antebellum period coal gained a steady comparative advantage as its relative price to consumers fell much faster

than wood. Anne Bezanson, Robert Davis Gray, and Miriam Hussey, *Wholesale Prices in Philadelphia, 1784–1861* (Philadelphia: University of Pennsylvania Press, 1936), 2:37, 167, 212.

6 Adams, "Warming the Poor," 81–88; Priscilla J. Brewer, *From Fireplace to Cookstove: Technology and the Domestic Ideal in America* (Syracuse, NY: Syracuse University Press, 2000), 98; Howell Harris, "Inventing the U.S. Stove Industry, C. 1815–1875: Making and Selling the First Universal Consumer Durable," *Business History Review* 82, no. 4 (2008).

7 George Derby, *An Inquiry into the Influence Upon Health of Anthracite Coal When Used as Fuel for Warming Dwelling-Houses* (Boston: A. Williams and Co., 1868), 6.

8 In 1860, Philadelphians likely consumed 1,134,000 tons of coal in addition to the amounts that were sent elsewhere. Richard G. Healey, *The Pennsylvania Anthracite Coal Industry, 1860–1902: Economic Cycles, Business Decision-Making and Regional Dynamics* (Scranton, PA: University of Scranton Press, 2007), 71.

9 Frederick Moore Binder, *Coal Age Empire: Pennsylvania Coal and Its Utilization to 1860* (Harrisburg, PA: Commonwealth of Pennsylvania, Pennsylvania Historical and Museum Commission, 1974), chap. 1; Derby, *Health of Anthracite Coal;* "The Coal Trade of 1855," *Miners' Journal,* January 12, 1856; "The Coal Trade," *Hazard's Register,* February 23, 1833.

10 Anecdotal evidence confirming that anthracite fires kept houses warmer is found in several testimonial letters. See, for instance, "Anthracite Coal, Versus Wood," *Hazard's Register,* November 15, 1834.

11 Ruth Schwartz Cowan, *More Work for Mother: The Ironies of Household Technology from the Open Hearth to the Microwave* (New York: Basic Books, 1983), 61.

12 Under good conditions in the nineteenth century, an acre of land could produce 30 cords of wood if clear-cut and would take 20 years to regrow. With poor soil or indifferent forestry practices, the yield would likely be lower. Thus, an estimate of 1.5 cords of wood per acre, or two-thirds an acre for one cord of wood is, if anything, an optimistic estimate. Michael Williams, *Americans and Their Forests: A Historical Geography* (Cambridge: Cambridge University Press, 1989), 106.

13 In 1839, 84 percent of the 54,000 newly constructed houses were made out of wood. Ibid., 147.

14 New York City grew even more quickly during this period, with 942,292 people in 1870, 1,206,299 in 1880, and 1,515,301 in 1890.

15 Diane Lindstrom, *Economic Development in the Philadelphia Region, 1810–1850* (New York: Columbia University Press, 1978), 48, footnote 101.

16 Healey, *Pennsylvania Anthracite Coal Industry,* 68.

17 Testimony of George Smith, John Morgan, and Daniel Colkglaser in Lehigh Coal & Navigation Company, *Facts Illustrative of the Character of the Anthracite, or Lehigh Coal, Found in the Great Mines at Mauch Chunk, in Possession of the Lehigh Coal and Navigation Company with Certificates from Various Manufacturers, and Others, Proving Its Decided Superiority over Every Other Kind of Fuel* (New York: Gray & Bunce, 1825), 5–6.

18 Ibid., 18.

19 Secretary of the Treasury, *Report on Steam Engines* (Washington, D.C.: Thomas Allen, printer, 1838), 379.

20 Philadelphia Committee on United States Census 1870, *Manufactures of the City of Philadelphia. Census of 1870* (Philadelphia: King & Baird, 1872), 27. By the 1890s, Atack, Bateman, and Weiss argue fuel consumption of steam engines had declined to two pounds per horsepower-hour. In 1870, it was most likely around three pounds. If the engines operated twelve hours a day, six days a week, the fuel consumption would be 278,969 tons ($6 \times 12 \times 5 \ 2 \times (3/2000) \times 49{,}674$). Jeremy Atack, Fred Bateman, and Thomas Weiss, "The Regional Diffusion and Adoption of the Steam Engine in American Manufacturing," *Journal of Economic History* 40, no. 2 (1980), 295.

21 Secretary of the Treasury, *Report on Steam Engines,* 156–57.

22 Oliver Evans, *The Abortion of the Young Steam Engineer's Guide* (Philadelphia: Fry and Kammerer, printer, 1805), 1.

23 Leo Marx, *The Machine in the Garden; Technology and the Pastoral Ideal in America* (New York: Oxford University Press, 1964); John F. Kasson, *Civilizing the Machine: Technology and Republican Values in America, 1776–1900* (New York: Grossman Publishers, 1976).

24 D. W. Meinig, *The Shaping of America: A Geographical Perspective on 500 Years of History,* vol. 2, *Continental America, 1800–67* (New Haven: Yale University Press, 1986), 397.

25 Vaclav Smil, *Energy in World History* (Boulder, CO: Westview Press, 1994), 161.

26 In 1840, there were 12 steam engines with a combined rating of 364 horsepower; 165 at 4,753 horsepower in 1850, and 320 at 18,500 by 1865. The Schuylkill Valley produced about 43 percent of the region's anthracite in 1865. *Eighth Annual Report Made by the Board of Trade to the Coal Mining Association of Schuylkill County* (Pottsville, PA: Benjamin Bannan, 1840); "Steam Engines in This Region," *Miners' Journal,* January 5, 1850; Samuel

Harries Daddow and Benjamin Bannan, *Coal, Iron, and Oil, or, the Practical American Miner: A Plain and Popular Work on Our Mines and Mineral Resources, and a Text-Book or Guide to Their Economical Development* (Pottsville, PA: Benjamin Bannan, 1866), 726.

27 Binder, *Coal Age Empire*, 86, 91; "Pine Lands of New Jersey," *Hazard's Register,* July 25, 1829.

28 Binder, *Coal Age Empire*, 90–93.

29 *Thirteenth Annual Report, Made by the Board of Trade, to the Coal Mining Association of Schuylkill County* (Pottsville, PA: Benjamin Bannan, 1845), 8–9; Binder, *Coal Age Empire*, 90, 92, 104–5; Secretary of the Navy, "In Compliance with a Resolution of the Senate, a Report of the Engineer-in-Chief of the Navy, on the Comparative Value of Anthracite and Bituminous Coals" (Washington, D.C., 1852), 5.

30 Binder, *Coal Age Empire*, 111. Three years earlier, the *Stourbridge Lion,* the first locomotive engine brought to the United States by the Delaware & Hudson Canal Company, also burned anthracite. However, the engine was too heavy for its tracks and only made a single journey. Hudson Coal Company, *The Story of Anthracite* (New York: Hudson Coal Company, 1932), 90.

31 The Reading Railroad in 1855 typically hauled trains weighing 740 tons at a speed of ten to twelve miles an hour; mules typically walked at about three miles an hour. G. A. Nicolls, "Anthracite Coal in Locomotives," *Miners' Journal,* January 27, 1855; John Nathan Hoffman, *Anthracite in the Lehigh Region of Pennsylvania, 1820–45* (Washington, D.C.: Smithsonian Institution Press, 1968), 112; "Coke and Anthracite for Locomotives," *Miners' Journal,* May 25, 1850.

32 Binder, *Coal Age Empire*, 96.

33 Wolfgang Schivelbusch, *The Railway Journey: The Industrialization of Time and Space in the 19th Century* (Berkeley: University of California Press, 1986).

34 Craig L. Bartholomew, Lance E. Metz, and Ann M. Bartholomew, *The Anthracite Iron Industry of the Lehigh Valley* (Easton, PA: Center for Canal History and Technology, 1988), 6.

35 Sieferle argues that there is a production limit of 2,000 tons of iron annually for a charcoal forge based on the limits of charcoal transport. Rolf Peter Sieferle, *The Subterranean Forest: Energy Systems and the Industrial Revolution* (Cambridge: White Horse Press, 2001), 64.

36 Thomas Childs Cochran, *Frontiers of Change: Early Industrialism in America* (New York: Oxford University Press, 1981), 93; Bartholomew, Metz, and Bartholomew, *Anthracite Iron Industry,* 21–27.

37 Binder, *Coal Age Empire*, 65; Bartholomew, Metz, and Bartholomew, *Anthracite Iron Industry*.

38 Anthracite iron production was 151,331 tons in 1847 and 519,211 in 1860; charcoal iron production was 219,674 in 1847 and 278,331 in 1860. Bartholomew, Metz, and Bartholomew, *Anthracite Iron Industry*, 52–53; Sam H. Schurr and Bruce Carlton Netschert, *Energy in the American Economy, 1850–1975: An Economic Study of Its History and Prospects* (Baltimore: Johns Hopkins Press, 1960), 66; *Proceedings of the American Iron and Steel Association at Philadelphia, Nov. 20, 1873* (Philadelphia: Chandler, 1873), 51.

39 Philadelphia Convention of Iron Masters, *Documents Relating to the Manufacture of Iron in Pennsylvania* (Philadelphia, 1850), 96.

40 I estimate total anthracite consumption in the iron industry in 1860 to have been approximately 1,715,000 tons. Total anthracite shipments that year were 7,808,255 tons. This estimate is based on 1,040,000 tons of anthracite to manufacture 519,211 tons of iron plus an additional 65 percent used to transform that iron into other products. Three points of data give credibility to the estimate of 65 percent additional consumption. First, in 1847 there was a total production of 151,331 tons of iron, and the entire industry was reported to have consumed 483,000 tons of anthracite. If roughly 300,000 tons were used to produce the iron, that leaves about 180,000 tons used in secondary processing, or an additional 60 percent. Second, in 1855 total iron production was 381,866 tons. Assuming that about half of this was made in the Lehigh and Schuylkill Valleys (190,000 tons), this would have required 380,000 tons of coal. Based on analysis of canal shipments, the regions consumed about 639,825 tons of coal in iron production, leaving a balance of 259,825 tons, or 68 percent more. Finally, in 1860 total iron production was 519,211 tons, with an estimated 260,000 produced in the Schuylkill and Lehigh regions. About 885,000 tons of coal were consumed in the region, which leaves a balance of about 365,000 tons of coal used in secondary iron operations, or 70 percent more than in iron production. Bartholomew, Metz, and Bartholomew, *Anthracite Iron Industry*, 52–53; *Proceedings of the Iron and Steel Association*, 51; Daddow and Bannan, *Coal, Iron, and Oil*, 698; "Henry Clay in Philadelphia," *Miners' Journal*, August 10, 1850; C. G. Childs, *The Coal and Iron Trade, Embracing Statistics of Pennsylvania* (Philadelphia: C. G. Childs, 1847), 24; Miners' Journal, *Coal Statistical Register for 1870* (Pottsville, PA: Miners' Journal Office, 1870).

41 Industry estimates at the time suggested that two tons of charcoal were needed to produce a ton of iron. Eight tons of wood were required to produce two tons of charcoal, because as much as 60 percent of the energy of the wood was lost as it was transformed into charcoal. Eight tons of wood are equivalent to 6.4 cords. In 1860, producing 519,211 tons of iron therefore would have required 3,322,950 cords of wood plus an additional 65 percent for secondary processing (2,159,918), for a total of 5,482,868 cords. With a sustainable yield of 1.5 cords per acre, this would have totaled 3,655,245 acres, or 5,711 square miles. In 1886, anthracite iron production was 2,099,597 tons; that year, an additional 459,557 tons of iron were produced with charcoal and 3,806,174 were produced with bituminous coal and coke. Pennsylvania's area is a little more than 46,000 square miles. Schurr and Netschert, *Energy in the American Economy,* 52, 66; Smil, *Energy in World History,* 117; Bartholomew, Metz, and Bartholomew, *Anthracite Iron Industry,* 53.

42 In 1847, the average charcoal furnace produced 730 tons while the average anthracite furnace produced 3,783 tons; by 1864, 90 anthracite furnaces produced 684,519 tons of iron, an average of more than 7,500 tons per enterprise. Daddow and Bannan, *Coal, Iron, and Oil,* 698; Bartholomew, Metz, and Bartholomew, *Anthracite Iron Industry,* 52–53; Childs, *Coal and Iron Trade,* 23.

43 The industry was concentrated into five distinct regions, each connected to one of the anthracite canals. The Lehigh Valley was the clear leader, with several of the largest iron furnaces. The Schuylkill Valley had many iron furnaces, particularly in Reading, Phoenixville, and the towns just outside of Philadelphia. The lower Susquehanna River area included furnaces in Harrisburg and Lancaster County. The upper Susquehanna River area included the iron furnaces of Wilkes-Barre and Scranton. The eastern region included the iron production of New Jersey and New York, most of which occurred along the Hudson River and Morris Canal. Daddow and Bannan, *Coal, Iron, and Oil,* 698; Richard Healey and Anne Knowles, "Geography, Timing, and Technology: A GIS-Based Analysis of Pennsylvania's Iron Industry, 1825–1875," *Journal of Economic History* 66, no. 3 (2006); Donald L. Miller and Richard E. Sharpless, *The Kingdom of Coal: Work, Enterprise, and Ethnic Communities in the Mine Fields* (Philadelphia: University of Pennsylvania Press, 1985), 64; *Proceedings of the Iron and Steel Association,* 49.

44 Total iron production in the Lehigh Valley in 1864 was 214,093 tons, while consuming 486,105 tons of anthracite. Daddow and Bannan, *Coal, Iron,*

and Oil, 698. Area information from Lehigh Valley Convention and Visitor's Bureau Home Page: http://www.lehighvalleypa.org/ [accessed September 18, 2008].

45 Anthony Brzyski, "The Lehigh Canal and Its Economic Impact on the Region through Which It Passed, 1818–1873," (Ph.D. diss., New York University, 1957), 711–22.

46 This tension between the interests of miners and transport companies gave rise to a significant fight between independent miners in the Schuylkill Valley and the Reading Railroad. The efforts by miners to restrict output, argues Yearley, led the Reading Railroad to enter the business of coal production. Clifton K. Yearley, *Enterprise and Anthracite: Economics and Democracy in Schuylkill County, 1820–1875* (Baltimore: Johns Hopkins Press, 1961), chap. 6.

47 "Report of the Committee of the Senate of Pennsylvania Upon the Subject of the Coal Trade" (Harrisburg, PA: Henry Welsh, 1834), 52, 61, 65, 56, 112.

48 Chester Lloyd Jones, *The Economic History of the Anthracite-Tidewater Canals* (Philadelphia: University of Pennsylvania Press, 1908), 63–65, 82–83, 113–15, 31–39.

49 For more information on the battle between the railroad and canal, see Miller and Sharpless, *Kingdom of Coal;* Jules Irwin Bogen, *The Anthracite Railroads: A Study in American Railroad Enterprise* (New York: The Ronald Press Company, 1927); Jones, *Economic History of the Anthracite-Tidewater Canals;* Yearley, *Enterprise and Anthracite.*

50 Ann M. Bartholomew and Lance E. Metz, *Delaware and Lehigh Canals* (Easton, PA: Center for Canal History and Technology, 1989), 142; Hudson Coal Company, *Story of Anthracite,* 99; Brzyski, "Lehigh Canal and Its Economic Impact," 594.

51 Jones, *Economic History of the Anthracite-Tidewater Canals;* Bogen, *Anthracite Railroads.*

52 Philadelphia and New York consumed more than half of the shipments of anthracite along the major carriers in 1855 and 1860. In 1855, they consumed 3,459,000 of the 6,374,179 tons shipped (54 percent) and in 1860, these two cities combined to absorb 4,789,000 out of 8,034,007 tons shipped (60 percent). Healey, *Pennsylvania Anthracite Coal Industry,* 71.

53 Ronald Filippelli, "The Schuylkill Navigation Company and Its Role in the Development of the Anthracite Coal Trade and Schuylkill County, 1815–1845" (M.A. thesis, Penn State University, 1966), 63; Miller and Sharpless, *Kingdom of Coal:* 46–50; Yearley, *Enterprise and Anthracite,* 31.

54 Burton W. Folsom, *Urban Capitalists: Entrepreneurs and City Growth in Pennsylvania's Lackawanna and Lehigh Regions, 1800–1920* (Scranton, PA: University of Scranton Press, 2001 [1981]).

55 Miners' Journal, *Coal Statistical Register for 1870;* Lehigh Coal & Navigation Company, *Report of the Board of Managers of the Lehigh Coal and Navigation Company, Presented to the Stockholders* (Philadelphia, 1828–1859).

56 Miners' Journal, *Coal Statistical Register for 1870.*

57 This estimate was a widely used metric in the British coal industry. E. A. Wrigley, *Continuity, Chance and Change: The Character of the Industrial Revolution in England* (Cambridge: Cambridge University Press, 1988), 56.

58 Lindstrom, *Economic Development in the Philadelphia Region,* 58.

59 Howard Benjamin Powell, *Philadelphia's First Fuel Crisis: Jacob Cist and the Developing Market for Pennsylvania Anthracite* (University Park, PA: Penn State University Press, 1978), 190; Binder, *Coal Age Empire,* 150.

60 Untitled article, *Miners' Journal,* April 9, 1831; "Rhode Island Manufactures," *Niles Weekly Register,* February 27, 1832; "Lowell Factories," *Niles Weekly Register,* November 8, 1834; Louis Hunter, *A History of Industrial Power in the United States, 1780–1930: Steam Power* (Charlottesville: University of Virginia Press, 1985), 416.

61 Of the 1,471,231 tons exported from Port Richmond, 770,006 went to New England, 594,537 to the mid-Atlantic, 89,456 to the South and West, and 17,232 to foreign ports (mostly in the Caribbean). "Coal Trade," *Miners' Journal,* December 29, 1855.

62 On regional differentiations during industrialization, see Walter Licht, *Industrializing America: The Nineteenth Century* (Baltimore: Johns Hopkins University Press, 1995).

63 Richard C. Taylor, *Establishment of an American Coal Trade with Europe* (Philadelphia, 1843).

64 Lindstrom, *Economic Development in the Philadelphia Region,* chap. 6.

65 The anthracite and iron industries faced decline, as did all businesses, during such episodes as the Panic of 1837, the general slow trade of the 1840s, and the depression in 1857. Anthracite iron manufacturers also experienced hard times when the United States temporarily removed its protective barriers on iron in the late 1840s.

66 Miller and Sharpless, *Kingdom of Coal,* 48; Yearley, *Enterprise and Anthracite,* chap. 1.

67 Thomas Dublin and Walter Licht, *The Face of Decline: The Pennsylvania Anthracite Region in the Twentieth Century* (Ithaca, NY: Cornell University

Press, 2005), chap. 8; Miller and Sharpless, *Kingdom of Coal,* Introduction, chap. 4.

68 Anthony Wallace, "The Perception of Risk in Nineteenth Century Anthracite Mining Operations," *Proceedings of the American Philosophical Society* 127, no. 2 (1983): 99.

69 Philadelphia had 99,003 industrial workers and a population of 565,529. New York had 102,969 workers with a population of 813,669. Meinig, *Shaping of America,* 2:384.

70 Only nine American cities had a population of greater than 100,000 people in 1860. John Andriot, *Population Abstract of the United States* (McLean, VA: Andriot Associates, 1980).

71 Cochran, *Frontiers of Change,* 112.

72 Licht, *Industrializing America,* chap. 1.

73 John McNeill notes that slavery was common in preindustrial times: "Slavery was the most efficient means by which the ambitious and powerful could become richer and more powerful. It was the answer to energy shortage. Slavery was widespread within the somatic energy regime, notably in those societies short on draft animals. They had no practical options for concentrating energy other than amassing human bodies." John Robert McNeill, *Something New under the Sun: An Environmental History of the Twentieth-Century World* (New York: W. W. Norton, 2000), 10–16. See also Robert Marks, *The Origins of the Modern World: A Global and Ecological Narrative* (Lanham, MD: Rowman & Littlefield, 2002), 56–57; Jean-Francois Mouhot, "Past Connections and Present Similarities in Slave Ownership and Fossil Fuel Usage," *Climatic Change* 105 (2011): 329–55.

74 The idea of energy slaves was introduced at least as early as 1880 by Emile Levasseur, a French demographer and economist. Wrigley, *Continuity, Chance, and Change,* 76. See also McNeill, *Something New under the Sun,* 15–16; Mohout, "Past Connections and Present Similarities."

75 After Pennsylvania (383), Louisiana (274) had more steam engines than any other state in the union at this date, with many more in states like Georgia (40) and South Carolina (40). Secretary of the Treasury, *Report on Steam Engines,* 379.

3 · Pennsylvania's Petroleum Boom

1 For details on Drake's discovery, see Daniel Yergin, *The Prize: The Epic Quest for Oil, Money, and Power* (New York: Simon & Schuster, 1991), 26–28. On the early history of the oil industry, see also Harold Francis

Williamson and Arnold Daum, *The American Petroleum Industry*, vol. 1, *The Age of Illumination 1859–1899* (Westport, CT: Greenwood Press, 1959); Brian Black, *Petrolia: The Landscape of America's First Oil Boom* (Baltimore: Johns Hopkins University Press, 2000); Paul Lucier, *Scientists & Swindlers: Consulting on Coal and Oil in America, 1820–1890* (Baltimore: Johns Hopkins University Press, 2008).

2 George Foster, *New York by Gas-Light* (New York: Dewitt & Davenport, 1850); A. Roger Ekirch, *At Day's Close: Night in Times Past* (New York: W. W. Norton, 2005); Wolfgang Schivelbusch, *Disenchanted Night: The Industrialization of Light in the Nineteenth Century* (Berkeley: University of California Press, 1988).

3 Richard Wolfson, *Energy, Environment, and Climate* (New York: W. W. Norton, 2008), 107.

4 Yergin, *The Prize*, 23–25.

5 Samuel Morton Peto, *The Resources and Prospects of America: Ascertained During a Visit to the States in the Autumn of 1865* (London: Alexander Strahan, 1866), 191.

6 Henry Erni, *Coal Oil and Petroleum: Their Origin, History, Geology, and Chemistry* (Philadelphia: H. C. Baird, 1865), 94–95.

7 Black, *Petrolia*, 23.

8 S. J. M. Eaton, *Petroleum: A History of the Oil Region of Venango County Pennsylvania* (Philadelphia: J. P. Skelley, 1866), 57.

9 Erni, *Coal Oil and Petroleum*, 65.

10 Christopher J. Castaneda, *Invisible Fuel: Manufactured and Natural Gas in America, 1800–2000* (New York: Twayne Publishers, 1999), 34.

11 Walter Sheldon Tower, *A History of the American Whale Fishery* (Philadelphia: University of Pennsylvania Press, 1907), 52.

12 Williamson and Daum, *American Petroleum Industry*, 1:56–58.

13 Yergin, *The Prize*, 19–20.

14 Benjamin Silliman, *Report on the Rock Oil, or Petroleum, from Venango Co., Pennsylvania: With Special Reference to Its Use for Illumination and Other Purposes* (New Haven: J. H. Benham, 1855), 17.

15 Yergin, *The Prize*, 26–28.

16 Ibid., chap. 1.

17 Ibid.

18 Eaton, *Petroleum*, 71.

19 Although most of the people in the oil business were men, nearly as many women came to the region as well. They were primarily employed in

activities that supported oil production, such as jobs in restaurants, hotels, and stores. Black, *Petrolia,* 117.

20 Yergin, *The Prize,* 30.

21 Eaton, *Petroleum,* 275.

22 Yergin, *The Prize,* 29.

23 Peto, *Resources and Prospects of America,* 203.

24 While merchants had shipped small amounts of oil for use in patent medicines before 1859, the scale of the trade was so small that it gave little incentive to invest in improved transport facilities.

25 Williamson and Daum, *American Petroleum Industry,* 1:185.

26 Ida M. Tarbell, *The History of the Standard Oil Company* (New York: McClure, Phillips & Co., 1904), 1:14.

27 The temporary dams provided a function similar to White's "bear-lock" gates discussed in Chapter 1.

28 Eaton, *Petroleum,* 165.

29 Arthur Menzies Johnson, "The Development of American Petroleum Pipelines: A Study in Private Enterprise and Public Policy, 1862–1906" (Ph.D diss., Vanderbilt University, published for the American Historical Association by Cornell University Press, 1956), 3.

30 Williamson and Daum, *American Petroleum Industry,* 1:168.

31 Eaton, *Petroleum,* 323.

32 Williamson and Daum, *American Petroleum Industry,* 1:107.

33 For instance, of the more than two million barrels produced in 1861, about 94,000 reached Pittsburgh by pond freshet, 135,000 reached the Sunbury & Erie railroad, and the Atlantic & Great Western railroad shipped 70,000 barrels. Ibid., 109.

34 Erni, *Coal Oil and Petroleum,* 107.

35 Eaton, *Petroleum,* 167.

36 J. T. Henry, *The Early and Later History of Petroleum, with Authentic Facts in Regard to Its Development in Western Pennsylvania* (Philadelphia: Jas B. Rodgers Co., 1873), 287.

37 Eaton, *Petroleum,* 160–61.

38 On the contemporary uncertainty surrounding oil production, see Black, *Petrolia;* Paul Sabin, "'A Dive into Nature's Great Grab-Bag': Nature, Gender and Capitalism in the Early Pennsylvania Oil Industry," *Pennsylvania History* 66, no. 4 (1999).

39 Williamson and Daum, *American Petroleum Industry,* 1:170.

40 Ibid., 170–75.

41 Similarly, William Cronon has shown that a system of water transport favored St. Louis for the trade of the Great Plains, while railroad networks favored Chicago. William Cronon, *Nature's Metropolis: Chicago and the Great West* (New York: W. W. Norton, 1991).

42 Williamson and Daum, *American Petroleum Industry*, 1:291.

43 Henry, *Early and Later History of Petroleum*, 315–24.

44 George H. Thurston, *Pittsburgh and Allegheny in the Centennial Year* (Pittsburgh: A. A. Anderson and Son, 1876), 209.

45 Allan Nevins, *Study in Power: John D. Rockefeller, Industrialist and Philanthropist* (New York: Scribner, 1953), 1:54.

46 Allan Nevins, *John D. Rockefeller: The Heroic Age of American Enterprise.* 2 vols. (New York: C. Scribner's Sons, 1941); Ron Chernow, *Titan: The Life of John D. Rockefeller, Sr.* (New York: Random House, 1998).

47 Rolland Harper Maybee, *Railroad Competition and the Oil Trade, 1855–1873* (Mt. Pleasant, MI: The Extension Press, 1940); Richard White, *Railroaded: The Transcontinentals and the Making of Modern America* (New York: W. W. Norton, 2011).

48 Tarbell, *History of Standard Oil*, 2:67.

49 James Deveraux, vice president of the Atlantic & Great Western Railroad later testified in court that if bulk shipments of oil could be guaranteed and run regularly, it would lower the capital costs of the railroad by several hundred thousand dollars, because fewer tank cars had to be purchased if they were used more efficiently. Therefore, it was logical for them to give special rates to any supplier that could provide these shipments. Testimony reprinted in ibid., 1:277–79.

50 Ibid., 2:11.

51 House of Representatives, "Report on Investigation of Trusts" (Washington, D.C.: Government Printing Office, 1888), 259–60.

52 Johnson, "Development of American Pipelines," 59–66. For details on the strike, see Walter Licht, *Industrializing America: The Nineteenth Century* (Baltimore: Johns Hopkins University Press, 1995), chap. 7.

53 Williamson and Daum, *American Petroleum Industry*, 1:437.

54 Tarbell estimated that after Standard Oil had eliminated its competitors, prices to consumers increased by a quarter to a third. Tarbell, *History of Standard Oil*, 2:59–60.

55 There are important distinctions between gathering pipelines and long-distance pipelines. Gathering pipelines were typically short in length with a small diameter, and their function was to take oil from the well to a

connection point where another transport system—either a railroad, canal/river barge, or long-distance pipeline—would ship the oil to its next destination. Long-distance pipelines were much longer in length, had greater diameters, and transported oil gathered at a central location long distances to sites where it would be refined. Van Syckel's pipeline was a gathering pipeline. The Tide-Water pipeline, discussed in the next chapter, was a long-distance pipeline.

56 Johnson, "Development of American Pipelines," 7.

57 *The Derrick's Hand-Book of Petroleum; a Complete Chronological and Statistical Review of Petroleum Developments from 1859 to 1899* (Oil City, PA: Derrick Publishing Company, 1898), 1:52.

58 Alfred Wilson Smiley, *A Few Scraps, Oily and Otherwise* (Oil City, PA: Derrick Publishing Company, 1907), 121.

59 Timothy Mitchell, *Carbon Democracy: Political Power in the Age of Oil* (London: Verso, 2011).

60 Henry, *Early and Later History of Petroleum,* 306.

61 Eaton, *Petroleum,* 223.

62 Lucier, *Swindlers & Scientists,* 233; Williamson and Daum, *American Petroleum Industry,* vol. 1.

63 Refiners later discovered that naphtha could be used to manufacture gas and benzine could replace turpentine in paints and varnishes. Eaton, *Petroleum,* 220.

64 On early oil refining, see Williamson and Daum, *American Petroleum Industry,* vol. 1, chap. 5, 9; Lucier, *Swindlers & Scientists,* chap. 7–9.

65 Erni, *Coal Oil and Petroleum,* 100.

66 Williamson and Daum, *American Petroleum Industry,* 1:320. On commodity standardization, see Cronon, *Nature's Metropolis,* chap. 3–5.

67 Eaton, *Petroleum,* 212.

68 Silliman, *Report on Rock Oil,* 17.

69 John Herbert A. Bone, *Petroleum and Petroleum Wells, with a Complete Guide Book and Description of the Oil Regions of Pennsylvania, West Virginia, Kentucky, and Ohio* (Philadelphia: J.B. Lippincott, 1865), 8.

70 Castaneda, *Invisible Fuel,* 35; Schivelbusch, *Disenchanted Night,* 40.

71 Erni, *Coal Oil and Petroleum,* 101.

72 Williamson and Daum, *American Petroleum Industry,* 1:524.

73 Ibid., chap. 20.

74 Ibid., 326.

75 Tower, *History of American Whaling,* 52; Lucier, *Swindlers & Scientists,* 154.

76 Robert B. Outland, *Tapping the Pines: The Naval Stores Industry in the American South* (Baton Rouge: Louisiana State University Press, 2004), 39.

77 At 1870 prices, kerosene had a cost of 2.0 cents per 1,000 lumen-hours while camphene cost 14.8 cents, manufactured gas an average of 24.1 cents, and sperm oil 40.1 cents. William D. Nordhaus, "Do Real-Output and Real-Wage Measures Capture Reality? The History of Lighting Suggests Not," in *The Economics of New Goods,* ed. Timothy F. Bresnahan and Robert J. Gordon (Chicago: University of Chicago Press, 1997), 35; Roger Fouquet and Peter J. G. Pearson, "Seven Centuries of Energy Services: The Price and Use of Light in the United Kingdom (1300–2000)," *The Energy Journal* 27, no. 1 (2006): 159–60.

78 Tower, *History of American Whaling,* chap. 6.

79 Ibid., 52.

80 Erni, *Coal Oil and Petroleum,* 89.

81 Henry, *Early and Later History of Petroleum,* 37. Paul Lucier cautions that while this transition occurred, it was not immediate and there was considerable resistance by some coal-oil refiners. Lucier, *Swindlers & Scientists,* chap. 8.

82 Williamson and Daum, *American Petroleum Industry,* 1:322, 328, 338, 489, 524–26, 740.

83 As quoted in Black, *Petrolia,* 27.

84 Henry, *Early and Later History of Petroleum,* 31.

85 Brian Bowers, *Lengthening the Day: A History of Lighting Technology* (Oxford: Oxford University Press, 1998), chap. 2.

86 Williamson and Daum, *American Petroleum Industry,* 1:30.

87 According to Alan Trachtenberg, "The spread of artificial illumination on streets and in homes, by means of gas, kerosene, and electricity, dramatically increased the practice, after 1870, of publishing evening newspapers in the afternoon, especially to catch homebound shoppers and workers and downtown evening crowds." Alan Trachtenberg, *The Incorporation of America: Culture and Society in the Gilded Age* (New York: Hill and Wang, 1982), 123–24.

88 *Chemical News,* 1864, x, 204. Reprinted in Stephen Farnum Peckham, *Report on the Production, Technology, and Uses of Petroleum and Its Products* (Washington, D.C.: Government Printing Office, 1885), 261.

89 Sam H. Schurr and Bruce Carlton Netschert, *Energy in the American Economy, 1850–1975: An Economic Study of Its History and Prospects* (Baltimore: Johns Hopkins Press, 1960), 99.

90 Peckham, *Report on Petroleum,* 195–96.

91 *Derrick's Hand-Book of Petroleum*, 2:402–4; Henry, *Early and Later History of Petroleum*, 474–77.

92 Lucier, *Swindlers & Scientists*, 224.

93 Erni, *Coal Oil and Petroleum*, 116.

94 Peto, *Resources and Prospects of America*, 193–94.

95 Eaton, *Petroleum*, 150–51.

96 For those accustomed to living within wooden homes heated with open flames, the fear of fire may have been a more accepted part of life than it is today. Black, *Petrolia*, 74–77.

97 Edmund Morris, *Derrick and Drill, or, an Insight into the Discovery, Development, and Present Condition and Future Prospects of Petroleum, in New York, Pennsylvania, Ohio, West Virginia, Etc.* (New York: James Miller, 1865), 192–93.

98 Black, *Petrolia*, 79.

99 Peckham, *Report on Petroleum*, 76.

100 Ibid., 138.

101 When the Exxon Valdez sank on a reef in 1989 in Alaska, it spilled an estimated 240,000 barrels of oil. Yergin, *The Prize*, 785.

102 "Where Stenches Abound," *New York Times*, March 27, 1881, 10.

103 Andrew Hurley, "Creating Ecological Wastelands: Oil Pollution in New York City, 1870–1900," *Journal of Urban History* 20, no. 3 (1994).

104 Jonathan Wlasiuk, "Refining Nature: Standard Oil and the Limits of Efficiency, 1863–1920" (Ph.D. diss., Case Western Reserve University, 2012), chap. 3.

105 Black, *Petrolia;* Sabin, "'A Dive into Nature's Grab-Bag.'"

106 Peto, *Resources and Prospects of America*, 196.

107 Black, *Petrolia*, 112.

108 Lucier, *Swindlers & Scientists*, 246–47; Trachtenberg, *Incorporation of America*.

109 Williamson and Daum, *American Petroleum Industry*, vol. 1, appendix E.

110 Sabin, "'A Dive into Nature's Grab-Bag.'"

4 · Pipelines and Power

1 "Tide-Water Items," *Titusville Morning Herald*, June 6, 1879; "The Oil Arrives," *Bradford Daily Era*, June 7, 1879.

2 Harold Francis Williamson and Arnold Daum, *The American Petroleum Industry* (Westport, CT: Greenwood Press, 1959), 1:485, 633; William D. Nordhaus, "Do Real-Output and Real-Wage Measures Capture Reality?

The History of Lighting Suggests Not," in *The Economics of New Goods*, ed. Timothy F. Bresnahan and Robert J. Gordon (Chicago: University of Chicago Press, 1997); Roger Fouquet and Peter J. G. Pearson, "Seven Centuries of Energy Services: The Price and Use of Light in the United Kingdom (1300–2000)," *The Energy Journal* 27, no. 1 (2006).

3 Arthur Menzies Johnson, "The Development of American Petroleum Pipelines: A Study in Private Enterprise and Public Policy, 1862–1906" (Ph.D diss., Vanderbilt University, published for the American Historical Association by Cornell University Press, 1956), chap. 2; Williamson and Daum, *American Petroleum Industry*, 1:405–12.

4 R. D. Benson, ed. *A Brief History of the Tide Water Companies* (Tide-Water Pipe Company, 1913), 8–9. Document accessed at Drake Well Museum, Titusville, Pennsylvania.

5 *The Derrick's Hand-Book of Petroleum; a Complete Chronological and Statistical Review of Petroleum Developments from 1859 to 1898* (Oil City, PA: Derrick Publishing Company, 1898), 1:270, 273.

6 Ibid., 1:301; Johnson, "Development of American Pipelines," 74; Williamson and Daum, *American Petroleum Industry*, 1:438.

7 Williamson and Daum, *American Petroleum Industry*, 1:444.

8 "Tidewater Pipe Line," *Titusville Morning Herald*, March 6, 1879, 1.

9 *The New York Graphic* reported that the project was "worthy . . . to be coupled with the Brooklyn Bridge, the blowing up of Hell Gate, and the tunnelling of the Hudson River." As cited in Ida M. Tarbell, *The History of the Standard Oil Company* (New York: McClure, Phillips & Co., 1904), 1:174. See also "The New Pipe Line," *Oil City Derrick*, January 7, 1879. The tongs were made by the Ames Manufacturing Company and had likely been designed while the men were planning the Seaboard Pipe Company. "Steam Pumps for the United and Machinery for the Tide-Water Pipe Line," *Titusville Morning Herald*, January 30, 1879; "Progress of the Tide-Water Pipe Line," *Bradford Daily Era*, December 14, 1878.

10 John Mills, *Heat* (Boston: American Printing and Engraving Co., 1890), 132.

11 Benson, *Brief History of the Tide Water Companies*, 27.

12 "Tide-Water Pipe Line," *Titusville Morning Herald*, April 9, 1879.

13 Benson, *Brief History of the Tide Water Companies*, 22–29.

14 "Independent oilmen" refers to those in the industry not affiliated with Standard Oil. Some outside the oil industry also opposed granting eminent domain privileges to pipeline companies since it could be seen as unfair to

ask property owners to be forced to sell land in order to address intra-industry struggles. Johnson, "Development of American Pipelines," chap. 2–3.

15 "Obstructing the Tide-Water," *Titusville Morning Herald,* April 17, 1879.

16 Letter from W. G. Warden to John D. Rockefeller, Sr., May 5, 1879, box 71, folder 526: "Warden, W. G., October 1877–February 1880," Papers of John D. Rockefeller, Sr., part 1: Business Correspondence, Rockefeller Foundation Archives, Rockefeller Archive Center, Sleepy Hollow, New York.

17 Benson, *Brief History of the Tide Water Companies,* 31–32.

18 Ibid., 13–14.

19 It is not surprising that many of the most negative articles appeared in the *Oil City Derrick,* which was controlled by Standard Oil. For instance, see these *Oil City Derrick* articles: "Mr. Zane on the Williamsport Pipe Line," December 30, 1878; " 'A Citizen' Has His Say About the Tidewater Line," May 27, 1879; untitled, June 11, 1879.

20 "Trouble in the Camp," *The McKean Miner,* March 6, 1879.

21 "An Important Decision," *Titusville Morning Herald,* March 13, 1879.

22 Benson, *Brief History of the Tide Water Companies,* 24.

23 "The Tidewater Line," *Oil City Derrick,* March 4, 1879, 2.

24 Benson, *Brief History of the Tide Water Companies,* 26–27.

25 "Reduction of Rates to the Seaboard," *Oil City Derrick,* June 23, 1879.

26 The estimate of $10,000,000 is likely an exaggeration. It came from Franklin Gowen's testimony, and he was prone to overstatement when it served his interests. However, the losses were significant enough that the railroads decided they needed to end the rate war. Henry Demarest Lloyd, *Wealth against Commonwealth* (Englewood Cliffs, NJ: Prentice-Hall, 1963 [1894]), 46.

27 "The New Oil Freights," *Titusville Morning Herald,* February 13, 1880.

28 Cornelius Vanderbilt at the Hepburn Committee hearings, New York Assembly, *Proceedings of the Special Committee on Railroads, Appointed to Investigate Alleged Abuses in the Management of Railroads Chartered in the State of New York,* 8 vols. (Albany, 1880), 2:1596.

29 As Arthur Johnson noted, "As long as [Standard Oil] had favorable rates from the railroads and its competitors had no alternative method for the long-distance carriage of crude, it had no incentive to build trunk pipelines." Johnson, "Development of American Pipelines," 100.

30 Williamson and Daum, *American Petroleum Industry,* 1:446–47; Johnson, "Development of American Pipelines," chap. 5. It was not until 1883 that Pennsylvania passed a bill giving pipeline entrepreneurs eminent domain

privileges, but because Standard Oil had already built sufficient pipeline capacity to handle output by this date, the law was not taken advantage of until nearly a decade later.

31 *Derrick's Hand-Book of Petroleum*, 1:318; Williamson and Daum, *American Petroleum Industry*, 1:448–49.

32 The pipeline was purchased for nearly $500,000, approximately the cost of construction. Ralph Willard Hidy and Muriel Hidy, *History of Standard Oil Company (New Jersey): Pioneering in Big Business, 1882–1911* (New York: Harper, 1955), 84; Williamson and Daum, *American Petroleum Industry*, 1:453.

33 Williamson and Daum, *American Petroleum Industry*, 1:449; Johnson, "Development of American Pipelines," 104, 126; Hidy and Hidy, *History of Standard Oil*, 82.

34 Ron Chernow, *Titan: The Life of John D. Rockefeller, Sr.* (New York: Random House, 1998), 211; Benson, *Brief History of the Tide Water Companies*, 19; *United States of America, Petitioner, V. The Standard Oil of New Jersey Et Al, Defendants*, 23 vols. (Washington, D.C.: Government Printing Office, 1908–1910), vol. 1, Petitioners' Testimony, 250.

35 Tarbell, *History of Standard Oil*, 2:17–20; Johnson, "Development of American Pipelines," 109–12; "The Standard Oil Company," *The New York Times*, February 20, 1883; "Blow at the Standard Oil Co.," *The New York Times*, March 17, 1883; Williamson and Daum, *American Petroleum Industry*, 1:454.

36 Williamson and Daum, *American Petroleum Industry*, 1:455.

37 Tarbell, *History of Standard Oil*, vol. 2, appendix 39B, 303.

38 Benson, *Brief History of the Tide Water Companies*, 16.

39 There is significant debate within the literature as to why the Tide-Water officials agreed to a settlement and the extent to which they betrayed the cause of independents. Some contend that Benson was angling for such a deal from the very early stages. Evidence for this view comes from a letter mailed to John D. Rockefeller from Daniel O'Day in 1880, where O'Day states that Benson took the initiative in reaching out to Standard Oil. As O'Day wrote to Rockefeller, "Yesterday . . . I met Benson on the train. We had a long talk about pipe line matters. He told me that he wanted to 'let the bars down,' as he expressed it for any overtures that might be made to his company, with a view of an adjustment of the pipe line questions. He said that he felt that the time had come when the companies should work together with a view of preventing other companies from engaging in the

business." Letter from Daniel O'Day to John D. Rockefeller, Sr., March 11, 1880, box 62, folder 459: "O'Day, D., 1880–1882," Papers of John D. Rockefeller, Sr., Part 1. On the other hand, Rockefeller's own reflections on the events show a distinct dislike for Benson and Gowen, implying that Benson did not take kindly to attempted negotiations. In contrast to those Tide-Water officials that Rockefeller worked with in 1883, he described Benson and Gowen as "unreasonable," operating with "a hostile spirit," and "vindictive." William O. Inglis, David Freeman Hawke, and Rockefeller Archive Center, *John D. Rockefeller Interview, 1917–1920* (Westport, CT: Meckler Pub. in association with the Rockefeller Archive Center, 1984). In reviewing the available sources, it seems the truth is somewhere in the middle. Without doubt, Benson and his associates created the Tide-Water Pipe Company to make money, not as a service to independent oil producers. On the other hand, based on the intensity of Rockefeller's dislike for Benson, it seems clear that he had little desire to see his company absorbed by Standard Oil. However, without complete control of his company and a contingent of stockholders seeking a deal with Standard Oil, it seems that Benson lacked the capacity to keep the company growing. It was reported, for instance, that Hopkins and Benson's son were in Europe in the summer of 1883 seeking to establish marketing outlets for the company's oil. *United States of America, Petitioner, V. The Standard Oil of New Jersey Et Al,* vol. 1, Petitioners' Testimony, 220. Developing such a system would have proved very capital-intensive at a time when the company's management was divided. In the end, it makes most sense to see Benson as a pragmatist whose desire to run a profitable business exceeded his opposition to Standard Oil.

40 Untitled article, *The New York Times,* October 17, 1883.

41 In this manner, it can be understood as an example of a disruptive technology as described by Clayton Christensen. Clayton M. Christensen, *The Innovator's Dilemma: When New Technologies Cause Great Firms to Fail* (Boston: Harvard Business School Press, 1997).

42 Allan Nevins, *Study in Power* (New York: Scribner, 1953), 1:345.

43 The competitive struggles of the Tide-Water pipeline dominate the narratives told by previous energy historians while the influence of pipelines on spatial politics and energy consumption has not been analyzed in-depth. Williamson and Daum, *American Petroleum Industry,* vol. 1; Nevins, *Study in Power;* Johnson, "Development of American Pipelines";

Daniel Yergin, *The Prize: The Epic Quest for Oil, Money, and Power* (New York: Simon & Schuster, 1991).

44 Williamson and Daum, *American Petroleum Industry*, 1:473, 627.

45 The costs of materials and labor in the Oil Regions were estimated to be 50 to 100 percent higher than in Philadelphia or New York. Nevins, *Study in Power*, 1:53. The daily capacity of Pittsburgh's refineries was estimated in 1895 to be 5,000 barrels, while national capacity exceeded 220,000 barrels. Williamson and Daum, *American Petroleum Industry*, 1:627.

46 In 1888, the daily capacity of Cleveland's refineries was estimated to be 25,310 barrels per day, of Philadelphia refineries 20,700, and of New York and New Jersey refineries 52,766. The national total was between 135,000 and 140,000 total barrels. Standard Oil was estimated to own or control 79 percent of these refineries, not including the output of the Tide-Water refineries, which produced approximately 5 percent of the total and were operating in coordination with Standard Oil. Williamson and Daum, *American Petroleum Industry*, 1:627.

47 There are no technical barriers to drawing off oil at intermediate points along the pipeline, particularly at pumping stations, but this was rarely done in practice. In addition, it was possible to reverse the flow of oil through pipelines but only by redesigning and relocating the pumping stations, an expensive and time-consuming process. I have found no evidence that this was ever attempted in the Pennsylvania pipelines during the nineteenth century.

48 Commentary in the *Butler Democratic Herald*, as cited in Johnson, "Development of American Pipelines," 45.

49 Hidy and Hidy, *History of Standard Oil*, 82. As Alfred Chandler demonstrated, the complexity of railroad operations gave a great impetus to the rise of large bureaucratic organizations. Alfred Dupont Chandler, *The Visible Hand: The Managerial Revolution in American Business* (Cambridge, MA: Belknap Press, 1977).

50 The chronology of the Oil Regions in *Derrick's Hand-Book of Petroleum* indicates burst pipes happened frequently, as evidenced in a report from March 5, 1885: "Eight-inch line of the Seaboard pipe line bursts on the farm of Abraham Kreider, near Wrightsville, N.Y., and the surrounding fields flooded with oil, which was fired by sparks from a passing locomotive and a terrific conflagration raged for 20 hours." Many other pipeline ruptures were reported over the next ten years. *Derrick's Hand-Book of Petroleum*, 1:385, 399, 417, 431, 454, 625.

51 R. A. Fisher, *Petroleum Versus Coal: Report of Prof. R. A. Fisher, Upon Experiments Undertaken to Determine the Relative Cost of Generating Steam, by Petroleum and Anthracite Coal* (New York: Jown W. Amerman, printer, 1864), 10.

52 "Petroleum Fuel for Steam Ships," *The Chemical News and Journal of Physical Science* 17, no. 440 (1868).

53 Stephen Farnum Peckham, *Report on the Production, Technology, and Uses of Petroleum and Its Products* (Washington, D.C.: Government Printing Office, 1885), 249.

54 Williamson and Daum, *American Petroleum Industry,* 1:485, 742–43.

55 From 1876 to 1880, the average annual value, in millions of dollars, was 183.5 for cotton, 134 for wheat, 66.7 for meat, and 43.8 for petroleum. Department of Commerce, "Statistical Abstract of the United States, 1946" (Washington, D.C., 1946), 904–5.

56 Williamson and Daum, *American Petroleum Industry,* 1:326.

57 A barrel of Pennsylvania crude oil has a heating value of 5,500,000 BTUs while a ton of anthracite produces 25,400,000 BTUs. Sam H. Schurr and Bruce Carlton Netschert, *Energy in the American Economy, 1850–1975: An Economic Study of Its History and Prospects* (Baltimore: Johns Hopkins Press, 1960), 499.

58 Anthracite price information from United States Geological Survey, *Mineral Resources of the United States, 1901* (Washington, D.C.: Government Printing Office, 1902), 301. Based on analysis of the Reading Railroad's receipts from coal shipments and the total supplies carried, the railroad charged approximately $1.30 per ton for transport, with a high charge of nearly $2.00 per ton in 1885 and a low of just over a $1.00 per ton in 1895. Richard G. Healey, *The Pennsylvania Anthracite Coal Industry, 1860–1902: Economic Cycles, Business Decision-Making and Regional Dynamics* (Scranton, PA: University of Scranton Press, 2007), 131, 136.

59 Richard White, *Railroaded: The Transcontinentals and the Making of Modern America* (New York: W. W. Norton, 2011), chap. 4.

60 In 1874, a proposal to regularize railroad rates recommended a price of $1.50 to New York and Philadelphia from the Oil Regions. In 1877, after the end of the rate war between Empire and Standard Oil, railroad rates of $1.15 per barrel from the Oil Regions to New York and $.75 to Philadelphia and Baltimore were announced. Standard Oil reportedly obtained a regular shipment rate of $.85 a barrel during the mid-1870s when others were paying $1.25. Johnson, "Development of American Pipelines," 36–38;

Derrick's Hand-Book of Petroleum, 1:288; "Mr. Gowen on the Standard Oil Company," *Oil, Paint, and Drug Reporter* 17, no. 11 (March 17, 1880): 304; "The Standard's Methods," *The New York Times*, January 12, 1883.

61 Williamson and Daum, *American Petroleum Industry*, 1:586.

62 Johnson, "Development of American Pipelines," 126–27.

63 *Derrick's Hand-Book of Petroleum*, 1:711.

64 Ohio State Geologist, Edward Francis Baxter Orton, and Stillman Williams Robinson, *First Annual Report of the Geological Survey of Ohio* (Columbus, OH: The Westbote Co., state printers, 1890), 46; Yergin, *The Prize*, 52; Williamson and Daum, *American Petroleum Industry*, vol. 1, chap. 22.

65 Yergin, *The Prize*, 52; United States Geological Survey, *Annual Report, Part 2* (Washington, D.C.: Government Printing Office, 1889), 62; *Derrick's Hand-Book of Petroleum*, 1:777, 815.

66 The United States Geological Survey reported, "The Standard Oil Company has planted in the new field more than $2,000,000, and it now avers through its representatives that it has made a great mistake, and declares that the numerous, extensive, and very costly experiments conducted by it in seeking to obtain from Lima crude an illuminating oil that will fairly compete with Pennsylvania oil in open market have resulted in complete and utter failure . . . Representatives of the company further declare that the only use that they have been able to find for Lima oil is for fuel, and to the introduction for this purpose they are now directing all their efforts." United States Geological Survey, *Annual Report, Part 2*, 624.

67 Hidy and Hidy, *History of Standard Oil*, 116.

68 The establishment of heat-intensive factories at the site of natural gas wells stands in contrast to the major pattern of mid-Atlantic industrial development during this period. Instead of moving the energy long distances to sites of consumption, some enterprises requiring massive quantities of heat moved to western Ohio. This development was, in large measure, the result of the difficulties of transporting natural gas. If the liquid nature of petroleum had confounded early oilmen due to its propensity to seep through barrels, evaporate, and run out of storage tanks, natural gas was many times more difficult to control. The gas flew out of wells, occupied so much space that building suitable storage was nearly impossible, and escaped through the joints in pipelines. As a result, until improved pipeline technology was developed in the 1920s, natural gas could not be profitably shipped more than short distances. Until these transport problems were addressed, natural gas was primarily used locally. Christopher J. Castaneda,

Invisible Fuel: Manufactured and Natural Gas in America, 1800–2000 (New York: Twayne Publishers, 1999), 85.

69 Ohio State Geologist, *First Annual Report,* chap. 3; Mills, *Heat,* 175; *Derrick's Hand-Book of Petroleum,* 1:794.

70 Williamson and Daum, *American Petroleum Industry,* 1:602–4.

71 Ibid., 616–19.

72 *Derrick's Hand-Book of Petroleum,* 1:80, 91, 131, 317, 456; *The Journal of the Iron and Steel Institute* (London: E. & F. N. Spon, 1883), 350, 360, 402; "Petroleum for the Locomotive," *Locomotive Firemen's Magazine* 11, no. 9 (1887); Mills, *Heat,* chap. 10–11; Sydney North, *Oil Fuel: Its Supply, Composition, and Application* (London: Charles Griffin and Company, 1905). Approximately 482,900 of 19,371,000 barrels of oil in 1884 were designated as fuel oil or residuum. In 1899, an estimated 8,239,100 of 48,932,000 barrels of oil were used as fuel oil or residuum. Williamson and Daum, *American Petroleum Industry,* 1:485, 678.

73 Schurr and Netschert, *Energy in the American Economy,* 105.

74 Yergin, *The Prize,* 87.

75 Harold F. Williamson et al., *The American Petroleum Industry: The Age of Energy 1899–1959* (Evanston, IL: Northwestern University Press, 1963), 75.

76 Merritt Roe Smith and Robert Martello, "Taking Stock of the Industrial Revolution in America," in *Reconceptualizing the Industrial Revolution,* ed. Jeff Horn, Leonard Rosenband, and Merritt Roe Smith (Cambridge, MA: MIT Press, 2010); Joel Mokyr, *The Lever of Riches: Technological Creativity and Economic Progress* (Oxford: Oxford University Press, 1990); Walter Licht, *Industrializing America: The Nineteenth Century* (Baltimore: Johns Hopkins University Press, 1995).

77 Anthracite coal production was 10,983,972 tons in 1860 and 57,367,915 tons in 1900. Pennsylvania bituminous production was 4,710,400 tons in 1860 and 79,842,326 tons in 1900. Howard Nicholas Eavenson, *The First Century and a Quarter of American Coal Industry* (Pittsburgh: Privately printed by the Baltimore Weekly Press, 1942), 431; United States Geological Survey, *Mineral Resources of the United States, 1901,* 292, 295.

78 The coal provided 3,539,753,000 million BTUs, which was equivalent to 169,317,564 cords of wood (assuming an average of 20,960,000 BTUs per cord). The sustainable yield of one cord of wood requires two-thirds of an acre (see page 254, note 12), therefore necessitating 112,878,376 acres, or 176,372 square miles (there are 640 acres in a square mile). As Pennsylvania's area is 46,055 square miles, this coal provided the heat equivalent of a forest nearly four times the state's total area.

79 Bryan Donkin, *A Text-Book on Gas, Oil, and Air Engines; or, Internal Combustion Motors without Boiler* (London: Charles Griffin and Company, 1896), 3.

80 Gardner Dexter Hiscox, *Gas, Gasoline, and Oil Vapor Engines* (New York: Norman W. Henley & Company, 1898), 5; William Robinson, *Gas and Petroleum Engines: A Practical Treatise on the Internal Combustion Engine* (London: E. & F. N. Spon, 1890); James J. Flink, *The Automobile Age* (Cambridge, MA: MIT Press, 1988).

81 Flink, *Automobile Age,* chap. 2; Williamson et al., *American Petroleum Industry,* 184–92.

82 Williamson et al., *American Petroleum Industry,* 2:168, 190.

83 Williamson and Daum, *American Petroleum Industry,* 1:521, 524, 681.

84 Bureau of Corporations, *Report of the Commissioner of Corporations on the Petroleum Industry* (Washington, D.C.: Government Printing Office, 1907), 1:40.

85 Donkin, *Text-Book on Engines,* 11.

86 Licht, *Industrializing America,* 102.

87 Overall population increased from 31,513,000 in 1860 to 76,094,000 in 1900 while the urban population increased from 6,217,000 to 30,160,000 in the same period. United States Bureau of the Census, *Historical Statistics of the United States, Colonial Times to 1970* (Washington, D.C.: Government Printing Office, 1975), part 1, 11–12.

88 In 1860, the total taxable wealth of the United States was $16,159,616,068; New York's share was $1,843,338,517 and Pennsylvania's was $1,416,501,818. In 1900, the total taxable wealth of the United States was $88,517,306,775, with manufacturing representing $2,541,046,639 of the total and railroads $9,035,732,000; New York's shares were $12,505,330,137 (taxable wealth), $385,789,387 (manufacturing), and $779,616,000 (railroads), respectively, and Pennsylvania's shares were $9,315,140,116, $392,150,856, and $1,136,410,000. Illinois was the next leading state in 1900 with an 8 percent share of total taxable wealth ($6,976,476,400), 8 percent share of manufacturing investment ($206,242,774), and 7 percent share of railroad property ($671,183,000). The combined taxable wealth of Florida, Georgia, North Carolina, and South Carolina was $2,459,403,587 in 1900 and $1,625,874,890 in 1860; their share of population decreased from 9.2 percent to 7.9 percent during this period. Department of Commerce and Labor and S. N. D. North, *Wealth, Debt, and Taxation: Special Reports of the Census Office* (Washington, D.C.: Government Printing Office, 1907), 36, 42–43.

89 On the significant social changes during the late nineteenth century and the various responses of Americans, see Licht, *Industrializing America;* Alan Trachtenberg, *The Incorporation of America: Culture and Society in the Gilded Age* (New York: Hill and Wang, 1982); Robert Wiebe, *The Search for Order, 1877–1920* (New York: Hill & Wang, 1967); Samuel Hays, *The Response to Industrialism, 1885–1914* (Chicago: University of Chicago Press, 1995 [1957]); Rebecca Edwards, *New Spirits: Americans in the Gilded Age, 1865–1905* (New York: Oxford University Press, 2006); Charles W. Calhoun, ed. *The Gilded Age: Essays on the Origins of Modern America* (Wilmington, DE: Scholarly Resources, 1996); Richard Bensel, *The Political Economy of American Industrialization, 1877–1900* (Cambridge: Cambridge University Press, 2000).

90 Yergin, *The Prize,* 100.

91 Chandler, *Visible Hand;* James Livingston, *Origins of the Federal Reserve System: Money, Class, and Corporate Capitalism, 1890–1913* (Ithaca, NY: Cornell University Press, 1986).

92 Herbert George Gutman, *Work, Culture, and Society in Industrializing America: Essays in American Working-Class and Social History* (New York: Knopf, distributed by Random House, 1976); David Montgomery, *The Fall of the House of Labor: The Workplace, the State, and American Labor Activism, 1865–1925* (Cambridge: Cambridge University Press, 1987).

93 Wiebe, *Search for Order, 1877–1920;* Henry Demarest Lloyd, *Wealth against Commonwealth* (New York: Harper & Brothers, 1894); Tarbell, *History of Standard Oil;* Hays, *Response to Industrialism, 1885–1914.*

5 · Taming the Susquehanna River

1 Bill Beck, *PP&L: 75 Years of Powering the Future: An Illustrated History of Pennsylvania Power & Light Co.* (Allentown, PA: Pennsylvania Power & Light, 1995), 81.

2 "Susquehanna Power in Use," *The New York Times,* October 15, 1910.

3 On electrification during this period, see Thomas Parke Hughes, *Networks of Power: Electrification in Western Society, 1880–1930* (Baltimore: Johns Hopkins University Press, 1983); David E. Nye, *Electrifying America: Social Meanings of a New Technology, 1880–1940* (Cambridge, MA: MIT Press, 1990); Paul Hirt, *The Wired Northwest: The History of Electric Power, 1870s–1970s* (Lawrence: University Press of Kansas, 2012); Harold L. Platt, *The Electric City: Energy and the Growth of the Chicago Area, 1880–1930*

(Chicago: University of Chicago Press, 1991); Mark H. Rose, *Cities of Light and Heat: Domesticating Gas and Electricity in Urban America* (University Park, PA: Penn State University Press, 1995); Ronald C. Tobey, *Technology as Freedom: The New Deal and the Electrical Modernization of the American Home* (Berkeley: University of California Press, 1996).

4 On dams and hydroelectricity, see Richard White, *The Organic Machine* (New York: Hill and Wang, 1995); Donald C. Jackson and David P. Billington, *Big Dams of the New Deal Era: A Confluence of Engineering and Politics* (Norman: University of Oklahoma Press, 2006); Sara Pritchard, *Confluence: The Nature of Technology and the Remaking of the Rhone* (Cambridge, MA: Harvard University Press, 2011); Donald Worster, *Rivers of Empire: Water, Aridity and the Growth of the American West* (New York: Pantheon Books, 1985); Louis C. Hunter and Lynwood Bryant, *A History of Industrial Power, 1780–1930*, vol. 3, *The Transmission of Power* (Cambridge, MA: MIT Press, 1991).

5 Wolfgang Schivelbusch, *Disenchanted Night: The Industrialization of Light in the Nineteenth Century* (Berkeley: University of California Press, 1988), 69.

6 United States Bureau of the Census, *Historical Statistics of the United States, Colonial Times to 1970* (Washington, D.C.: Government Printing Office, 1975), part 2, 827.

7 A. Roger Ekirch, *At Day's Close: Night in Times Past* (New York: Norton, 2005); Schivelbusch, *Disenchanted Night,* chap. 2; Peter C. Baldwin, *In the Watches of the Night: Life in the Nocturnal City* (Chicago: University of Chicago Press, 2012).

8 Nye, *Electrifying America,* chap. 2.

9 National Electric Light Association, *Ornamental Street Lighting: A Municipal Investment and Its Return* (New York: National Electric Light Association, 1912), 37.

10 Nye, *Electrifying America,* chap. 2.

11 National Electric Light Association, *Ornamental Street Lighting,* 17, 8.

12 Nye, *Electrifying America,* 193.

13 In 1899, industry used 30 percent of its electricity for power, 10 percent for materials conversion, and 60 percent for support services (including lighting and information processing). As there were relatively few applications for electric information processing in 1899, the vast majority of support services likely represented lighting. Sam H. Schurr et al., eds., *Electricity in the American Economy: Agent of Technological Progress* (New York: Greenwood Press, 1990), 295.

14 Sam Bass Warner, *Streetcar Suburbs: The Process of Growth in Boston, 1870–1900* (Cambridge, MA: Harvard University Press, 1962), 15.

15 Philadelphia's population increased from 408,762 in 1850 to 1,293,697 in 1900; Baltimore's from 169,054 in 1850 to 508,957 in 1900; Boston's from 136,881 in 1850 to 560,892 in 1900; and New York City's from 515,547 in 1850 to 3,347,202 in 1900. John Andriot, *Population Abstract of the United States* (McLean, VA: Andriot Associates, 1980).

16 Five miles per hour was the maximum average speed for horse-drawn omnibuses. Riders also had to allocate a few minutes to walk to an omnibus stop, wait for a ride, and then walk to their final destination. Charles W. Cheape, *Moving the Masses: Urban Public Transit in New York, Boston, and Philadelphia, 1880–1912* (Cambridge, MA: Harvard University Press, 1980), 4; Warner, *Streetcar Suburbs*, 16; Clay McShane and Joel Tarr, *The Horse in the City: Living Machines in the Nineteenth Century* (Baltimore: Johns Hopkins University Press, 2007); Eugene Griffin, "Three Years' Development of Electric Railways," in *Proceedings of the Fourteenth Convention,* ed. National Electric Light Association (New York: James Kempster Printing Company, 1892).

17 Cheape, *Moving the Masses*, 2–5.

18 Warner estimates that streetcars could consistently travel twice as fast and carry three times as many passengers as could horse-draw trolleys. Warner, *Streetcar Suburbs*, 28.

19 Nye, *Electrifying America*, 89, 96.

20 In 1902, streetcar companies consumed more than 2,651 million kilowatt-hours of electricity out of a total of 6,029 million kilowatt-hours. United States Bureau of the Census, *Census of Electrical Industries: Street Railways* (Washington, D.C.: Government Printing Office, 1905); Cheape, *Moving the Masses*, 6.

21 White, *Organic Machine*.

22 Susan Q. Stranahan, *Susquehanna, River of Dreams* (Baltimore: Johns Hopkins University Press, 1993), chap. 1.

23 Ibid.

24 "A Short Story of the History of the Susquehanna River in Lancaster County," August 3, 1943, Pennsylvania Power & Light Collection, Pennsylvania Water & Power Company Files, accession 1552, box 149, folder 3, Hagley Museum and Library, Wilmington, Delaware.

25 Stranahan, *Susquehanna*, 27.

26 R. L. Thomas, "The Development of a Regional Power System," June 6, 1935, Pennsylvania Power & Light Collection, Pennsylvania Water & Power Company Files, accession 1552, box 149, folder 14.

27 Along the Susquehanna's tributaries, these sites included the Rock Hill and
    Wabank plants on Conestoga Creek (1896–97) the Colemanville plant on
    Pequea Creek (1896) and the Delta Electric Power Co. plant on Muddy
    Creek (1896). Each produced between 500 and 1,000 kilowatts (a kilowatt
    is equal to about 1.33 horsepower). R. L. Thomas, "The Development of a
    Regional Power System," June 6, 1935, Pennsylvania Power & Light
    Collection, Pennsylvania Water & Power Company Files, accession 1552,
    box 149, folder 14.
28 United States Bureau of the Census, *Census of Electrical Industries: Central
    Electric Light and Power Stations, 1902* (Washington, D.C.: Government
    Printing Office, 1905), 67.
29 Hunter and Bryant, *History of Industrial Power*, 3:254–72.
30 The transmission line in 1896 only had a capacity of 1,000 hp at a time
    when the powerhouse was producing fifteen times as much energy.
    Hughes, *Networks of Power*, 265.
31 Ibid., chap. 10; Hirt, *Wired Northwest*, chap. 2.
32 McCall Ferry Power Company engineers Boyd Ehle and Robert Anderson
    had led surveys of the river in 1901. Affidavit of Robert Anderson, Septem-
    ber 30, 1926, 1, Pennsylvania Power & Light Collection, Pennsylvania
    Water & Power Company Files, accession 1962, box 215, folder 13. From
    1902, Cary T. Hutchinson, one of the company's directors, had purchased
    many land rights along the river. In addition to the efforts of the McCall
    Ferry Power Company, James Harlow and the Susquehanna Electric Power
    Company purchased properties in the same area, as did the agents of the
    Susquehanna Power Company, an organization with connections to New
    York financiers. Boyd Ehle, "Later Achievements of Engineers on the
    Lower Susquehanna—Harnessing the River," *The Cornell Civil Engineer* 37,
    no. 4 (1929); R. L. Thomas, "The Development of a Regional Power
    System," June 6, 1935, Pennsylvania Power & Light Collection, Pennsylva-
    nia Water & Power Company Files, accession 1552, box 149, folder 14;
    "Amended Bill of Complaint, Answer, Decree Appointing Receiver and
    Certificate of Clerk of Court as to Entry of Bond of Receiver," Circuit
    Court of the United States (Eastern District of Pennsylvania), April
    Sessions, 1909, no. 329, 26, in *McCall Ferry Power Company Reorganization,
    1908–1910*, Pennsylvania Power & Light Collection, Pennsylvania Water &
    Power Company Files, accession 1962.
33 "A Gigantic Operation," *Lancaster New Era*, April 30, 1906.
34 "Don't Give Up the River," *York Dispatch*, March 26, 1906.

35 Other notable engineers associated with the McCall Ferry Power Company included George S. Morrison, Cary T. Hutchinson, Boyd Ehle, F. Q. Blackwell, and Charles Main.

36 "York to Have Power from McCall's Ferry," *York Gazette,* July 6, 1906.

37 "Developing Electricity from the Susquehanna," *Manufacturers' Record* 50, no. 12 (October 4, 1906).

38 "Four Men Drowned," *York Springs Comet,* April 12, 1906.

39 "York to Have Power from McCall's Ferry," *York Gazette,* July 6, 1906.

40 Such practices may have been brought by engineers from their experiences working on the Panama Canal, where pay grades were structured by national background. Julie Greene, *The Canal Builders: Making America's Empire at the Panama Canal* (New York: Penguin, 2009).

41 In the next decade, the ability of electric motors and wires to provide power to several motors more efficiently would be a major factor in the rapid spread of electricity and the eclipse of compressed air. L. R. Chadwick, "Air Power in the Construction of the McCall Ferry Dam," *Mine and Quarry* 11, no. 2 (1907); Hunter and Bryant, *History of Industrial Power,* vol. 3, chap. 3.

42 H. H. McClune, "Letters from the People: The McCall's Ferry Power Plant," *York Gazette,* May 21, 1906.

43 "Wonders of the New Dam," *Lancaster New Era,* July 28, 1906.

44 "Alderman Aughenbaugh Insists that Power Company Dam Will Destroy Fish," *York Gazette,* April 2, 1906; "Don't Give Up the River," *York Dispatch,* March 27, 1906.

45 "The Wonderful Promise of the Dam Builders," *Lancaster Morning News,* April 30, 1906.

46 "The Great River Work," *Lancaster New Era,* March 13, 1906.

47 "A Halt Called in River Steal," unknown newspaper, June 21, 1906, Pennsylvania Power & Light Collection, Pennsylvania Water & Power Company Files, accession 1962: *McCall Ferry Power Co Scrap Book,* 12.

48 "Don't Give Up the River," *York Dispatch,* March 27, 1906.

49 "Mr. Blair Talks of Dam, A Reply to Mr. Hutchinson," *York Dispatch,* April 8, 1906.

50 "Letters from the People—The McCall's Ferry Power Plant, by H. H. McClune," *York Gazette,* May 21, 1906.

51 "Carson Visits Dam Site," unknown newspaper, August 11, 1906, Pennsylvania Power & Light Collection, Pennsylvania Water & Power Company Files, accession 1962: *McCall Ferry Power Co Scrap Book,* 21.

52 Theodore Steinberg, *Nature Incorporated: Industrialization and the Waters of New England* (Cambridge: Cambridge University Press, 1991).

53 "M'Call's Ferry Is in Danger," *Wilmington Evening Journal,* August 15, 1906.

54 Pennsylvania Power & Light Collection, Pennsylvania Water & Power Company Files, accession 1962, box 35, folder: "McCall Ferry Power Company—Decree of Court of Common Pleas—Dauphin County Dated January 14, 1907."

55 "A Dry Fishway," *Lancaster New Era,* May 21, 1915; "No Adequate Fishway Can Be Built for Use of Shad, Says Buller," *Lancaster New Era,* June 14, 1915; "Legislators Visit Big Dam at Holtwood on Fishing Proposition," *Lancaster New Era,* April 5, 1917; "Thousands of Shad and Other Food Fish Killed by Power Co," *Lancaster Intelligencer,* August 7, 1917.

56 Pennsylvania Water & Power Company, *Holtwood Power Development* (Baltimore: Peters Publishing & Printing Co., 1920).

57 The McCall Ferry Power Company was able to purchase the property rights of the Susquehanna Electric Power Company. However, it had more difficulty acquiring the rights of the Susquehanna Power Company. Eventually, the two parties divided their land holdings, giving the McCall Ferry Power Company the rights to lands at McCall's Ferry and the Susquehanna Power Company the rights to lands near Conowingo, Maryland. "Making a Great River Work for Men," *Baltimore Sun,* February 20, 1910; R. L. Thomas, "The Development of a Regional Power System," June 6, 1935, Pennsylvania Power & Light Collection, Pennsylvania Water & Power Company Files, accession 1552, box 149, folder 14, 7.

58 "The Land Damage Cases," October 19, 1906, Pennsylvania Power & Light Collection, Pennsylvania Water & Power Company Files, accession 1962: *McCall Ferry Power Co Scrap Book,* 19, and "Railroad Work Stopped," *Lancaster Intelligencer,* Oct. 12, 1906.

59 "'White Coal' From the Susquehanna," *Lancaster New Era?,* March 4, 1908, Pennsylvania Power & Light Collection, Pennsylvania Water & Power Company Files, accession 1962: *McCall Ferry Power Co Scrap Book,* 33.

60 J. E. Aldred, "Memorandum Re: Talk by R. L. Thomas, June 6, 1935," September 13, 1935, Pennsylvania Power & Light Collection, Pennsylvania Water & Power Company Files, accession 1552, box 149, folder 14, 1; "Certificate of Organization," Pennsylvania Power & Light Collection,

Pennsylvania Water & Power Company Files, accession 1552, box 142, folder 142, 1–2.

61 Pennsylvania Water & Power Company, *Description and Views* (New York: E. F. Fitch, 1912).

62 Ten other transmission lines were operating in the United States at or above 70,000 volts in 1910. None were in the mid-Atlantic and all were connected to hydroelectric dams. Four were in California, two in Michigan, two in Montana, one in Colorado, and one between North and South Carolina. "Transmission Systems of the World Operating at and above 70,000 Volts, Ranked According to Operating Voltage," in *Census of Electrical Industries: Central Electric Light and Power Stations and Street and Electric Railways, 1912* (Washington, D.C.: Government Printing Office, 1915).

63 For example, landowners J. Edward and Dora Webster sued the company in the Circuit Court of Harford County, but lost the case in February 1910 when the Court of Appeals maintained the verdict. The decision is reprinted in William M. McKinney and H. Noyes Greene, eds., *The American and English Annotated Cases,* (Northport, NY: Edward Thompson Company, 1911), 21:357–65. Two weeks later, the company began condemnation proceedings against William J. Barton and Hugh C. Whiteford. As a newspaper noted, "It is understood that similar steps will be taken in other cases where the company and landowners cannot get together on figures." Untitled article, *Bel Air Aegis,* May 18, 1910.

64 The McCall Ferry Power Company was reported to be behind a bill introduced to the Pennsylvania legislature in 1909 that sought to give utilities eminent domain privileges. "Combine to Control Electric Power," *Philadelphia Public Ledger,* January 19, 1909. Aldred was said to be pushing for similar legislation a few months later, after he took control of the project. "Electric Eminent Domain," *Philadelphia Public Ledger,* March 31, 1909. However, a general ruling on eminent domain was not issued during this period, in no small part because some utilities opposed the bill. The Philadelphia Electric Company, for example, opposed the measures because it feared that they would make it easier for the hydro-electric dam company to cut into its business in the towns surrounding Philadelphia.

65 "Susquehanna Transmission Company," *Electrical World* 56, no. 4 (1910); "McCall Ferry-Baltimore Transmission Line," *Electrical World* 56, no. 8 (1910).

66 Aluminum had about 60 percent of the conductivity and 60 percent of the weight of copper. National Electric Light Association, *Handbook on Overhead Line Construction* (Philadelphia: National Electric Light Association, 1914). Its cost was reported in 1910 to be "not very much greater" than copper. "Aluminum Versus Copper Cables," *Electrical World* 56, no. 24 (1910); "Aluminum Conductors," *Electrical World* 56, no. 7 (1910). A survey of 55 transmission wires built before 1915 shows that 41 lines were made of copper, 3 of copper and aluminum combined, and 9 of aluminum; 2 did not report the wire material. Two of the nine companies using aluminum wires were the Pennsylvania Water & Power Company and Shawinigan Water & Power Company. "Transmission Systems of the World," *Census of Electrical Industries, 1912.*

67 The aluminum cost $100, and the total price of the cap was $225. The average wage of a worker on the Washington Monument was $1/day; highly skilled laborers were paid $2/day. George Binczewski, "The Point of a Monument: A History of the Aluminum Cap of the Washington Monument," *JOM* 47, no. 11 (1995).

68 Pennsylvania Water & Power Company, *Holtwood Power Development* (Holtwood: Pennsylvania Water & Power Company, 1922), 16; Pennsylvania Water & Power Company, *1913 Annual Report,* 7. The complete set of annual reports for the Pennsylvania Water & Power Company is available at the Hagley Museum and Library, Wilmington, Delaware.

69 Hunter and Bryant, *History of Industrial Power,* 3:123–24.

70 William Wister Haines, *Slim* (Boston: Little, Brown, and Company, 1934).

71 According to newspaper reports, Vickers had planted three sticks of dynamite to remove rocks for the base of a tower. He approached the tower after the initial explosion, but apparently the third stick of dynamite had not yet blasted. It went off as he neared the tower, killing him instantly. "Fatal Accident on New Power Line," *Bel Air Aegis,* June 10, 1910.

72 Pennsylvania Water & Power Company, *Holtwood Power Development,* 16.

73 "Susquehanna Transmission Company," *Electrical World* 56, no. 4 (1910).

74 White, *Organic Machine.*

75 Thomson King, *Consolidated of Baltimore, 1816–1950: A History of Consolidated Gas Electric Light and Power Company of Baltimore* (Baltimore: Consolidated Gas Electric Light and Power Co., 1950), 184.

76 J. E. Aldred, "Memorandum Re: Talk by R. L. Thomas, June 6, 1935," September 13, 1935, Pennsylvania Power & Light Collection, Pennsylvania Water & Power Company Files, accession 1552, box 149, folder 14, 2.

77 Pennsylvania Water & Power Company, Corporate Minutes, vol. 1,
    1910–1919, January 14, 1910, 20–22, Pennsylvania Power & Light Collec-
    tion, Pennsylvania Water & Power Company Files, accession 1552, V 590.

78 Pennsylvania Water & Power Company, Corporate Minutes, vol. 1,
    1910–1919, October 14, 1910, 79–80, Pennsylvania Power & Light Collec-
    tion, Pennsylvania Water & Power Company Files, accession 1552, V 590.

79 In 1922, PWP officials confirmed that they received an average of between
    3.5 and 4 mils per kwh during this ten-year contract. A mil is a thou-
    sandth of a dollar, or a tenth of a cent. Pennsylvania Water & Power
    Company, *1919 Annual Report;* "Memorandum on Alternative Set-up of
    Power Relations between Baltimore and Conowingo," February 14, 1922,
    Pennsylvania Power & Light Collection, Pennsylvania Water & Power
    Company Files, accession 1962, box 32. In 1908, Consolidated received
    an average rate of 4.75 cents per kwh sold. King, *Consolidated of Balti-
    more,* 172.

80 In 1917, the average cost per kwh of large plants (producing more than
    50,000,000 kwh/year) was 5.04 mils (versus less than 3.5 for Holtwood
    Dam). Medium-size plants (producing between 5,000,000 and
    10,000,000 kwh/year) had costs of 25.72 mils. United States Bureau of
    the Census, *Census of Electrical Industries: Central Electric Light and
    Power Stations, 1917* (Washington, D.C.: Government Printing Office,
    1920), 141.

81 Pennsylvania Water & Power Company, Corporate Minutes, vol. 1,
    1910–1919, February 10, 1911, 83–85, 101–3, 109, Pennsylvania Power & Light
    Collection, Pennsylvania Water & Power Company Files, accession 1552,
    V 590; Pennsylvania Water & Power Company, *First Annual Report,* 1910;
    "Pennsylvania Water & Power Company," *Electrical World* 56, no. 3 (1910);
    Pennsylvania Water & Power Company, *Description and Views.*

82 Consolidated Gas Electric Light and Power Company, *1925 Annual Report,
    Year Book,* 10. Annual reports for Consolidated are available at the Harvard
    Baker Library, Boston, Massachusetts.

83 King, *Consolidated of Baltimore,* 194, 203. The company had 16,605
    electrical customers in 1910 and 32,342 in 1913. Consolidated Gas Electric
    Light and Power Company, *1923 Annual Report, Year Book,* 8.

84 Industry produced 58.2 percent of the electricity compared with 41.8
    percent by utilities. Schurr et al., *Electricity in the American Economy,*
    appendix 2, 388, 423.

85 King, *Consolidated of Baltimore,* 202.

86 Ibid., 187.

87 J. Edward Aldred and Ernest V. Illmer, *Industrial Survey of Baltimore* (Baltimore: 1915) v, vi.

88 Consolidated Gas Electric Light and Power Company, *1923 Annual Report, Year Book*, 8.

89 Consolidated Gas Electric Light and Power Company, *1924 Annual Report, Year Book*, 17.

90 Pennsylvania Water & Power Company, *1913 Annual Report*, 9.

91 Bernard Baruch, *American Industry in War: A Report of the War Industries Board* (Washington, D.C.: Government Printing Office, 1921), 145.

92 Pennsylvania Water & Power Company, *1918 Annual Report*.

93 Lancaster's consumption increased from approximately 20,000,000 kwh in 1911 to 71,400,000 in 1920. R. L. Thomas and A. P. Rusk, "Report on Business and Property of Edison Electric Company of Lancaster, PA," March 26, 1924, Pennsylvania Power & Light Collection, Pennsylvania Water & Power Company Files, accession 1552, box 149, folder 21; memo, "Minutes of Meeting at Lancaster, Friday, October 13, 1924," November 3, 1924, Pennsylvania Power & Light Collection, Pennsylvania Water & Power Company Files, accession 1552, box 149, folder 24.

94 In 1920, Consolidated had 79,469 consumers in a city of 733,826 residents with an average consumption of 431 kwh. Nicholas B. Wainwright, *History of the Philadelphia Electric Company, 1881–1961* (Philadelphia: Philadelphia Electric Company, 1961), 147–48, 390; Consolidated Gas Electric Light and Power Company, *1928 Annual Report*, 6.

95 Steinberg, *Nature Incorporated*.

96 Pennsylvania Water & Power Company Files, accession 1552, V 590, Pennsylvania Water & Power Company Minutes, vol. 1, 1910–1919, notes from January 14, 1910.

97 Pennsylvania Water & Power Company, *1912 Annual Report*.

98 Pennsylvania Water & Power Company, *1933 Annual Report, Year Book*, 26–27. The 1921 Superpower Survey reported that "the Susquehanna has no favorable sites for storage reservoirs." William S. Murray et al., "A Superpower System for the Region between Boston and Washington" (Washington, D.C.: Government Printing Office, 1921), 195.

99 Pennsylvania Water & Power Company, *1911 Annual Report*.

100 Pennsylvania Water & Power Company, *1913 Annual Report*.

101 Pennsylvania Water & Power Company, *1914 Annual Report*, 7.

102 Pennsylvania Water & Power Company, *1940 Annual Report*, 39–41.

103 The creation of the Contingency Fund, later renamed the Equalization Reserve in 1928, is first discussed in the company's 1913 Annual Report. It

was abandoned in 1931 when sufficient steam capacity allowed for more precise planning.

104 Pennsylvania Water & Power Company, *1931 Annual Report, Year Book*.

105 In 1900, the price in cents per 1,000 lumen-hours of electricity was 2.692; in 1920, it was 0.630. Kerosene lamps circa 1880 cost 3.479 cents. William D. Nordhaus, "Do Real-Output and Real-Wage Measures Capture Reality? The History of Lighting Suggests Not," in *The Economics of New Goods,* ed. Timothy F. Bresnahan and Robert J. Gordon (Chicago: University of Chicago Press, 1997), 49.

106 David E. Nye, *America's Assembly Line* (Cambridge, MA: MIT Press, 2013), 27. Original citation is to Harley W. Barclay, *Ford Production Methods* (New York: Harper, 1936), 205.

107 Cheape, *Moving the Masses,* 2.

108 Griffin, "Development of Electric Railways," 237, 238.

109 In 1924, Consolidated provided industrial power to 29 railroad companies, 18 shipyards, 153 metal companies, 41 chemical manufactures, and 31 textile companies using 10,130 hp. Overall, the company was supplying industrial power to 3,323 companies with a connected load of 433,076 hp. Consolidated Gas Electric Light and Power Company, *1924 Annual Report, Year Book,* 20.

6 · The Electrification of America

1 Nicholas B. Wainwright, *History of the Philadelphia Electric Company, 1881–1961* (Philadelphia: Philadelphia Electric Company, 1961), chap. 10.

2 In 1899, 475,000 hp out of 9,811,000 hp of the nation's industrial motors were electrical (4.8 percent); in 1914, 8.4 million out of 21.6 million were electrical (39 percent); in 1919, 15.6 million out of 28.4 million were electrical (55 percent). Sam H. Schurr and Bruce Carlton Netschert, *Energy in the American Economy, 1850–1975: An Economic Study of Its History and Prospects* (Baltimore: Johns Hopkins Press, 1960), 187.

3 Louis C. Hunter and Lynwood Bryant, *A History of Industrial Power, 1780–1930,* vol. 3: *The Transmission of Power* (Cambridge, MA: MIT Press, 1991), chap. 3; Warren D. Devine Jr., "Electrified Mechanical Drive: The Historical Power Distribution Revolution," in *Electricity in the American Economy,* ed. Sam H. Schurr et al. (New York: Greenwood Press, 1990).

4 Hunter and Bryant, *History of Industrial Power,* 3:115–16.

5 Devine Jr., "Electrified Mechanical Drive."

6 David E. Nye, *America's Assembly Line* (Cambridge, MA: MIT Press, 2013), 21–27; Lindy Biggs, *The Rational Factory: Architecture, Technology, and Work in America's Age of Mass Production* (Baltimore: Johns Hopkins University Press, 1996).

7 Nye, *America's Assembly Line,* chap. 2.

8 Ibid.; David E. Nye, *Electrifying America: Social Meanings of a New Technology, 1880–1940* (Cambridge, MA: MIT Press, 1990), chap. 5. On shifts in American production techniques during this period, see David A. Hounshell, *From the American System to Mass Production, 1800–1932: The Development of Manufacturing Technology in the United States* (Baltimore: Johns Hopkins University Press, 1984).

9 United States Bureau of the Census, *Historical Statistics of the United States, Colonial Times to 1970* (Washington, D.C.: Government Printing Office, 1975), part 2, 828; Pennsylvania Giant Power Survey Board, *Report of the Giant Power Survey Board to the General Assembly of the Commonwealth of Pennsylvania* (Harrisburg, PA: Telegraph Printing Company, printer, 1925); Warren D. Devine Jr., "Coal Mining: Underground and Surface Mechanization," in Schurr et al., eds., *Electricity in the American Economy;* Hunter and Bryant, *History of Industrial Power,* vol. 3, chap. 7–9.

10 Warren D. Devine Jr., "Early Developments in Electroprocessing," in Schurr et al., eds., *Electricity in the American Economy.*

11 Schurr et al., eds., *Electricity in the American Economy,* 295.

12 In 1910, manufacturers generated 59.5 percent of their electricity and purchased 40.5 percent from utilities; in 1920, they generated 44.3 percent and purchased 55.7 percent. By 1929, the ratio was 36.2 percent to 63.8 percent. Ibid., appendix 2, 423.

13 The nation's total industrial capacity increased by approximately 6,800,000 hp from 21,565,000 hp in 1914 to 28,397,000 hp in 1919, while electrical capacity increased by more than 7,200,000 hp (from 8,392,000 in 1914 to 15,612,000 in 1919). Ibid., 187.

14 Thomas Parke Hughes, *Networks of Power: Electrification in Western Society, 1880–1930* (Baltimore: Johns Hopkins University Press, 1983), chap. 11.

15 Robert Wiebe, *The Search for Order, 1877–1920* (New York: Hill & Wang, 1967); Ellis Hawley, *The Great War and the Search for a Modern Order, a History of the American People and Their Institutions, 1917–1933* (New York: St. Martin's Press, 1979); Daniel T. Rodgers, *Atlantic Crossings: Social Politics in a Progressive Age* (Cambridge, MA: Harvard University Press, 1998).

16 Brian Balogh, *A Government Out of Sight: The Mystery of National Authority in Nineteenth-Century America* (Cambridge: Cambridge University Press, 2009).

17 Martin V. Melosi, *Coping with Abundance: Energy and Environment in Industrial America* (New York: Knopf, 1985), chap. 4–5.

18 Bernard Baruch, *American Industry in War: A Report of the War Industries Board* (Washington, D.C.: Government Printing Office, 1921), 279–86; Hughes, *Networks of Power,* 279; Hawley, *Great War and Search for Order.*

19 Hughes, *Networks of Power,* 292.

20 On the history of Superpower, Giant Power, and the PNJ Interconnection, see ibid; Bayla Singer, "Power to the People: The Pennsylvania-New Jersey-Maryland Interconnection, 1925–1970" (Ph.D. diss., University of Pennsylvania, 1983); Ronald C. Tobey, *Technology as Freedom: The New Deal and the Electrical Modernization of the American Home* (Berkeley: University of California Press, 1996).

21 Several of the engineers and executives associated with hydroelectric projects on the Susquehanna were consultants to the Superpower project, including Boyd Ehle, Cary T. Hutchinson, and J. A. Walls.

22 In the 1910s, the electric industry required over $2 billion in capital annually, more than any industry other than the railroads. Richard F. Hirsh, *Power Loss: The Origins of Deregulation and Restructuring in the American Electric Utility System* (Cambridge, MA: MIT Press, 1999), 34.

23 William S. Murray et al., "A Superpower System for the Region between Boston and Washington" (Washington, D.C.: Government Printing Office, 1921), 11–12.

24 Singer, "Power to the People," 47.

25 Pennsylvania Giant Power Survey Board, *Giant Power Report,* "Governor's Message of Transmittal," viii.

26 Ibid., iii–xiii.

27 Ibid.

28 In 1925, 178,666 of Pennsylvania's 202,250 farms lacked electric service, 12,452 were supplied by utilities, and 11,132 operated their own generators either independently or in collectives. Ibid., "General Report of Director," 37.

29 Ibid., "Governor's Message of Transmittal," vii, xi.

30 Ibid., "General Report of Director," 24.

31 "Pinchot Takes a Radical Stand," *Electrical World* 85, no. 8 (1925); William S. Murray, "To the Editor of Electrical World," *Electrical World* 85, no. 10 (1925).

32 For a thorough analysis of the reasons behind Giant Power's legislative defeat, see Thomas Parke Hughes, "Technology and Public Policy: The Failure of Giant Power," *Proceedings of the Institute of Electrical and Electronics Engineers* 64 (1976): 1361–71.

33 Morris Cooke was appointed the first head of the Rural Electrification Administration. Tobey, *Technology as Freedom.*

34 Hughes, *Networks of Power*, 331.

35 James Harlow was a key actor in surveying sites for hydroelectric facilities below Holtwood. Boyd Ehle, "Later Achievements of Engineers on the Lower Susquehanna—Harnessing the River," *The Cornell Civil Engineer* 37, no. 4 (1929).

36 Hughes, *Networks of Power*, 328–29; Wainwright, *History of Philadelphia Electric Company,* chap. 12.

37 These peaks would come between midnight and six a.m. during times of high river flow. W. C. L. Elgin, "Conowingo Hydroelectric Project with Particular Reference to Interconnection," *AIEE Transactions* 47 (1928): 380–81.

38 Wainwright, *History of Philadelphia Electric Company,* 264.

39 Singer, "Power to the People," 154–67.

40 W. C. L. Elgin, "Pennsylvania-New Jersey Interconnection," *Electrical World* 91, no. 8 (1928).

41 Engineer J. A. Walls was one of the advisors to the Superpower Survey. "Memorandum—Discussion with Dr. C. T. Hutchinson, This Morning," November 17, 1921, Pennsylvania Power & Light Collection, Pennsylvania Water & Power Company Files, accession 1962, box 32: Correspondence & Data exchanged with Dr. C.T.H. and notes on Discussions, Hagley Museum and Library, Wilmington, Delaware; Pennsylvania Water & Power Company, *Holtwood Power Development* (Holtwood: Pennsylvania Water & Power Company, 1922).

42 Pennsylvania Water & Power Company, *1924 Annual Report.* The company's annual reports are available at the Hagley Museum and Library, Wilmington, Delaware.

43 R. L. Thomas, "The Development of a Regional Power System," June 6, 1935, Pennsylvania Power & Light Collection, Pennsylvania Water & Power Company Files, accession 1552, box 149, folder 14, 14.

44 Pennsylvania Water & Power Company, *1931 Annual Report;* Pennsylvania Water & Power Company and Safe Harbor Water Power Corporation, *The Safe Harbor Hydroelectric Development: A Digest of the Solutions of Its Engineering Problems* (Baltimore: Barton-Gillet, printer, 1936).

45 Pennsylvania Water & Power Company, *1932 Annual Report.*

46 In 1954, Holtwood and Safe Harbor were acquired by Pennsylvania Power & Light, and at that point, they became integrated into the PNJ Interconnection. Singer, "Power to the People," chap. 5.

47 Farley Osgood, "Discussion: Papers on Interconnection and Its Effect on Power Development," *AIEE Transactions* 47 (1928): 413.

48 Electricity production increased from 5,969 million kwh in 1902 to 114,637 million kwh in 1930 while overall energy consumption increased from 8,715 trillion BTUs in 1902 to 22,253 trillion BTUs in 1930. Part of the reason overall energy growth was slower than the growth of electrification is due to the increasing efficiency of coal-fired steam plants. It took seven or more pounds of coal to produce a kilowatt-hour at the turn of the century; by 1927 the average was 1.84, thereby giving Americans access to more electricity while consuming less coal. Schurr and Netschert, *Energy in the American Economy,* 182; United States Bureau of the Census, *Census of Electrical Industries: Central Electric Light and Power Stations, 1927* (Washington, D.C.: Government Printing Office, 1930), 68.

49 In 1929, the nation had installed 41,122,000 hp, and 33,844,000 hp was electrified (82.3 percent). Schurr and Netschert, *Energy in the American Economy,* 187. In 1930, industrial consumers used more than 61 billion kwh, compared to about 14 billion kwh for commercial enterprises and 11 billion kwh for residential users. United States Bureau of the Census, *Historical Statistics,* part 2, 828.

50 Utilities defended these practices by noting that industrial consumers used much more electricity, thereby allowing utilities to invest in larger and more efficient equipment. Bureau of the Census, *1927 Electrical Census,* 57.

51 Rural Electrification Administration and David Cushman Coyle, *Electric Power on the Farm: The Story of Electricity, Its Usefulness on Farms, and the Movement to Electrify Rural America* (Washington, D.C.: Government Printing Office, 1936), 72.

52 In 1929, 22,458 laborers in Philadelphia worked in 774 establishments manufacturing ready-made clothing. The whole industry was powered by 3,866 hp of prime movers, a ratio of roughly 1 hp per 6 workers. Pennsylvania Department of Internal Affairs, *Report on Productive Industries, Public Utilities and Miscellaneous Statistics of the Commonwealth of Pennsylvania for the Years 1929 and 1930* (Harrisburg, PA: Bureau of Statistics, 1931), 233–38.

53 The Gross National Product increased from $140 billion in 1920 to $204 billion in 1929 as measured in 1958 dollars. United States Bureau of the Census, *Historical Statistics,* part 1, 224.

54 Gasoline output of American refineries increased from 12.9 million barrels in 1909 to 432.2 million in 1930. Schurr and Netschert, *Energy in the American Economy,* 93.

55 In 1927, 33.5 billion of the 63.5 billion kwh sold by utilities in the nation were purchased by industrial consumers (53 percent of the total). 10 billion kwh (30 percent) were consumed in the mid-Atlantic. In addition, mid-Atlantic industries likely consumed at least an additional 6 billion kwh of electricity produced by factories. (The mid-Atlantic produced 28.5 billion kwh from all sources, with 19 billion kwh produced by utilities and 3.5 billion kwh by street railways; the vast majority of the balance was likely produced by industries for their own use.) Bureau of the Census, *1927 Electrical Census,* 41, 47, 51, 78.

56 Pennsylvania Giant Power Survey Board, *Giant Power Report,* 78.

57 Consolidated Gas Electric Light and Power Company, *1924 Annual Report: Year Book,* 20. Consolidated annual reports are available at the Harvard Baker Library, Boston, Massachusetts.

58 Nye, *America's Assembly Line,* 53.

59 Ibid., chap. 5.

60 The electricity used in homes between 1900 and 1930 was a small fraction of the total produced. In 1912, about 4 percent of electricity was used in homes (.9 billion kwh out of a total of 25 billion kwh); in 1920, about 6 percent was used in homes (3.2 billion kwh of 57 billion kwh); in 1930, about 9 percent was used in homes (11 billion kwh out of 116 billion kwh). United States Bureau of the Census, *Historical Statistics,* part 2, 828.

61 Pennsylvania Giant Power Survey Board, *Giant Power Report:* "Governor's Message of Transmittal," v.

62 Harold L. Platt, *The Electric City: Energy and the Growth of the Chicago Area, 1880–1930* (Chicago: University of Chicago Press, 1991), 241.

63 Nye, *Electrifying America,* 395n50.

64 Consolidated Gas Electric Light and Power Company, *1923 Annual Report: Year Book,* 62.

65 PECO's electrification rate is based on the company's report that there were over 2,000,000 people living in its service area and 102,464 were customers. Assuming the average household had six residents, this provides

an adoption rate of 35 percent. Wainwright, *History of the Philadelphia Electric Company,* 147–48. Consolidated estimates from Consolidated Gas Electric Light and Power Company, *1927 Annual Report: Year Book,* 18.

66 Only one-third of American homes had wiring sufficient to power large electric appliances in 1929. Tobey, *Technology as Freedom,* 33.

67 34.3 percent of electrified homes had washing machines in 1922, 38.4 percent in 1929. Ibid., 26.

68 Wainwright, *History of Philadelphia Electric Company,* 196.

69 The actual numbers were 97.2 percent for irons, 49.8 percent for toasters, 48.8 percent for washing machines, 48.3 percent for vacuum cleaners, 41.6 percent for clocks, 34.2 percent for refrigerators, 31.6 percent for percolators, 19.7 percent for waffle irons, 18.4 percent for heaters, 14.9 percent for hot plates, and 6.8 percent for ranges. Rural Electrification Administration and Coyle, *Electric Power on the Farm,* 124.

70 Consolidated Gas Electric Light and Power Company, *1923 Annual Report: Year Book,* 61.

71 Mark H. Rose, *Cities of Light and Heat: Domesticating Gas and Electricity in Urban America* (University Park, PA: Penn State University Press, 1995); Tobey, *Technology as Freedom.*

72 Ruth Schwartz Cowan, *More Work for Mother: The Ironies of Household Technology from the Open Hearth to the Microwave* (New York: Basic Books, 1983).

73 In 1920, the national average was 339 kwh, which increased to 805 kwh in 1937. United States Bureau of the Census, *Historical Statistics,* part 2, 827; Consolidated Gas Electric Light and Power Company, *1928 Annual Report,* 6, and *1937 Annual Report,* 8.

74 United States Bureau of the Census, *Historical Statistics,* part 2, 827.

75 Calvin Burwell and Blair Swezey, "The Home: Evolving Technologies for Satisfying Human Wants," in Schurr et al., eds., *Electricity in the American Economy,* 250.

76 Nye, *Electrifying America,* chap. 3.

77 Susan J. Douglas, *Inventing American Broadcasting, 1899–1922* (Baltimore: Johns Hopkins University Press, 1987), 303.

78 Nye, *Electrifying America,* 282–83.

79 Tobey, *Technology as Freedom,* 23.

80 Melosi, *Coping with Abundance,* 114–16; Platt, *The Electric City,* 246–47; Lizabeth Cohen, *Making a New Deal: Industrial Workers in Chicago, 1919–1939* (Cambridge: Cambridge University Press, 1990), 120–25.

81 The population of the United States grew from 76,212,168 in 1900 to 123,202,264 in 1930. Energy production grew from 8,715 trillion BTUs in 1902 to 22,253 trillion BTUs in 1930. Schurr and Netschert, *Energy in the American Economy,* 182.

82 Electricity production grew from 5,969 million kwh in 1902 to 114,637 million kwh in 1930. Ibid; Nye, *America's Assembly Line,* 53.

83 In 1899, an average of 2.14 hp was available to each worker and 0.1 hp was electrified; in 1925, 4.25 hp was available to each worker and 3.12 hp was electrified. National Electric Light Association, *The Electric Light and Power Industry in the United States* (New York: National Electric Light Association, 1928), 87.

84 Melosi, *Coping with Abundance,* 118.

85 William S. Murray, *Superpower, Its Genesis and Future* (New York: McGraw-Hill, 1925), 188–89.

86 Paul Hirt, *The Wired Northwest: The History of Electric Power, 1870s–1970s* (Lawrence: University Press of Kansas, 2012), 89–95.

87 The population of the South Atlantic, East South Central, and West South Central states in 1927 contained 36,889,000 out of a national total of 118,628,000. Collectively, they generated 14.5 billion kwh out of a national total of 74.5 billion kwh. United States Bureau of the Census, *1927 Electrical Census,* 41, 47.

88 Ibid., 53.

89 In 1930, 68,955,000 Americans lived in urban areas while 53,820,000 lived in rural areas. New York had 10,522,000 urban residents and 2,066,000 rural ones; in Pennsylvania the ratio was 6,534,000 to 3,098,000. Bureau of the Census, *Historical Statistics,* part 1, 11, 32–33.

90 In 1930, manufacturing produced $18.3 billion in value compared to $6.4 billion in agriculture, forestry, and fisheries. Ibid., 239.

Conclusion

1 In 1950, America produced 334 billion kwh of electricity; in 2000, the total was 3,802 billion kwh. In the same period, oil consumption grew from 13,315 to 38,264 quadrillion BTUs and coal consumption grew from 12,347 to 22,580 quadrillion BTUs. Energy Information Administration, "Annual Energy Review" (Washington, D.C., 2008), 9, 227. On the twentieth century as a period of intensified activity in energy and other domains, see John Robert McNeill, *Something New under the Sun: An Environmental History of the Twentieth-Century World* (New York: W. W. Norton, 2000).

2 Mark Fiege, *The Republic of Nature: An Environmental History of the United States* (Seattle: University of Washington Press, 2012), chap. 6.

3 Brian Frehner, *Finding Oil: The Nature of Petroleum Geology, 1859–1920* (Lincoln: University of Nebraska Press, 2011).

4 The exhaustibility of fossil fuels was apparent to some historical actors, though most were inclined to focus on the relative abundance of supplies. The most famous historical expression of these limits came from William Stanley Jevons in Britain in 1865. His book *The Coal Question* used new statistical methods to warn that British coal reserves would be depleted sooner than most expected. Though there were brief moments in American history where concerns over resource shortages raised questions of sustainability, such as in the 1920s when discoveries of oil were slowing, questions of scarcity received did not receive great attention. William Stanley Jevons, *The Coal Question; an Enquiry Concerning the Progress of the Nation, and the Probable Exhaustion of Our Coal-Mines* (London: Macmillan, 1865).

5 Scylla (a six-headed hydra) and Charybdis (a whirlpool) are mythical monsters best known from Homer's *Odyssey*. They guard a narrow strait, thereby forcing ships to choose one peril or the other. Just as Odysseus was faced with sacrificing six men or risking his entire ship, we must choose between the costs of higher-priced energy and the costs of climate change.

6 The distinction between accumulative, distributive, and communicative systems is useful in this regard. Daniel Jonsson, "Sustainable Infrasystem Synergies: A Conceptual Framework," *Journal of Urban Technology* 7, no. 3 (2000).

7 Edmund Russell et al., "The Nature of Power: Synthesizing the History of Technology and Environmental History," *Technology and Culture* 52, no. 2 (2011).

8 This includes natural gas and nuclear power as well as coal and oil. Uranium is a stock, comparable to fossil fuels, that is consumed in the process of fission. Nuclear fusion technically offers the potential of a renewable stock of energy, but all attempts to harness this process to produce electricity have failed dramatically.

9 This hybrid future is not the same as the "advanced organic economy" articulated by E. A. Wrigley. He noted that between 1600 and 1800 the increasing use of draft animals and fertilizers greatly increased the productivity of the land, thereby creating a new stage of the organic economy but one that still relied primarily on photosynthesis and metabolism. The post-mineral future is likely to involve a much greater reliance on

energy converters developed in the past century. E. A. Wrigley, *Continuity, Chance and Change: The Character of the Industrial Revolution in England* (Cambridge: Cambridge University Press, 1988), chap. 2.

10 Adam Smith's parable of the pin-makers, the first chapter of *The Wealth of Nations,* captures the logic of production in an organic energy regime. Smith's pin-makers increased their profits through division of labor and the adoption of more efficient processes, thereby saving the application of energy. By contrast, the economic growth that was most characteristic of industrialization was based on the substitution of fossil fuels for other production inputs like labor or capital. Adam Smith, *An Inquiry into the Nature and Causes of the Wealth of Nations,* 3 vols. (Dublin: Whitestone, 1776).

Acknowledgments

WRITING MAY BE a solitary process, but I have not taken the journey alone. It is a great pleasure to acknowledge the abundance of family, friends, colleagues, and institutions that have sustained me along the way. My parents paved the way for me in this endeavor, giving me a strong intellectual background and the freedom to pursue my dreams; Nick Jones read and commented on the entire manuscript, sometimes reading chapters multiple times; and Sue Jones proofread the final draft. My extended family has offered companionship, meals, and places to stay on research trips and vacations. My friends have provided fun, distraction, and balance. Lola has slept at my feet for much of this project, and it turns out that I needed all those walks around the block just as much as she did. Lindsey has been a true partner throughout, sharing the ups and downs of life and patiently abiding the vagaries of the writing process. Her love, support, and understanding are deeply appreciated.

A young scholar could not ask for a better cast of faculty mentors than I have had. When I was an undergraduate, Robert McGinn at Stanford University inspired me to ask critical questions about the role of science and technology in society. His passion and backing led me to the University of Pennsylvania History and Sociology of Science Department for my graduate work, where this project was first conceived. Ruth Schwartz Cowan was a terrific advisor—challenging, insightful, and supportive. Her insistence on sound thinking, clear writing, and attention to detail saved me from numerous blunders. Walter Licht helped me think broadly about the links between energy and transport and shared his deep knowledge of mid-Atlantic history. John McNeill of Georgetown University was gracious with his time and feedback, emphasizing the importance of writing for wide audiences. Sheila Jasanoff hosted me for two stimulating years at Harvard University full of rousing debate and critical inquiry. At the University of California–Berkeley, David Winickoff was a welcoming and encouraging mentor. Finally, Robert Kohler nurtured this book from its earliest days at the University of Pennsylvania. His intellectual engagement, interest in the big picture, and incisive feedback on several drafts have been more valuable than I can express. It is with great pleasure that I dedicate this work to him.

I have also been blessed with a large number of supportive colleagues along the way. The graduate students and faculty at the University of Pennsylvania History and Sociology of Science Department provided a dynamic intellectual environment through seminars, workshops, writing groups, and hallway chats. At Harvard University, I enjoyed the company of two communities: the postdoctoral fellows at the Center for the Environment and the members of the Harvard STS Program. My time at Berkeley was enhanced by participating in the Winickoff Lab and attending events at the Center for Science, Technology, Medicine, and Society. And my new colleagues at Arizona State University have graciously allowed me to lock myself in my office while completing this work. I'd like to offer particular thanks to members of the writing groups I have participated in over the past several years: Daniel Barber, Robert Chester, Bartow Elmore, Adam Ewing, Joanna Guldi, Matthew Hersch, Eric Hintz, Lauren Hirshberg, Emily Pawley, Jebediah Purdy, Trygve Throntveit, and Roger Turner. In addition, I have appreciated the generous encouragement and feedback from Sean Adams, Brian Balogh, Margaret Curnutte, Samuel Weiss Evans, Barbara Hahn, Paul Hirt, Martin Melosi, Tyler Priest, Fred Quivik, Peter Shulman, and Joel Tarr. At the proofreading stage, I was graciously assisted by Javiera Barandiaran, Catherine Boleyn, Maria Bowman, Margaret Copeland, Leah Grossman, Caroline Jack, Kathy Jacobson, Nathan Jones, Laura Nelson, Lynn Plait, Sid Plait, Carl Roose, and Marcia Treece. William Nelson produced the maps that illustrate this work. At Harvard University Press, I'd like to thank Kathleen McDermott for her support throughout the process and the three reviewers for their insightful comments.

The work of history would not be possible without the help of countless librarians and archivists, and this project is no exception. I am deeply appreciative of the assistance from Christopher Baer and the archival staff of the Hagley Museum and

Library in Wilmington, Delaware; Susan Beates at the Drake Well Museum in Titusville, Pennsylvania; Darwin Stapleton and the staff at the Rockefeller Archive Center in Sleepy Hollow, New York; Connie King and the staff at the Library Company of Philadelphia; and the many archivists who helped me find sources at the Historical Society of Pennsylvania in Philadelphia. The librarians and interlibrary loan staff at Penn, Harvard, and Berkeley tracked down numerous works for me during the research process.

Finally, I am happy to acknowledge the generous financial support of numerous institutions. The University of Pennsylvania provided funding for five years of graduate work, a Teece Summer Fellowship, and several research trips. Grants from the Hagley Museum and Library and the Philadelphia Area Consortium for the History of Science covered additional research and travel expenses. I am also grateful for a fellowship from the Miller Center of Public Affairs at the University of Virginia and for postdoctoral funding from the Ziff Fund at the Harvard University Center for the Environment and the S. V. Ciriacy-Wantrup Fellowship in Natural Resource Economics and Political Economy at the University of California–Berkeley, which gave me the focused time necessary to complete the book revisions.

Index